Now publisher of **National Review,** William A. Rusher served as Associate Counsel to the Senate Internal Security Subcommittee in 1956-57 — a period during which the Subcommittee was engaged in some of its most dramatic and "controversial" investigations.

Mr. Rusher was born in Chicago in 1923 and received his early education in New York State. After graduating from Princeton's School of Public and International Affairs at the age of 20, he served three years with the Air Force and was discharged with the rank of Captain in 1946. Two years later he graduated from Harvard Law School and entered a large Wall Street law firm, specializing in litigation. In 1955, Mr. Rusher left his firm to become Special Counsel to the Finance Committee of the New York State Senate, and the following year lent his talents to the U.S. Senate's investigations of domestic Communism. A familiar figure on late-night TV and radio, Mr. Rusher is author of many articles and has played an active role in national politics. He has traveled extensively in Europe, Africa, South America and the Far East, and logs thousands of miles a year on speaking tours in the U.S. Mr. Rusher is single, and lives in New York City.

Special Counsel

SPECIAL
COUNSEL

BY

WILLIAM A. RUSHER

ARLINGTON HOUSE

New Rochelle, New York

For my Mother

For my mother

Foreword

This book is the story of my seventeen months as a special counsel to the Internal Security Subcommittee of the United States Senate in the years 1956-57. As such, it is primarily an account of the activities of the Subcommittee: the way it worked, the hearings it held, the controversies in which it became embroiled.

There are many ways in which such a story could have been written. Various friends urged me to lay heavier stress on the dramatic elements in the composition, the so-called "human interest" aspects. Others called for a tough-minded exposition of the powers and duties of Congressional investigating committees, a book that might, perhaps, even break new ground in this field, and end by helping to expand the scope of their work.

But neither of these was the kind of book I had in mind, or the kind I have persisted in writing. The idea of telling, in book form, the story of those seventeen months first occurred to me in the spring of 1965, when I was having a relaxed chat one evening with two intelligent young people who could not themselves recall those (relatively!) far-off days. I recognized the intrinsic fascination of the subject-matter but sensed that my young listeners would neither understand nor respect a hot-eyed, fist-pounding approach to it. Moreover, I was myself more than a little exhausted by the raging emotions of these old controversies. So I simply let the story tell itself; and that, in general, is what I have tried to do in this book.

For all that, I think the reader will find it exciting enough. There are spies in these pages, and traitors; there are defectors and redefectors; there are suicides and perjurers; there are brave men and pathetic psychotics; there is even a sidelong glance at beauty, and an unexpected touch of humor. The tone of the book may disappoint those anti-Communists who "like their doctrine hot"; and it may equally fail to live up to the carefully nurtured expectations of those critics of Congressional investigations who regard the whole process as diabolical. But if I have not labored in vain, it will interest those for whom it is primarily intended: namely, people who are too young to remember the mid-

1950's at all, or who, whatever their age, are sufficiently detached, now, from the controversies of that era to view it with a modest objectivity.

The book's myriad faults are wholly my responsibility. Its merits, such as they may be, are in large measure due to the many friends who have encouraged me: my unfailingly kind and thoughtful publisher, Neil McCaffrey; Ruth Matthews, who checked the manuscript for accuracy; my valued colleague Wm. F. Buckley Jr., who donated long hours of his time to that sort of gentle yet penetrating criticism, both substantive and stylistic, that is so much better than mere praise; Agatha Schmidt and Philip McCombs, who conducted the often intricate research upon which many of the factual statements are based; Daniel J. McGrath and Frank A. Shepherd, who reviewed and commented upon the manuscript as a whole; Noel and Elaine Busby, who photostated the entire first and second drafts; and lastly, my tireless and uncomplaining secretary Ann Turner, who typed and re-typed the manuscript repeatedly—yet never forgot, even once, to spur me on with a smile.

William A. Rusher

New York City
July 1967

Contents

Contents

Special Counsel

1

The Subcommittee,
the Senators,
and the Staff

The plane banked over the lordly Capitol and the other familiar landmarks of Washington and settled toward the runway of National Airport. It was Monday evening, March 5, 1956, and I was beginning a new life. The pre-war college years at Princeton; the war itself, during which I had served with the Air Force in India; the return to books—and more books, and still more books—at Harvard Law School in the immediate postwar years: all these were far behind me. Between them and that night in 1956 lay more than seven years as an attorney with Shearman & Sterling & Wright, Wall Street's largest law firm.

As the plane taxied toward the terminal, I looked back—not for the first time, or the last—across those seven years. There is a case to be made against working for one of the great Wall Street "law factories," but I had never regretted it for a moment. The matters on which I was engaged in those years customarily involved millions of dollars, and some of America's largest and most prestigious corporations. My colleagues and superiors were supremely intelligent men, superbly trained to manage such affairs. What the experience lacked in breadth, it more than made up in depth—in precision, in thoughtfulness, in care.

But now it was all behind me: the sedate conferences behind paneled doors; the delicately nuanced letters and affidavits; the silent victories and muted defeats of corporate law practice. Ahead—dead ahead—lay savage controversy, charge and countercharge, heated denials, shouting headlines, popping flashbulbs. In the morning I was to be sworn in as a special counsel to the Internal Security Subcommittee of the United States Senate—the body charged by the Senate with the investigation of internal security problems, and especially the problem of domestic Communism.

Beside me in the plane, as we unsnapped our safety belts and prepared to disembark, was the man who had caused the sea-change in my life: Robert Morris, at forty-one just beginning his second tour of duty as chief counsel to the Subcommittee. I—nine years his junior—was to be his associate, and for a time the only other lawyer active on the staff. We had met in New York early in the 1950's, after Morris' first hitch with the Subcommittee and while he was serving as a judge of the Municipal Court. We had become fast friends. Often, late in the evening, when his work at the court was finished, I would drop in at his home on East 64th Street and listen to his tales of the fascinating life he had led: in Naval Intelligence during the war; as minority (i.e., Republican) counsel to the Tydings Committee, investigating the early charges of Senator Joseph McCarthy in 1950; and above all with the Internal Security Subcommittee under its late, great founder and first chairman, Senator Pat McCarran. When he returned to the Subcommittee early in 1956, at the bipartisan invitation of its new chairman, Senator James Eastland, and its ranking minority member, Senator William Jenner, Bob Morris asked me to come with him. I submitted my resignation to Shearman & Sterling & Wright, and went.

Both Houses of Congress necessarily conduct most of their business through committees, each charged with a major area of national concern. Each committee, in turn, is usually authorized to establish temporary or permanent subcommittees to deal with separate aspects of its field. In the Senate, in 1956, the powerful Judiciary Committee had no less than fourteen subcommittees. Of these, the largest and most important, in terms of staff and public notoriety, was the Subcommittee to Investigate the Administration of the Internal Security Act and Other Internal Security Laws—known for short (or at any rate shorter) as the Internal Security Subcommittee, and hereinafter often further abbreviated as the ISSC.

The Subcommittee was first created by Senate Resolution 366 of the 81st Congress, which was adopted on December 21, 1950. Under the terms of that resolution, the Internal Security Subcommittee was

. . . authorized and directed to make a complete and continuing study and investigation of (1) the administration, operation, and enforcement of the Internal Security Act of 1950; (2) the administration, operation and enforcement of other laws relating to espionage, sabotage, and infiltration by persons who are or may be under the domination of the foreign government or organizations controlling the world Communist movement or any other movement seeking to overthrow the Government of the United States by force and violence. . . .

The . . . subcommittee . . . is authorized to sit and act at such places and times during the sessions, recesses, and adjourned periods of the Senate, to hold such hearings, to require by subpoenas or otherwise the attendance of such witnesses and the production of such books, papers and documents, to administer such oaths, to take such testimony, to procure such printing and binding, and, within the amount appropriated therefor, to make such expenditures as it deems advisable. . . .

A majority of the members of the . . . subcommittee . . . shall constitute a quorum for the transaction of business, except that a lesser number, to be fixed by such subcommittee, shall constitute a quorum for the purpose of administering oaths and taking sworn testimony. . . .

The . . . subcommittee shall have the power to employ and fix the compensation of such officers, experts, and employees as it deems necessary in the performance of its duties, and is authorized to utilize the services, information, facilities, and personnel of the various departments and agencies of the Government to the extent that such services, information, facilities, and personnel, in the opinion of the heads of such departments and agencies, can be furnished without undue interference with the performance of the work and duties of such departments and agencies.

From time to time people unfamiliar with the constitutional separation of powers among the three branches of the federal government quite sincerely wonder why the investigation of such matters as domestic Communism must be undertaken by Congress at all, why Congress, in the famous phrase, doesn't just "leave it to the FBI." The answer, of course, lies in an understanding of the separate functions of the legislative branch (i.e., Congress) and the executive branch (of which the FBI is a part). It is one of the major functions of the executive branch to enforce *existing* laws, but it is the sole prerogative of Congress to pass *new* laws. Neither branch can perform its task without adequate investigatory power: the Justice Department (through the FBI) must have the necessary power to investigate violations of existing laws; but the Congress must have a separate and in some ways broader power to investigate activities which may *not* now be crimes—if only to determine whether they should be declared unlawful, or be otherwise controlled by legislation. No amount of investigation by the FBI could conceivably replace this investigatory obligation of the Congress, unless we were willing to authorize the FBI to investigate presently lawful acts on its

own initiative and make reports to the Congress on its findings, a procedure which critics of the Congressional committees would be the first to
deplore.*

By tradition, as if to underline the importance attached to the ISSC, it
had always been chaired by the chairman of the full Judiciary Committee: Senator McCarran from its founding in 1951 to 1953; Senator
Jenner during the Republican 83rd Congress from 1953 to 1955; and
Senator Eastland from 1955 onward. But the daily work of the Subcommittee was carried on by its counsel (one or more lawyers; in this
case, Bob Morris and me) and a staff of investigators, researchers,
clerks, etc. The entire annual budget of the Subcommittee in the years
1956 and 1957 was $290,000—less than the cost of half a dozen World
War II landing craft, or (to put it another way) not much more than the
Ford Foundation donated in 1956 alone to the Business Administration
Program of the University of Rangoon.

The ISSC was, to be sure, not the only Congressional committee
charged with the investigation of Communism. Across the Hill, in the
House of Representatives, the Committee on Un-American Activities
had been ceaselessly active since 1938, and in 1945 had achieved the
status of a separate standing committee of the House. Even in the
Senate, the Government Operations Committee, under the chairmanship of Senator McCarthy from 1953 to 1955, had busied itself in this
field. But the investigations of the House Committee were the House of
Representatives' own affair, and the mandate of the Senate's Government Operations Committee was manifestly inadequate for the investigation of Communist activities beyond the sphere of "government operations" or plausibly related areas. So, increasingly—and especially after
the Democratic victory of November 1954 took the chairmanship of the
Government Operations Committee from McCarthy—the Internal Security Subcommittee of the Judiciary Committee had become the Senate's favored instrument in this delicate field.

And it *was* a delicate field. It is sometimes charged that the chairmen
and members of the various Congressional committees investigating
Communism have lusted after the publicity that attends their work. If
so, they have been fools, for these committees have been the graveyards
of more public men than any comparable institutions in our nation's
history. Merely to list the names of their chairmen is to call a melan-
choly roll of ruined careers. Martin Dies, first chairman of HCUA—

* For a brilliant exposition of the theory and practice of Congressional investigations, see James Burnham's chapter on "The Investigating Power of Congress"
in *The Committee and Its Critics*, a study of the House Committee on Un-American Activities, edited by Wm. F. Buckley Jr. (Chicago: Henry Regnery Co., 1962).

denigrated and retired from Congress; J. Parnell Thomas, his Republican successor in the immediate postwar years—jailed for accepting kickbacks from his staff (the only Congressman in modern times to go to prison for that particular offense, though not, it is safe to say, the only one to commit it); Joseph McCarthy, the gaudiest gladiator of them all—officially "condemned" by his senatorial colleagues, and soon to die at 48, a broken man; Harold Velde and Francis Walter of HCUA, Pat McCarran, William Jenner, and James Eastland of the ISSC—one dead, one retired, three (as of 1956) hanging grimly on: each the possessor of a name that the American left, Communist and otherwise, reviled at every opportunity.

Why hasten to board a vessel so manifestly doomed? By March 1956, the condemnation of McCarthy—in effect, the pronouncement of the American society that the investigation of domestic Communism had gone too far—was already fifteen months in the past. The American people, who had reacted with shock and dismay to the 1950 conviction of Alger Hiss and the subsequent disclosures of deep Communist penetrations of the American society, were very plainly tired of the subject. The fire was over. Why leave a comfortable Wall Street job to poke among the ashes?

I am no more idealistic—or, to put it another way, no more a slave to my convictions—than most men. But I had been fascinated by the great story of domestic Communism's amazingly successful infiltration of the American society, as it came to light under the probing of the 80th Congress in 1948. I had read every published account of the two trials and final conviction of Alger Hiss. I had read Whittaker Chambers' monumental *Witness*—the Alpha and Omega, for me and for thousands of others, of a true insight into the mind of an American Communist. Many Americans were comfortably blinkered on the subject ("Freddie Field comes from a fine family—a *fine* family. Nobody can tell *me* he's a Communist"). But somehow, from the very start, I had been able to put myself in the place of these sick and outraged people, and to understand how (if not in a moral sense why) they had come to be what they were, the dedicated agents of a theory of history which has decreed America's doom. On those late evenings in Bob Morris' home I had even come to know some of the actors in this fantastic drama, when they dropped in to visit him: ex-Communists, now the wisest and most impassioned foes of the conspiracy they had abjured; their *quondam* enemies, still fighting the good fight; and the investigators, men who, like Bob, had become experts in this arcane field, and who now struggled to bring to light the fantastic story of what the forces of Communism had achieved —were still achieving—in America.

It was one of these investigators that I aspired to be. With the caricatures of the job I had chosen, I had simply nothing to do. I realized that all Congressional investigators of Communism were—falsely—supposed to be hard-eyed smear artists, seeking to crucify hapless professors of English for the crime of having read John Stuart Mill. I also knew the truth: that men like Bob Morris were veritable connoisseurs of Communism, able to distinguish between the subtlest shades of the numerous creeds sheltered in that vast temple; men, moreover, with a profound compassion for human frailties and a tremendous confidence in the regenerative power of the human spirit. By continuing the investigation of domestic Communism they were arming America with priceless knowledge of its foe—"building a record," as lawyers would say, on which all could draw—contemporary America, if it chose to do so; history, if it did not.

Beyond that, I felt, as many young Americans were beginning to feel, a powerful need to become personally engaged in the great struggle between world Communism and the forces of freedom. Heretofore, in my spare time, I had busied myself with routine politics, serving as a Republican precinct captain in my Manhattan district and climbing the ladder of Young Republican activities to membership on the Executive Committee of the Young Republican National Federation. But now, in March 1956, a Republican President had completed three years in office, and it was plain that nothing fundamental had changed. On the contrary, the Communist conquest of the world was proceeding with appalling efficiency. Before Eisenhower's second term was over, the uprising of free Hungary would be smashed by Soviet tanks, Khrushchev would be America's honored guest at Camp David, Cuba would be in Communist hands, and all central Africa would be reeling under a carefully coordinated Communist onslaught. Domestically, moreover, the aggressive investigation of Communist activities had been all but halted at the demand of America's frightened liberals. Just when catharsis seemed possible, when a symbolic gesture from the newly mandated Chief Executive could have reordered our national life to eliminate or at least reduce the influence of those elements in it which had unforgivably trafficked with the Communists, his innate amiability had decreed otherwise. Under the rubric of "unity," a tremendous crime against America was to be ignored.

I remembered the words of a friend of mine who, as an intelligence officer at the close of World War II, had witnessed the forced repatriation to Russia of the survivors of "Vlasov's Army"—the anti-Communist Russians who had fought with the Germans against Stalin, and who had finally surrendered to the Americans. Under the (secret) Treaty of

Halle, signed by General Eisenhower with his Soviet counterparts, these men had simply been herded into trucks and shoved across the zonal border into Stalin's waiting grasp. Some—the lucky ones—had managed to slit their wrists in time, with broken pieces of glass. The rest were never heard from again. "I knew then," said my friend, who before the war had taught English at a small Midwestern college, "that I couldn't spend the rest of my life footnoting Chaucer."

Nor could I spend mine disentangling the silken ropes that cumbered American business. It was late, but I would do what I could.

A taxi sped us through the darkness to Bob Morris' little apartment on Capitol Hill. Bathed in floodlights, the great dome of the Capitol seemed to float above us. I remembered the words of Goethe:

> Heard are the voices,
> Heard are the sages—
> The worlds and the ages:
> Choose well; your choice is
> Brief, and yet endless.
> Here eyes do regard you
> In eternity's stillness.
> Here is all fullness,
> Ye brave, to reward you.
> *Work, and despair not.*

In March 1956 the Internal Security Subcommittee consisted of nine senators, five Democrats and four Republicans. The Democrats were, in order of seniority: James O. Eastland (Mississippi), Olin D. Johnston (South Carolina), John L. McClellan (Arkansas), Thomas C. Hennings, Jr. (Missouri) and Price Daniel (Texas). The Republicans were: William E. Jenner (Indiana), Arthur V. Watkins (Utah), Herman Welker (Idaho) and John Marshall Butler (Maryland).

Not all of these senators were equally active in the work of the Subcommittee, by any means. On the Democratic side, Eastland as chairman naturally took a lively interest and frequently presided over hearings. So, to a lesser degree, did Johnston. McClellan would occasionally take on the burden of chairing a session, but he was one of the great "work horses" of the Senate (to use Senator Carl Hayden's apt term, which he carefully distinguished from the "show horses") and was usually too busy with other committees and subcommittees of which he was chairman to spare us much time. Hennings and Daniel might as well not have been on the Subcommittee at all. On the Republican side, the load was divided more equally. Senators Jenner, Welker and Watkins— more or less in that order—all attended or presided over hearings with reasonable frequency; Senator Butler, less often. However, it should be understood that the members of the Senate tacitly agree among themselves to divide up the work of the many scores of subcommittees, and it may well be that Senator Hennings (for instance) was pulling his full weight somewhere else, out of my line of vision.

Naturally too, the senior members of a Senate committee or subcommittee (in both parties) tend to control its work. In ours, the two leading personalities were unquestionably Senators Eastland and Jenner; and it was a happy fact that they got along together extremely well, and that no flavor of partisanship was ever permitted to creep into our activities. This was, of course, crucially important in the case of a subcommittee as "sensitive" as the ISSC and was a proud tradition which had been handed down from the date of its founding, in 1951, under Senator Pat McCarran. McCarran (a Democrat) had hired Bob Morris (a Republican) as chief counsel. When Morris left, Jay Sourwine (a Democrat) replaced him. The rest of the staff was equally bipartisan; Bob's secretary was a Democrat, mine a Republican. Our Subcommittee records clerk was the wife of Robert ("Bobby") Baker, the Secretary to the Democratic majority of the Senate, who was then (if we had only known it) just beginning his climb to power, wealth—and a criminal conviction for tax evasion. Most of the staff, as far as we knew, were apolitical, or at least discreet. All, needless to say, had undergone a rigorous security check and received full clearance.

Over the years I have had frequent occasion to note the highly unfavorable public image of Senator Eastland, not only or even primarily because of his work as chairman of the ISSC (if the criticisms are to be taken at face value), but because of his segregationist views. Yet it is certainly true that a great many other Southern senators held equally objectionable views on that subject, while somehow managing to escape comparably savage criticism for maintaining them. No doubt the fact that Eastland was chairman of the Senate Judiciary Committee, through which all civil-rights legislation had to pass, and that he used his powers as chairman to the full to obstruct or delay such legislation, made him a natural high-priority target of the civil-rights lobby. But I personally do not doubt that the sincere criticisms of Eastland were multiplied in the echo chambers of the Communist Party and its sympathizers for reasons that had no relation whatever to civil rights. The Communists would have attacked *any* chairman of the hated Subcommittee with any stick that came to hand.

Certainly there was nothing very offensive about Eastland personally. His usual manner was taciturn and gruff, and he had a way of staring at you noncommittally through his glasses that could be strangely disconcerting. But his attitude toward witnesses, even when he knew they were Communists bent on denouncing him, was imperturbable; and in his actions (so far as I was in a position to judge them), as distinguished from his manner, he could be genuinely kind. He had, I noticed, one apparently inflexible rule which I am sure his critics never suspected, and that was: in personal relations, never speak ill of anyone. I remember, for example, the day I reported to him that the administrative assistant to Senator *X* was deliberately delaying some action on his chief's part that Eastland ardently desired. This particular AA was widely regarded as the most obnoxious bastard on Capitol Hill—I had never heard anyone say a kind word for him, and I knew that Eastland knew his characteristics and reputation. When I paused for Eastland's comment, he blinked his eyes owlishly and began, "That man . . ." My hopes soared—was I to hear Eastland criticize somebody at last? But, after a moment, he ended lamely, ". . . is not in the right job."

A cigar was as much a part of Eastland's equipment as of Churchill's. He smoked incessantly, allowing the ashes to fall where they might. On the floor around the swivel chair in which he sat in his office, there was a permanent corona of stale cigar ashes, extending perhaps a foot in all directions.

He was, of course, a member of the powerful clique of Southern Democratic senators who, by virtue of their committee chairmanships, control so much of the business of the Senate. But he was not its leader, nor even (so far as I could tell) one of its stronger figures. He seemed content to be in on its caucuses, and to take his cue from others, most notably from Senate majority leader Lyndon Johnson. On more than one occasion when Bob Morris or I needed urgently to see Eastland on Subcommittee business, we would learn that he had left his office suddenly some minutes before—not (we soon learned to realize) to go to the floor of the Senate, or to any committee meeting, but to attend a secret council of war of his Southern peers in one of the private senatorial offices that honeycomb Capitol Hill's northern flank.

As an investigator of domestic Communism Eastland must be relegated distinctly to the middle rank, not nearly so competent or venturesome as his predecessor, Senator Pat McCarran, or HCUA's Representative Francis Walter, but abler than a number of chairman in HCUA's long history, and (for that matter) abler than Senator McCarthy as well. I will have more to say about McCarthy later on; for the moment, and apropos of Eastland, I will only note that Eastland came to regret that he had joined his fellow Democratic senators in their unanimous front against McCarthy on the famous condemnation resolution of December 1954. In the last year or two of McCarthy's life they became fast friends.

One final vignette may perhaps serve to illuminate another aspect of this complex Mississippian's personality. Years after I had left the Subcommittee, I was having dinner with a friend one evening at Duke Ziebert's famous steak house on L Street in Washington. I noticed Senator Eastland and some friends a few tables away and pointed him out to my dinner companion. As we glanced at him, I saw another figure rise from a nearby table and go over to say hello to Eastland. To my astonishment, I recognized the visitor as Joseph Forer, senior partner of Forer & Rein, the Communist Party's leading law firm in Washington. On literally dozens of occasions, Forer had accompanied Communists subpoenaed to appear before our Subcommittee; and he had also represented the Communist Party (successfully) on various appeals to the U. S. Supreme Court. Now Eastland shook Forer's hand cordially, introduced him to the others at his table, and invited him to pull up a chair and join them—which is exactly what Forer did! When my friend and I tottered out, the arch-segregationist "Red-baiter" and the Communist Party's lawyer were chatting cozily together.

Our other active Democrat, Olin Johnston, now dead, was a less interesting personality. Ponderous in the old Southern senatorial style, with a mind far more crafty than quick, he only once evinced a really serious interest in our Subcommittee's work. That was when he urged us, strenuously and repeatedly, to look into the question of alleged Communist subversion in Puerto Rico. Morris and I were puzzled at Johnston's insistence on this score, but loyally made a preliminary investigation of the matter—only to find, and report to Johnston, that Communism did not appear to be a special problem in Puerto Rico at that time.*

Of Senator McClellan, as I have already said, we saw less, and only one incident concerning him stands out in my memory. One afternoon we badly wanted to take the testimony of a friendly witness in executive session, but could find no senator available to formalize the proceeding

---

* I am bound to say that, some years later, I read with interest (though, to be sure, with caution) the assertion of Arturo Espaillat, Trujillo's paymaster to U.S. politicians, that the Dominican dictator had paid $75,000 to Olin Johnston in 1957 in an effort to stimulate American interest in the problem of Communism in the Caribbean. Espaillat first told of the alleged payment to Johnston in 1962, in an article in the Toronto *Globe and Mail*, and he repeated the story in 1963 in his book *Trujillo: The Last Caesar*. (The book, however, described the recipient of the $75,000 only as "a powerful Atlantic seaboard senator.") The charge received gingerly mention in one or two U.S. papers, but the American press in general would not touch it. Johnston simply ignored it, and he died in 1965 with the accusation unproved.

by his physical presence. At last, in response to Bob Morris' piteous importunings, Senator McClellan agreed to preside, and I was dispatched posthaste to his office with the witness and a shorthand reporter. We found the Senator in conference with Robert Kennedy (now New York's junior senator), who at the time was assistant counsel to the Permanent Investigation Subcommittee of McClellan's Government Operations Committee. Evidently their business (which probably concerned their then current investigation of corrupt labor unions) was urgent too, for McClellan swore in my witness, listened as I started interrogating him in a little window alcove of the office, and then began strolling back and forth between the alcove and his desk, beside which Kennedy was seated. It was a rather weird experience for me, questioning a witness as my chairman divided his attention between our hearing and his conference with Kennedy; but I was grateful to McClellan for taking on the hearing at all, amid his other pressing business. Moreover, half of John McClellan's time and attention were worth more than the undiluted devotion of many a less competent member of the Senate. This craggy, humorless Arkansan is, in my opinion, one of the ablest and hardest-working senators of them all.

Among the Republicans on the Subcommittee, first place indisputably belonged to William Jenner. I have no idea when he was nicknamed "Wild Bill," but no one who knew him ever doubted why. A short, wiry man with piercing black eyes, he possessed a fiery temper and one of the gamiest vocabularies in the United States Senate. He reminded one of a bantam rooster, and of his devotion to the anti-Communist cause there was no doubt whatever. There seemed no question, either, of his popularity in Indiana—where, as Westbrook Pegler once noted, men take off their neckties without untying the knot. It was told of Jenner that once, as a member of the Indiana State Senate, he tried and failed three times, during an excited session, to obtain recognition from the President *pro tem* of the Senate. Finally he picked up a heavy book and threw it squarely at the man's head. When it landed, Jenner yelled, "There, you sonofabitch; do you see me now?" That was Bill Jenner.

Jenner retired from the Senate in 1958—not because he feared he would lose if he ran for reelection (even his worst enemies conceded him an excellent chance to win), but because he and his wife genuinely preferred life back home in Indiana to life in Washington. Aware of newspaper reports that he was thinking of retiring, I once presumed to encourage him to stay on. I had run into him at Washington's National Airport, where it developed that we were booked on the same plane to New Orleans for the Subcommittee's hearings there (see Chapter 2). (As I paused to buy a quarter's worth of life insurance at a machine, I asked the senator whether he wanted to do likewise. Jenner, who had a wicked sense of humor, replied, "Naw, Rusher, if I die my wife'll just marry some no-good bastard and he'll get it all.") On the plane, I gently urged him to run again, but he was gloomy and tired: "Aw, Rusher, the newspapers beat your brains out, and the slick magazines beat your brains out, and you get awful tired. The other day my son Billy came home from school and said, 'Dad, we were reading in *Time* magazine today where it said there are 46 Republican senators and William Jenner. Does that mean you're like Wayne Morse?' And boy," Jenner groaned, "that hurts." In a minute or two he brightened: "Still, I don't know. Probably somebody'll say something that'll make me mad, and I'll run." I had to let it go at that, but it was not to be.

Arthur Watkins, the second ranking Republican on the Subcommittee, was a grave and dignified man with silver-white hair who had once been a district judge in Utah. I have no doubt that his personal instincts were profoundly conservative, but either political opportunism or stark necessity had made him painfully subservient to the Eisenhower administration and, more generally, to the liberal pressures that rain down constantly upon every senator. In sessions of the full Judiciary Committee (which were normally held every Monday morning, and which I customarily attended to watch over the fortunes of legislation reported by our Subcommittee to the full Committee), it was no unusual thing to see Watkins literally stall important votes to gain time within which to obtain his marching orders from the White House.

Watkins had chaired the 1954 senatorial inquiry into McCarthy's conduct and then had voted, with 21 other Republican senators (out of 48), for the resolution condemning the Wisconsan, and I suspect that as time went on he may have become obsessed with the need to justify his action. Certainly that is the only way I can explain his strange behavior one day early in 1957, not long before McCarthy's death, when I took to his office some Subcommittee document that needed his signature. He knew me only as a junior counsel to the Subcommittee, and I do not suppose we had exchanged more than a dozen words of personal conversation during the year I had been on its staff. Yet on this particular day, as I sat across his big desk with the document in my hand, he began obscurely to reminisce—about McCarthy, about the condemnation resolution, about why he had voted as he had. Gradually it seemed to me that I faded entirely from his vision—or, perhaps more accurately, that I grew in his eyes into a symbol of all the people who disapproved of his action. On and on he rambled, justifying, explaining, almost pleading. Although privately I had only contempt for his weakness, both on the McCarthy vote and in general, I was far too diplomatic to reveal my attitude to a man who, after all, was a member of the Subcommittee. I confined myself to avoiding any substantive approval of the points he was making so passionately and merely murmured politely from time to time: "Hm . . . I see . . . Oh? . . . Really?" At last, exhausted, he stopped; I obtained the desired signature, and left.

Herman Welker was a man much more in the Jenner mold, fiery, outspoken, pugnacious. In meetings of the full Judiciary Committee I often saw him bury his head in his arms on the green baize of the long table around which the senators met, and I supposed—as I am sure many others supposed—that he was suffering from a hangover. The truth, though I did not know it (and I believe he did not know it himself), was that his headaches were the first symptom of the brain tumor that was to kill him in October 1957. In retrospect, I believe that the pain he was enduring was responsible for the often sharp way in which he treated members of the Subcommittee staff, including me. Certainly I treasure the memory of a day when, apparently with nothing much on his mind, he dropped into the little office I shared with Bob Morris and found me there alone. That day, at least, he was at peace; and I found him, to my astonishment, one of the most charming personalities I had ever met. We must have chatted for a half hour or more, as he described to me various experiences he had had as an Air Force enlisted man in World War II. When he finally left, I understood at last why the people of Idaho had made him their senator. In the election of 1956 he ran again and was defeated by a young Boise attorney, Frank Church, in a campaign fetid with totally false rumors of Welker's alcoholism. Less than a year later he was dead.

Of Senators Butler, Hennings, and Daniel I simply did not see enough to form any valid opinion; and the same was true of Senators Sam J. Ervin Jr. of North Carolina and Matthew A. Neely of West Virginia, who replaced Hennings and Daniel in the reshuffle of committee assignments that occurred with the opening of the new (85th) Congress in January 1957. The replacement of Welker by Senator Roman L. Hruska of Nebraska, however, provided us with a powerful addition to our tiny band of able and willing senators. This tall, square-jawed prairie lawyer with the deliberate manner and the easy smile impressed me enormously. Without fanfare or grandstanding, but with consummate care and skill, he would plan and conduct major investigations, laying the legal foundations for his questions like a master mason laying stones. And yet, whatever the pressures, he always had a kind word and a ready smile for the Subcommittee staff. It is no accident that this quiet, unassuming man, whose name is not even yet well known to most Americans, is widely acknowledged as the probable successor to Everett

Dirksen one of these days as the leader of the Republican Party in the U.S. Senate.

From my vantage point with the Subcommittee, the only other senators I saw at close range were those who, though not on the ISSC, were members of its parent Judiciary Committee. Of those whom I saw in action repeatedly in the Committee's Monday sessions (which were closed to outsiders), mental snapshots of only three remain: Estes Kefauver of Tennessee, stolidly chewing on a cigar which he customarily not only did not light but *did not remove from its cellophane sheath*; magnificent old Joseph O'Mahoney of Wyoming, with that majestic silver mane, and his Irish eyes dancing under great, bushy eyebrows, captivating his fellow senators with samples of the ornate speaking style he had mastered so superbly; Everett Dirksen—the Wonderful Wizard of Ooze—pouring his unctuous bass-baritone voice like a lubricant over any problem that threatened to become abrasive. The United States Senate may have its full share of heroes and rascals, but it is never, or at any rate only very rarely, dull.

Senators not on the Judiciary Committee were little more than newspaper-familiar faces to me. Occasionally I would see Vice President Nixon hurrying along a hall, his dark eyes looking out noncommittally from beneath heavy brows; he planned to be elected President in 1960 and had a lot on his mind. So did Senator John F. Kennedy of Massachusetts—striding along there, looking very young, with hips incredibly slimmer than the shoulders he carried hunched forward, like a football lineman. Of majority leader Lyndon Johnson I saw next to nothing, save when business took me over to the Senate floor or the cloakrooms. There often he could be seen, his arm resting persuasively on some colleague's shoulder as he asked a legislative favor. Once in a while, in an elevator or on the little subway that runs between the Senate Office Building and the Senate wing of the Capitol, I would share a ride with Senator Hubert Humphrey of Minnesota, whose expression, I am sorry to say, always struck me as almost unbelievably calculating. Certainly, as Carlyle said of the procession of the Commons Deputies from Versailles to Notre Dame on May 4, 1789, "there was Futurity enough" on the Senate side of Capitol Hill in those years 1956 and 1957. It billowed about us like a sea.

And then there was the man I was closer to than any other, the chief counsel of the Subcommittee, Robert Morris. Of medium height, with sandy hair and a cherubic red face, he reminded one of Churchill's dictum: "All babies look like me." Like the typical stage Irishman, he had obviously kissed the Blarney Stone, and his hearty, genial manner was studded with humorous remarks, extravagant compliments and infectious laughter. On the other hand, as is common among extrovert personalities, he also suffered periods of depression, fortunately not long, and certainly never long enough to impair materially his high appetite for action. In these Blue Periods, as I called them, he seldom realized that he was simply passing through a personality phase, and was quite likely to ascribe his gloom to some exterior circumstance, usually the highly unsatisfactory State of the Nation. "Come on, Bob," I once joshed him over the phone, diagnosing a recurrence of this sort of depression, "you sound lower than a turtle's toenails." But he refused to be amused, and shot back: "Well, seeing the way things are going, aren't *you* lower than a toetle's turnails?—I mean a turtle's toenails?" I laughed aloud at the spoonerism, but I couldn't persuade him to join me.

Luckily such episodes were rare. Working with Bob Morris seemed to me a high and exciting calling. On the subject of Morris' character and basic qualities, I can do no better than to quote from an article I wrote in 1960 for *National Review*:

What quality distinguishes him? Not personality—he is almost the typical warm-hearted Irishman, but no more so than a thousand others. Not intellect—though serious-minded, he is not by temperament attuned to the life of the mind. Not any special expertise—while he is surely one of the half-dozen best-informed men in America on the question of internal security, we all know men almost equally adept in their chosen fields. No: what sets Robert Morris apart is a trait of *character,* more important than warm-heartedness, more fundamental than intellect, more necessary than expertise. I shall call it, for want of a better phrase, an invincible innocence of spirit.

Anyone familiar with the ways of the world will know what I mean when I speak of the manner in which politics commonly corrupts men. Even making all due allowances for natural differences of attitude and temperament, it remains true that a steady diet of political infighting tends to coarsen, and ultimately to cheapen, most participants. They approach politics as reasonably honorable citizens, and by imperceptible degrees it sucks them into its vortex. The plainly right shades into the nearly wrong; the inexcusable slowly becomes the barely permissible. At last the best of men become very nearly the worst, and behave—usually in the name of some long-forgotten virtue—in ways that would shame a pain-crazed rattlesnake.

But here and there, now and then, some individual defies the pattern, and succeeds in the teeth of the seemingly universal Gresham's Law of politics. A Taft, a Goldwater, a Bracken Lee makes the truth pay off, for a change, and gladdens the hearts of millions who supposed that honesty could never again win an election.

That is the kind of cloth Bob Morris is cut from.

I doubt that it has ever seriously occurred to him to prosper personally, politically and financially, by consenting to "go along" with policies that he knows to be popular but considers harmful to the national interest. I saw some variant of that suggestion made to him a hundred times, and his response was always the same. The round cherubic face grew somber, the mouth tightened to a determined little line, and he slowly shook his head. That was all. In extreme cases one might hear a little grunt—a pathetic sound that somehow always reminded me of a game but winded boxer taking a body blow. But never was there a pause that could have been construed as an instant's hesitation, or even a worldly smile to signify that he had heard the wings of temptation rustling by.

As an investigator of domestic Communism, Morris compiled a record of performance that is, I believe, unique. He was a key figure in every investigation described in this book, as well as in scores of others —dating back to the 1940 Rapp-Coudert inquiry into communism in the public schools of New York, the ISSC's famous Institute of Pacific Relations hearings of 1951-52, and its investigation of Communist infiltration among American members of the UN staff in 1952-53. His chief talents lay in the pace he maintained, which exhausted just about everybody else, from the senators on the Subcommittee to the Communists they were investigating; in the care with which, nevertheless, he avoided pitfalls, booby-traps and soft shoulders; and in his unerring nose for the key point in a mass of heterogeneous information. His questioning methods, on the other hand, were distressingly casual—a world away from the glacial precision of Jay Sourwine, for example, who had each question typed in advance on a 3 x 5 card and turned them over, one by one, as the questions were answered. I remember one occasion on which Morris had questioned an elderly female Communist in public session for perhaps half an hour, eliciting considerable useful information despite her frequent grandmotherly recourse to the Fifth Amendment. He was about to wind up when a friendly newspaper reporter handed me a note: "For God's sake have him ask her whether she's a Communist." I passed the note along to Bob, who hurriedly put the question—and got another plea of the Fifth. He had almost forgotten the most important question of all! Despite such lapses, it was in no small part thanks to the skill of Robert Morris that the House of Delegates of the American Bar Association in 1959 commended the Senate Internal Security Subcommittee for its work over the years.

One other figure on the staff requires mention here: Ben Mandel, our Research Director. Thirty years before I went to work for the Subcommittee, Mandel himself had been a Communist—indeed, as he was always the first to remind us, a member of the Central Committee of the CPUSA. But he had broken with the Party in the explosion that followed Stalin's decision against the "Lovestoneites" (i.e., those Communists who, like Mandel, were supporters of Jay Lovestone) and in favor of the faction headed by William Z. Foster; and before many years had passed, Ben Mandel was one of the most knowledgeable and persistent researchers into the dark recesses of domestic Communism. He had been the ISSC's Research Director from its inception, and his efforts were certainly indispensable to us. As may be imagined, it was tremendously useful to have on the staff a man who was himself a former Communist, and who was thus able to talk with genuine understanding to other ex-Communists giving, perhaps, their first public testimony on the subject. Wiry, dark-eyed and still black-haired as he neared seventy, Ben Mandel seemed to defy both Communism and time.

As for me, I quickly found a small bachelor apartment on Capitol Hill, scarcely a block east of the huge Senate Office Building. (The so-called "New" Senate Office Building was just a hole in the ground in those days. By the time I left in July 1957 it was nearing completion.) I would usually have my breakfast at home, then report to the little room on the mezzanine of the rotunda at the main entrance of the Senate Office Building which served as an office for Morris and me and our two secretaries. The rest of the Subcommittee staff—researchers, investigators, clerks, etc.—was housed in larger but no more palatial quarters on the ground floor of the building.

Hearings, if any were scheduled, would ordinarily be held in two parts: first an "executive" or secret session, to test the responses of a potentially hostile witness—a session confined to the presiding senator and staff members, the witness, his attorney and a stenographer, and usually held in the senator's private office; and then a public session, held at a previously announced time in one of the large hearing-rooms scattered through the Senate Office Building.

Most often, perhaps, but by no means invariably, our public sessions were held in the ornate Caucus Room, not far from the entrance rotunda. (This room had become familiar to millions of Americans in 1954, when the Watkins Committee's hearings on Senator McCarthy were held there.) In the front of the room was a long green-baize table at which sat the presiding senator, any other senators present, and counsel. Facing this table was a smaller one, for the witness and his lawyer. Both tables were equipped with microphones. On either side of the smaller table, and running at right angles to it, were tables for the press.

Our hearings were routinely covered by all of the wire services, and usually also by several of the more conscientious reporters posted to Capitol Hill by individual newspapers and magazines. The rest of the room was filled with benches for spectators. Like the courthouses in any city, the hearing rooms on Capitol Hill have their buffs who regularly attend the public sessions. In addition, of course, whenever a particularly newsworthy hearing was to be held, the usual ranks would be swollen by an influx of comparative strangers—Senate staff members, curious Washingtonians and just plain tourists, as well as impassioned fans or critics of the announced witness. Well-known Communist personalities—for example, Eugene Dennis, the Party's General Secretary —could always count on an enthusiastic claque, as well as a booing corps. It was the job of the uniformed Capitol police to keep these various factions under control, and they did their job well.

When no hearings were being held, my over-all assignment was to assist Morris in directing, under the senators, the daily work of the Subcommittee. In particular, I was responsible for the legislation which had been referred to the ISSC and which was, after all, its principal *raison d'être*. This involved obtaining the approval of the members of the Subcommittee for bills to be reported to the full Committee on the Judiciary, and then appearing before the Committee itself, at its regular executive sessions each Monday morning at 11, to make the actual reports. This latter was an awesome duty, especially in the beginning. I was, after all, just one subcommittee counsel among several, all more experienced than I, sitting along the wall paralleling the long table which dominated the Judiciary Committee's own permanent meeting room. The senators, perhaps a dozen altogether, were ranged along the sides of the table in ascending order of seniority, with Senator Eastland presiding at its head amid a veritable moonscape of cigar ashes. When a bill reported from the Internal Security Subcommittee was called up for discussion, I was expected to give a succinct description of it and answer any questions the senators might have concerning it. My responsibilities included not only bills, but also resolutions citing for contempt of the Senate those witnesses who had refused to answer our questions and who had explicitly declined to rely on the Fifth Amendment as their ground for refusal. Several such citations were pending in the Subcommittee when I became associate counsel, and one of my earliest tasks was to put these before the full Committee. In addition, I was called on to prepare and report on the citations for contempt that were promptly earned by Herman Liveright and Pauline Feuer in our New Orleans hearings in April (see Chapter 2) 1956. For the rest, aside from hearings, my office day consisted of conferences, phone calls and correspondence on Subcommittee business. (Several extreme examples of the range of matters we coped with are offered in Chapter 11, "Far Out—And Still Further," pp. 277-283.)

Lunch was usually a quick affair, in a cafeteria maintained in the basement of the Senate Office Building for the myriad employees it takes to operate the vast and complex machine known as the United States Senate. We naturally tend to think of the Senate as consisting of just 100 men (96 in those days), and in a narrow sense of course this is true. But behind each senator—answering his mail, staffing his office, handling his business and political affairs, and in general running his life—are anywhere from 10 to 30 or 40 full-time employees. In addition, every standing committee and most major subcommittees (such as the ISSC) have their own separate staffs. Finally there are the people who work directly for the Senate as a whole, from the parliamentarian all the way down to the page boys, and the huge maintenance corps necessary to service the Senate Office Building: postal and telephone employees, police guards, even barbers. If I was feeling more than ordinarily hungry, or less hurried or a little more prosperous than usual, I would hop the famous subway from the Senate Office Building to the Senate wing of the Capitol for lunch in the Senate Family Dining Room.

The subway was an experience all by itself. Installed for the convenience of senators, and running through a spacious tunnel in a gentle *S* from the Office Building to the Senate wing of the Capitol, it was one of the most popular tourist attractions in Washington—certainly for children, whose eyes invariably popped as one of the noisy, rickety little vehicles sped them the few hundred feet from one building to the other. And I will confess that the ride never quite lost its glamor for me either, as I slouched casually onto a seat beside (say) Senator Dirksen and whizzed off on business of the United States Senate. For some reason, members of the House of Representatives had not yet (as of 1956) been favored with a similar device, though their office buildings were just as distant as that of the senators, and a similar airy tunnel, through which they were compelled to trudge, linked them too with the Capitol. Probably they prided themselves (quite mistakenly, in some cases) on a greater agility. The Senate, in return, condescended by naming one of its major committees the Senate "Foreign Relations" Committee, in contradistinction to the House "Foreign Affairs" Committee. ("Senators," one would tell you with a twinkle, "are too old to have affairs.")

The Senate Family Dining Room in the Capitol was a comparatively small and (during the lunch hour) crowded place, whose great asset was the fact that, unlike the Office Building's cafeteria, it was served by the central kitchen in the Senate wing and thus enjoyed the same menu as the nearby Members' Dining Room. Luckily it was by no means confined to senators' families; staff members were welcome, and I availed myself generously of the privilege. Everyone has heard of the famous Senate bean soup, served daily by that busy kitchen, and I cheerfully concede its excellence. But for me and for many others, the really supreme accomplishment of the Senate's talented chefs is Senate rum pie. If I am ever sentenced to be executed, I plan to ask for it as the dessert of my final meal. Unfortunately the execution will have to be scheduled rather carefully, for Senate rum pie is prepared and served only on Wednesdays. Why this should be, I do not know; conceivably, the Senate would stop working altogether and turn to sheer gluttony if it were served every day. Anyway, across the years it shimmers in my memory —that flaky crust, that creamy golden filling, that feather-light meringue topping. To paraphrase Izaak Walton's Dr. Boteler, doubtless God could have made a better pie, but doubtless God never did.

One unexpected and (to me) precious attribute of my job was the "privilege of the Floor"—the right, when business required it, to go onto the floor of the Senate while the body was in session. It was not a privilege to be abused; in theory I was required to obtain separate written authorization for each visit (unlike the senators' administrative assistants, who had blanket authorization). But the officials who guarded the main entrance from the Reception Room soon learned to recognize me, and in time I was striding quite casually around those august precincts. Directly behind the rostrum, running the length of the chamber, was a narrow corridor known as the Writing Room because it contained a number of desks well stocked with Senate note paper. More important, it also contained AP and UP tickers, so the senators could keep a sharp eye on the news (including, of course, any that they themselves happened to make). Behind this corridor, at each end, were ornate reception rooms, known as the President's Room and the Vice President's Room, used only for the occasional ceremonial visit of a well-connected troop of Boy Scouts or whatnot. Between these was a large and restful chamber, well supplied with commodious sofas and over-stuffed chairs, where senators—and senators *only*—repaired to rest, meditate, nap or (as the case might be) merely let their blood pressure return to normal. More than once I peered into its somnolent gloom in search of some senator, but I cannot recall ever disturbing one there and I am not sure I would have dared. Across the Senate chamber, facing the rostrum, twin doors on either side of the central entrance led into the Minority and Majority Cloakrooms—L-shaped lobbies with sofas, desks, and phone booths, where Democrats retired to plot against Republicans, and vice versa. These "cloakrooms" have passed into the language, but personally I never found them half so redolent of portent as the thoroughly bipartisan retreat behind the Writing Room, where a famous and powerful figure dozed on every sofa.

The greatest thrill of all, of course, was to walk through the swinging doors that led from the Writing Room onto the Senate floor. Bathed in a uniform and comfortable light, tastefully carpeted and appointed, with a small mahogany desk for every member, the United States Senate is a genuinely impressive place. What makes it especially so, of course, are the galleries—the seats for the press, for special guests, and for ordinary citizens, that rise on all four sides from the top of the paneled walls, giving anyone on the floor a quite personal and physical sensation of being carefully watched. It was a wonderful experience to step into the chamber during a Senate debate, pausing for a moment to listen to the speaker (usually, for some strange reason, Senator Morse of Oregon), gaze up at the galleries with their spellbound spectators, and then find one's senator and transact one's business. It was all very leisurely, save when a teen-aged page in his black suit came running at the beckon of a senatorial hand. But for all the air of indolence it was a busy and knowing place. Guided by the majority leader or his deputy, monitored by a vigilant minority, impeccably advised by a parliamentarian in constant attendance, faithfully transcribed by relays of swift stenographers, and of course instantly reported by the world's press, the United States Senate moved through its business day like some huge, well-run luxury liner. From time to time a peremptory buzzer would ring, not only in the Senate chamber, but in every office and corridor of the Senate Office Building across the park. Then the elevators and the little subway would be congested with senators hurrying to the chamber for a quorum call or a vote.

The bit of business I liked best, however, was still more formal. In the midst of a debate, the center door facing the rostrum would suddenly swing open to admit a messenger from the House of Representatives or from the President, bearing some official communication. The presiding officer would interrupt the discussion to recognize the intruder, who would bow low and say: "Mr. President, I have a message from the House of Representatives [or from the President of the United States]." A page would dash forward, take the document from the messenger, and convey it to the rostrum, where its receipt would be noted formally in the Record. Another low bow, and the messenger was gone.

For dinner I would usually go to the Capitol Hill Club, a club for Republicans only, that occupied a modest building on the House side of Capitol Hill. Walking slowly home again after a good meal, I would often stroll through the Capitol grounds and along the magnificent Olmsted Terraces that adorn the Western facade of the great building. There, below me, the vast Mall stretched away toward the sunset, punctuated in the distance by the Washington Monument's stately obelisk and, directly behind it, by the lower outline of the Lincoln Memorial. It was impossible not to feel, in such surroundings, a profound sense of obligation. I certainly felt it, and hoped fervently that I was discharging mine.

The social life of Washington notoriously leaves a great deal to be desired. In the words of one cynic, "there's one thing you can say about Washington: no matter how hot it gets during the day, there's never anything to do at night." The diplomatic corps is, of course, an exception to this rule, and no doubt there are others. But for a junior counsel to a Senate subcommittee in the years 1956-57, the boredom was fairly acute. One almost shining moment does stand out in my memory, however, and deserves recording here. Not long after I arrived in Washington I was invited (at the suggestion of Bob Morris, I am sure) to attend a dinner in honor of the visting English writer, Rebecca West. Miss West (she had not yet become, by royal decree, Dame Rebecca) had been lecturing at Yale and was now making a triumphal progress down the East coast. I was enormously excited at the prospect of meeting and talking with her, for I had long considered her (and still do) one of the finest living craftsmen of the English language. Her study of *The Meaning of Treason*, in particular, had fascinated me, and I was sure that my professional preoccupation with Communist subversion would provide the basis for a long and enjoyable talk with my heroine.

It was, as Beatrice Lillie remarked of another occasion, a marvelous party: in the form of a Hawaiian *luau,* complete with a glorious whole roast pig and subtly powerful drinks sipped through straws inserted in a coconut shell. It was also very crowded, and I consoled myself with a coconut-shell cocktail while what seemed like all Washington swarmed around the guest of honor. Another coconut, and I pressed into the swarm. A couple of coconuts later it was apparent that I was not going to have any very lengthy discussion with Miss West that day; there were just too many competitors for her attention. Then, rather suddenly, she was taking her leave. Coconut in hand, I joined the ragged line of those waiting to bid her good night. Slowly she worked her way toward me. If a long conversation was out of the question, at least there might be a brief but memorable encounter between kindred spirits. At last—the electric moment!—we stood face to face, and she clasped my hand.

"Miss West . . ." I began, a bit thickly.

"Good night," she smiled politely—and was gone.

A word in conclusion about the House of Representatives. When one reflects that the Senate and House are, after all, simply two different aspects of a single vast legislative process, it is incredible how little they have to do with each other in their daily operations. On the Senate side of Capitol Hill, whole weeks passed during which we shuttled back and forth between the Senate wing of the Capitol and the Senate Office Building and gave scarcely a thought to that other and even larger organization, in many respects our twin, that was living a separate life of its own just a few hundred feet away on the other side of the Capitol rotunda. In the Senate Internal Security Subcommittee, although we maintained personally cordial relations with the members and staff of HCUA, we actually knew very little more of their plans and actions than any citizen could read in the Washington newspapers. On both sides a courteous effort was made to avoid poaching on either subject matter or witnesses; but that was the usual extent of our liaison. Between the committees, and indeed between the two Houses of Congress as a whole (or rather as two wholes), the relationship was not far different from that between the United States and some close and powerful ally, like (say) Britain.

Such, then, were the scenes among which I was to move and work for seventeen hectic months. My bosses and colleagues came from all over the United States, and from almost every conceivable cultural, social and economic background. They differed widely on domestic politics, but all were agreed on the deadly seriousness of the Communist challenge, and on the deep necessity for America to confront it, understand it, and overcome it. I was proud to do what I could to help them.

2

In Sleepy Old
New Orleans

But just how much remained to be done, in that year 1956, in the matter of investigating domestic Communism? Granted, there had been a remarkable degree of Communist penetration in the 1930's and 1940's, not only into government, but into the labor unions, the entertainment industry, the press, the churches, even into business. In 1945, in the field of government alone, the Assistant Secretary of the Treasury (Harry Dexter White) was an agent of the Soviet Union; the Director of the Office of Special Political Affairs of the Department of State was Alger Hiss; the Deputy Chief of the Presentation Branch of the Office of Strategic Services (Carl Aldo Marzani) was a secret Communist; and that was just scratching the surface. But all that was eleven years in the past. Since then there had been an enormous wave of investigations and exposures; a huge public outcry; a major revision—indeed, several successive revisions—of the Executive Orders governing security; and not least, several major pieces of legislation, drafted by the Congressional investigating committees themselves, with a view to obstructing Communist activities. Surely the worst was over? Surely we could afford to relax now? Perhaps the worst was over, but evidence was not long in coming that we could ill afford to relax.

Sometime in 1955 or 1956, before I went down to Washington, Chairman Eastland had instructed the Subcommittee to investigate the matter of Communist activity in New Orleans. I have no idea why he chose New Orleans. It is the nearest really large city to the Senator's home bailiwick, Mississippi; perhaps that explained his interest. For our present purposes the point is precisely the *random* quality of the selection. There was nothing about New Orleans in 1956 to suggest that this sleepy, rather patrician old metropolis was a hotbed of Communist activity, nor do I mean to imply that it was in any way exceptionally so. Whatever degree of Communist activity existed in New Orleans in 1956 could, so far as the Subcommittee knew, equally well exist in any other city in America of comparable size.

The Subcommittee's investigators submerged. Their methods did not differ significantly from those of all the other investigators who, over the years, have sought to discover the facts about the domestic Communist movement. But I do want to salute at this point the prodigies accomplished by our tiny investigative staff. During most of my service with the Subcommittee it consisted of just two men: Frank Schroeder, a knowledgeable old pro, who seemed, to my innocent eyes, to know where just about all the bodies in America were buried; and Ed Duffy, a keen-eyed man in his thirties, who rarely missed a trick. Quietly, efficiently they moved through the shadowy underworld of Communist activity, bringing us what we—and America—needed to know.

In due course they surfaced again, recommending that we subpoena certain individuals—surely the strangest catch ever hauled in by New Orleans fishermen. Slowly it became apparent that the Subcommittee's investigators had come upon nothing less than a "professional unit" of the Communist Party, banded together for the study of Marxism, for mutual support, and (where appropriate) for concerted action. The terminology of subversion is a language all its own, the mastery of which is fortunately not necessary here. A "professional unit" or "professional branch," however, is the Party's term for a white-collar cell, consisting of professional people. It was just such a group that Herbert Philbrick, with the foreknowledge and approval of the FBI, infiltrated in Boston in 1947.

The New Orleans hearings began in Washington on March 19, 1956, with the appearance, under subpoena, before the Subcommittee of Herman Liveright, the Program Director of WDSU-TV, New Orleans' largest television station. Though the Internal Security Subcommittee had nine members, testimony could lawfully be taken (and ordinarily was) when only one of the members was present. (See the text of the resolution creating the Subcommittee, which is quoted on pp. 14-15.) This procedure, which is entirely customary in the Senate, was forced on us by the circumstance that each senator was on several subcommittees, and that all of them had to divide their time between the work of their various subcommittees, the meetings of the full committees to which they belonged, the sessions of the Senate itself and the not inconsiderable demands of their constituents. In this particular case, the morning (it being a Monday) had been consumed with the regular weekly meeting of the Judiciary Committee. Morris and I had attended, to report on matters concerning the Subcommittee. Then, after a quick lunch, we had convened an executive session of the Subcommittee before Senator Eastland, at which Liveright was briefly questioned.

As I have already explained, this preliminary executive session (which was standard procedure in our Subcommittee) served to sound out a witness before he was heard in public. It was also a signal protection to any witness who genuinely desired to cooperate but feared publicity. If the witness testified freely in executive session, and if it was possible—with due regard to the paramount importance of the Subcommittee's legislative function—to spare him the ordeal of public testimony, the matter ended there, with the witness' sworn testimony on permanent record but available only to the Subcommittee. (See, for example, "The Case of the Missing Witness," p. 266.) If, however, as often happened, the witness refused to answer relevant questions concerning Communist activities, either on grounds of the Fifth Amendment (against self-incrimination) or otherwise, then the executive session would adjourn and a public session would promptly be held. The witness' refusal to answer would thus be on the public record.

In the executive session Liveright, a swarthy, intense man, who was accompanied by his attorney, Philip Wittenberg, had refused to answer a whole array of questions, submitting a lengthy legal memorandum in justification of his refusal. At 3:30, therefore, again before Senator Eastland, the public session began. Bob Morris started it by reading the general statement of the purpose of the series of hearings of which this was one, a series entitled "Scope of Soviet Activity in the United States"*:

> MR. MORRIS. Mr. Chairman, before commencing the interrogation of this particular witness this afternoon, I would like to restate again for the record the purpose of the particular series of hearings being held by the Internal Security Subcommittee. I read now from the opening statement of the chairman:
>
>> We shall try to determine to what extent Soviet power operates through the Communist Party here and to what extent other organizations have been devised to effectuate its purposes. We shall study

---

* All testimony quoted in this chapter may be found in Parts 11, 12 and 13 of the published transcripts of the Subcommittee's hearings on "Scope of Soviet Activity in the United States," U.S. Government Printing Office, 1956.

the structural revisions that the Communists have made in their network in order to avoid detection, and endeavor to trace the movement of individual agents through these changing structures.

Under consideration during these hearings will be the activities of Soviet agents and agencies registered with the Department of Justice and such other agents or agencies not now registered whose activities may warrant legislative action.

We shall endeavor to determine to what extent this Soviet activity here is calculated to contribute to Soviet expansion abroad and to what extent it is working to undermine the structure and the composition of our own Government here. [As] the facts bearing on these issues are gathered in the public record of this subcommittee, [they] will enable it to make recommendations or determinations as to whether the Internal Security Act of 1950 and other existing laws should be repealed, amended or revised, or new laws enacted.

This witness is being called here this afternoon, Senator, in the course of that particular set or series of hearings.

Morris then took Liveright swiftly through his biography—backward from his television job in New Orleans, to a roughly similar job with WJZ-TV (later WABC-TV) in New York, and then still further back to various jobs in publishing houses and the like, in the 1930's and 1940's. The witness was extremely choosy about which questions he answered, repeatedly citing his memorandum of law (which he was allowed to file with the Subcommittee, and which was printed verbatim as an appendix to the transcript of his public testimony). But the crunch was not long in coming:

MR. MORRIS. Mr. Chairman, this committee has been informed that Mr. Liveright and his wife were active in the Communist Party of New York City, and that at the time and date they moved to the South, they were formally asked by their Communist Party superiors to keep away from formal associations with the Communist Party at that time in their activities.
CHAIRMAN EASTLAND. That was in New Orleans?
MR. MORRIS. In New Orleans.
The purpose of subpoenaing this witness and asking him the following questions is to determine to what extent Mr. Liveright's activities have been carried out in New Orleans in the framework of the Communist Party and to what extent they have been carried out in some other framework.

More succinctly, Morris' point was that, according to information received by the Subcommittee, Liveright had been ordered to avoid *open*

Communist activities in New Orleans, in favor of quieter kinds. But Liveright was in no mood to discuss the matter:

> MR. LIVERIGHT. Sir, may I stand on the objection that I have already submitted, on the grounds that, as it states in the objection, this is an inquiry into my political beliefs?

Eastland promptly moved to make clear on the public record what had become apparent in the executive session:

> CHAIRMAN EASTLAND. Now, you do not object on the grounds of the Fifth Amendment that your testimony may tend to incriminate you?
> MR. LIVERIGHT. No, sir; I do not.
> CHAIRMAN EASTLAND. You do not.
> I order and direct you, sir, to answer the question. It is a question that is pertinent to this inquiry.
> MR. LIVERIGHT. Sir, I must still stand on the objection as submitted.

The legal significance of this colloquy was tremendous. Under the decided cases, Liveright had a perfect right to refuse to answer any of the Subcommittee's questions *if* he "pleaded the Fifth Amendment," i.e., if he would, in effect, assert that a truthful answer to the question would furnish a link in a chain of evidence that might be used to convict him of a crime. While mere membership in the Communist Party was not (and still is not) a crime under federal law, the Smith Act and various other laws define crimes (such as advocating the violent overthrow of the government) of which Communist Party membership might be partial evidence. Accordingly, the fact of such membership, or other facts pointing toward it, can properly be withheld without legal penalty, *if* the witness will avail himself of the Fifth Amendment's privilege against self-incrimination. On the other hand, this particular escape route is understandably unpopular, since the Senate and the world at large are perfectly free to draw what inferences they choose from the witness' plea of the Fifth. In Liveright's case, the towering fact was precisely that he had *not* pleaded the Fifth. His memorandum of law, no doubt prepared by his attorney Mr. Wittenberg, set forth a carefully considered argument that he was privileged to refuse to answer because the questions sought to inquire into his political beliefs, and were accordingly improper under his interpretation of the First (free speech) Amendment. But the First Amendment had never been recognized by the courts as a valid excuse for declining to answer the questions of a Congressional investigating committee. Accordingly, if he refused to answer and yet would not plead the Fifth, Liveright was in grave danger of being cited and convicted for contempt of the United States Senate.

Citation for contempt is the Senate's normal method of punishing a witness' refusal to give testimony to which the Senate is legally entitled. It is a necessary corollary of the power to subpoena—indeed, of the power to investigate at all. Once a witness has been clearly directed to answer, and has clearly refused, the contempt has been established. The investigating body (committee or subcommittee) adopts a resolution citing the witness for contempt; the citation in due course is approved by the Senate as a whole; and the matter is then referred to the U.S. Attorney for the district in which the contempt occurred, who obtains an indictment and, if all goes well, a conviction—leading to a fine, a jail sentence, or both. Nor was this procedure honored only in the breach; numerous convictions had been obtained over the years, and there were several citations pending that very day against witnesses who had refused to answer questions put by the ISSC. Liveright and his attorney were well aware of all this; they had calculated the risks and decided to defy the Subcommittee on the gamble that they could get the courts to break new ground: specifically, to recognize the First Amendment as a valid ground for a refusal to answer. Hence the deadly and delicate minuet between Senator Eastland and Bob Morris, on the one hand, and Messrs. Liveright and Wittenberg, on the other. There was jail in the very air as they proceeded, with Chairman Eastland conducting the questioning himself:

CHAIRMAN EASTLAND. . . . Now, have you affiliated with a Communist cell in the city of New Orleans, composed of professional people?
MR. LIVERIGHT. Sir, I still have to stand on this objection.
CHAIRMAN EASTLAND. You decline to answer the question?
MR. LIVERIGHT. On the basis of the aforementioned objection; yes, sir.
CHAIRMAN EASTLAND. I order and direct you to answer the question, sir.
MR. LIVERIGHT. I must stand on the objection as submitted.
CHAIRMAN EASTLAND. Did you ever live at 333 Ware Street, New Orleans?
MR. LIVERIGHT. May I consult counsel, please?
CHAIRMAN EASTLAND. Yes.
(The witness consults with his attorney.)
MR. LIVERIGHT. I will have to stand on the objections as read, Your Honor.
CHAIRMAN EASTLAND. I order and direct you to answer the question.
MR. LIVERIGHT. I am sorry, sir. I will have to stand on the objections.

CHAIRMAN EASTLAND. And it does not include the Fifth Amendment?
MR. LIVERIGHT. No, sir.

There was more of the same, but the main thrust of the questions and answers was blindingly clear: Herman Liveright, Program Director of New Orleans' largest television station, would not answer questions concerning Communist Party membership or Communist activities—in New York or New Orleans, in his home or elsewhere.*

Having laid this solid foundation for a closer look at New Orleans (and thoroughly astonished the people of that city in the bargain), the Subcommittee swiftly scheduled further hearings in New Orleans itself. On Thursday morning, April 5, flanked by Senators Jenner and Watkins, Chairman Eastland gaveled the Subcommittee to order in a humid, crowded federal courtroom in the U.S. Post Office Building in downtown New Orleans. The proceedings were televised by WDSU-TV, whose Program Director had started the fireworks. Sitting behind the senators, I gazed out over the scene—a large crowd of curiosity-seekers, a generous supply of bailiffs and federal marshals, and a tense and hostile batch of subpoenaed witnesses, accompanied by wary counsel.

The first witness to be called was Richard Feise. Morris quickly established that Feise, a native of Madison, Wisconsin, had graduated from Johns Hopkins University in 1935, had then successively been employed by the National Research Project of the WPA (in Toledo), by the Textile Workers Organizing Committee (in Boston), as an economist with the War Labor Board, as Director of Industrial Relations for Higgins Industries (the great landing-craft builders, in New Orleans), and for the past six years as secretary of Port Travel Service, one of the eight travel agencies in New Orleans, the hub of much travel to and from the Caribbean and South America.

And now approached the Moment of Truth. The Subcommittee had already heard Feise in executive session and knew that, for whatever

---

* Mr. Liveright ultimately won his gamble. Twice convicted of contempt of the Senate, he was twice freed by higher courts, most recently on April 29, 1965, by the United States Court of Appeals for the District of Columbia, which reversed his second conviction on the highly technical ground that the subpoena served on him was invalid because it was issued without obtaining the formal approval of a majority of the Subcommittee in advance. The Subcommittee, as we have seen, normally acted on the initiative of its chairman, and the other members never gave the slightest sign that they objected to this procedure—let alone to the New Orleans hearings, at which Eastland was (exceptionally) accompanied by two other members. Moreover, the Subcommittee members unanimously endorsed the very contempt citation thrown out by the Court. The Court's decision is to be understood as a result which it wished to reach on far broader grounds, but chose to base on a handy technicality.

reasons of policy or preference, he would not emulate Liveright and refuse to plead the Fifth. But Feise too had a lengthy statement to read, in which the crucial plea of the Fifth was made just once, surrounded (and hopefully obscured) by a great deal of legal parsley about the Ninth and Tenth Amendments and copious judicial quotations. The Subcommittee's task at this point was to ask the key questions about Communist activity and establish quite clearly Feise's refusal to answer them *on the ground of potential self-incrimination.* Morris proceeded directly:

MR. MORRIS. Mr. Feise, have you been the head of the professional branch of the Communist Party here in New Orleans?

MR. FEISE. Have I been what?

MR. MORRIS. The head of the professional branch of the Communist Party in New Orleans.

MR. FEISE. Mr. Chairman, I object to that question, and I don't think I should answer it. And I don't think I should answer it on the following grounds:

That it is an inquiry into my political beliefs.

CHAIRMAN EASTLAND. That is your first ground, that it is inquiring into your political beliefs?

MR. FEISE. Into my political beliefs.

CHAIRMAN EASTLAND. That is overruled.

MR. FEISE. It is an inquiry into my personal and private affairs.

CHAIRMAN EASTLAND. That is overruled.

MR. FEISE. And it is an inquiry into an individual's associational activities, with an implication about them.

CHAIRMAN EASTLAND. That is overruled.

MR. FEISE. I further object on the following grounds:

Any investigation into my political beliefs, any other personal and private affairs, and my associational activities, is an inquiry into personal and private affairs which is, I feel, beyond the powers of this Subcommittee. And in saying this, I rely not only upon my own opinion, but upon statements contained in the opinions of the Supreme Court of the United States.

For example, among others, in "United States v. Rumely," the Supreme Court of the United States said, in a concurring opinion by Mr. Justice Douglas—

CHAIRMAN EASTLAND. How long is that statement, sir?

MR. FEISE. It is not very long—well—

CHAIRMAN EASTLAND. Answer my question. How long is the statement?

MR. FEISE. It is 9 pages, Senator.

CHAIRMAN EASTLAND. State your grounds, now, and I will let you put that in the record.

MR. FEISE. Well, in addition to the grounds I have already stated, I also

think I should refuse to answer this question on the grounds stated in the Fifth Amendment—
CHAIRMAN EASTLAND. Yes.
MR. FEISE. To the Constitution.
CHAIRMAN EASTLAND. Now, by that you mean that your testimony might tend to incriminate you; is that correct? Do you think your testimony would tend to incriminate you?
MR. FEISE. Yes. That is why the Fifth Amendment is used.

To all further inquiries concerning Communist activities, Feise steadfastly refused to respond, stubbornly pleading the First Amendment and various other inadequate defenses, but always, under careful questioning, falling back on the trusty (if damaging) Fifth. Thus, when Morris took over the interrogation and alluded to certain information received by the Subcommittee, Feise replied according to his formula:

MR. MORRIS. Mr. Feise, to your knowledge, have plans been made within the professional group of the Communist Party here in New Orleans to have you replaced with Mr. Liveright, Mr. Herman Liveright, as head of the—in other words, to have Mr. Liveright take your place as head of the professional group here in New Orleans?
MR. FEISE. I couldn't possibly answer a question like that.
MR. MORRIS. Why not?
MR. FEISE. For the same grounds that I just stated.
MR. MORRIS. Among those grounds, do you claim your privilege under the Fifth Amendment to the Constitution?
MR. FEISE. Yes sir; I do.
MR. MORRIS. To your knowledge, has Junesh Jenkins been liaison between you, as head of the professional group of the Communist Party here in New Orleans, and the Communist Party organization?
MR. FEISE. I refuse to answer that on the same grounds, including—
MR. MORRIS. Mr. Feise, do you recall—
CHAIRMAN EASTLAND. What are the grounds? Let him state his grounds.
MR. FEISE. The grounds stated in my objection, which is part of the record.
CHAIRMAN EASTLAND. Every ground except the Fifth Amendment is overruled. If you avail yourself of the Fifth Amendment, that is your right, sir.
MR. FEISE. Senator, I am availing myself of the First Amendment, as I said.
SENATOR JENNER. That has been overruled, Mr. Chairman.
CHAIRMAN EASTLAND. That has been overruled.
MR. FEISE. But I reiterate it, nevertheless, because I think it is a fine amendment, and I think it ought to be kept alive. And I also avail myself of the Fifth Amendment.

Those interested in the further testimony of Richard Feise are referred to Part 12 of the Hearings of the ISSC on "Scope of Soviet Activity in the United States," pp. 587-610. It was plain to everyone in the courtroom that the Communist Party had a handy means of solving its travel problems, if any, as far as New Orleans (and much of Latin America) was concerned.

The next witness was Winifred Feise, Richard's wife. She admitted to being assistant librarian of the Isidore Newman School in New Orleans, but drew the line at saying whether she had been an officer of the Parent-Teachers Association of Jefferson Parish (i.e., County) "because it is a question into my associational activities." Senator Eastland nonetheless pressed the question:

CHAIRMAN EASTLAND. Do you avail yourself of the Fifth Amendment?

MRS. FEISE. Senator—

CHAIRMAN EASTLAND. Wait; just answer the question.

MRS. FEISE. Senator, you called these hearings, and I would like to answer that question so that it can be well understood.

CHAIRMAN EASTLAND. Answer—wait just a minute, now. Answer my question: Do you avail yourself of the Fifth Amendment?

MRS. FEISE. I certainly do avail myself of the Fifth, First, Fourth, Eighth, Ninth, the Bill of Rights, which gives an innocent citizen protection, in the Constitution of the United States.

The Subcommittee, temporarily interrupting Mrs. Feise's testimony (or lack of it), swiftly put on the stand Mrs. Lois Wolsch, the president of the PTA of Jefferson Parish:

MR. MORRIS. Do you recognize the witness, Mrs. Richard Feise, Mrs. Winifred Feise, who has just testified before this Subcommittee?

MRS. WOLSCH. Yes, I do.

MR. MORRIS. Who is she?

MRS. WOLSCH. She is at present—well, I tell you, she had asked me to relieve her of her duties because of a coming baby about September. She was my legislative chairman for the unit.

Prior to that, she was vice president—

MR. MORRIS. She was legislative chairman of the unit?

MRS. WOLSCH. Yes, for our schools.

MR. MORRIS. Do you have anything in your files that would indicate her activity in that organization?

MRS. WOLSCH. Here I have—these records that I have here are when she was vice president, for the years of 1953-54, and 1954-55.

MR. MORRIS. And these records, together with your knowledge and your experience with this woman, indicate very clearly that she has been active in the Parent-Teachers Association of Jefferson County?

MRS. WOLSCH. Yes.

MR. MORRIS. There is no doubt about it at all, is there?

MRS. WOLSCH. No.

Back, then, to Mrs. Feise:

> MR. MORRIS. Mrs. Feise, have you been active in the professional branch of the Communist Party in New Orleans?
>
> (The witness conferred with her counsel.)
>
> MRS. FEISE. I refer to the objections which you already have written into the record, and I stand on the First and Fifth Amendments, of my refusal to answer that question.

And so it went, for several more pages—monotonous invocations of the Fifth Amendment whenever a question touched on possible Communist activity. Mrs. Feise would not discuss her years as a student at the University of Chicago, or whether she had worked for the Communist Party among church groups, or what she and her husband had been doing on a trip to Europe in 1951. Bob Morris, sure that the record was clear, finally asked her to step down.

Next to testify was Mrs. Pauline Feuer, a hard-faced woman who, like Herman Liveright but unlike Mr. and Mrs. Feise, had decided not to cooperate and *not* to plead the Fifth. Since her decision ultimately led to her conviction for contempt of the Senate, it may be useful to quote portions of her lengthy interrogation. One interesting variant was her eagerness to testify that "I am not [carefully in the *present* tense] a member of the Communist Party." As to the past, however, she was much less voluble, and Senator Jenner sought to pin her down:

> SENATOR JENNER. Mr. Chairman, may I ask a question?
>
> CHAIRMAN EASTLAND. All right.
>
> SENATOR JENNER. I think maybe we can clear this matter up. Are you now or have you ever been a member of the Communist Party?
>
> (The witness conferred with her counsel.)
>
> MRS. FEUER. I am not a Communist. I refuse to answer on the same grounds in these [referring to a legal memorandum she had submitted]. You are asking me when I stopped beating my children.
>
> SENATOR JENNER. Mr. Chairman, I request that you order and direct the witness to answer the question: Are you now or have you ever been a member of the Communist Party?
>
> CHAIRMAN EASTLAND. Yes. She is ordered and directed to answer the question.
>
> MRS. FEUER. How many times am I going to be asked the same one,

when I have given you my refusal on this? I am not a Communist, and I refuse to answer on the basis of this thing here.

CHAIRMAN EASTLAND. As I understand it, you refuse to answer—you state you are not a Communist at the present time, but you refuse to answer as to whether you have previously been a member of the Communist Party.

(The witness conferred with her counsel.)

SENATOR JENNER. Let the record show, Mr. Chairman, that the witness, before responding to this simple question, confers with her attorney.

CHAIRMAN EASTLAND. All right.

MRS. FEUER. Pardon me, I didn't hear you.

SENATOR JENNER. It is just a matter for the record.

MRS. FEUER. I will simply state, I stand on my refusal as stated in my brief.

MR. MORRIS. Your refusal does not include your privilege against self-incrimination?

MRS. FEUER. Pardon me?

MR. MORRIS. Your refusal is not based upon your privilege against self-incrimination?

MRS. FEUER. It is not based on that, Mr. Morris.

MR. MORRIS. Mr. Chairman, I therefore suggest you direct the witness to answer the question.

CHAIRMAN EASTLAND. She is again directed and ordered to answer the question, under penalty of contempt of the United States Senate.

MR. MORRIS. Mrs. Feuer, did you attend meetings—

SENATOR JENNER. Wait a minute.

MR. MORRIS. Excuse me, Senator.

MRS. FEUER. I refuse to answer the question on the grounds I have stated there. I think this is the fifth refusal, Senator.

CHAIRMAN EASTLAND. All right.

MR. MORRIS. Mrs. Feuer, have you attended meetings at the home of Herman Liveright in New Orleans?

(The witness conferred with her counsel.)

MRS. FEUER. As a matter of principle—I have nothing to hide, and as a matter of principle, I refuse to answer that question.

CHAIRMAN EASTLAND. You are ordered and directed to answer the question.

MRS. FEUER. I refuse on the grounds stated.

MR. MORRIS. These grounds do not include your privilege under the Fifth Amendment?

MRS. FEUER. They do not include the Fifth Amendment.

CHAIRMAN EASTLAND. They are pertinent to this inquiry, ma'am, and you are directed, under penalty of contempt, to answer the question.

MRS. FEUER. I am very cognizant of that, and I refuse on the basis stated in the document you have in front of you.

But it was not merely Mrs. Feuer's stubbornness about the past that interested the Subcommittee. It had in its possession a letter published in the *New Orleans Item* for October 13, 1953, in which she had signed herself, "Mrs. Joseph Feuer, Chairman, National Legislation, Louisiana Parent-Teacher Association." As to this:

> MR. MORRIS. All right.
> Were you a member of the Communist Party on October 13, 1953, when this particular letter appeared in the *New Orleans Item*?

But there was simply no doing business with the lady:

> MRS. FEUER. I am not a Communist. I will not be impugned, and I am not answering that question.
> MR. MORRIS. That was not the question.
> CHAIRMAN EASTLAND. Yes, but you are dodging. Now, answer his question. He asked you if you were a Communist at the time that letter appeared in the *New Orleans Item* in 1953.
> MRS. FEUER. I want no tags of dodging put on me.
> CHAIRMAN EASTLAND. Answer the question.
> MRS. FEUER. I am [not] going to answer the question. Put a tag of "principles" on my stand, if you please. I refuse to answer that question.

One last question suggested the reason for Mrs. Feuer's infatuation with the present tense when asked about Communist Party membership:

> MR. MORRIS. Mrs. Feuer, were you a member of the Communist Party when you were served with a subpoena last week by this committee?
> MRS. FEUER. I have said I am not a member of the Communist Party.
> SENATOR JENNER. That is not responsive.
> CHAIRMAN EASTLAND. I understand it is not responsive. I will order her to answer it.
> MRS. FEUER. I object to that. This is an invasion into my political beliefs, my personal and private affairs, my associational activities. And I am very tired, gentlemen; it is in the record.
> CHAIRMAN EASTLAND. That is overruled.*

Next witness: Betty Liveright, the blonde wife of Herman, who fanned herself in the humid courtroom atmosphere with a paperbound copy of *The Fifth Amendment Today* by my old Harvard Law mentor,

---

* On October 3, 1961, in the U.S. District Court for the Southern District of Louisiana, Pauline Feuer pleaded *nolo contendere* to a charge of contempt of the Senate and received a suspended sentence of a year in jail and a $200 fine. Ironically, if she had contested the indictment and appealed her conviction, it seems likely that she would have beaten the rap altogether—as Herman Liveright did, and on the same technical ground. (See footnote, p. 42.)

Dean Erwin Griswold. Evidently she had also studied it well, for (unlike her husband) she invoked it liberally. When Morris had established that she had helped to produce "Tulane Close-Up," a public service TV program of Tulane University, on her husband's television station, he came straight to the point:

> MR. MORRIS. Mrs. Liveright, have you been active in the professional branch of the Communist Party in New Orleans?
> MRS. LIVERIGHT. May I consult with my attorney?
> (The witness conferred with her counsel.)
> MRS. LIVERIGHT. I refuse to answer on the grounds stated in my objection [another legal memorandum, identical with Richard Feise's].
> MR. MORRIS. And does that include your objection—your privilege under the Fifth Amendment against self-incrimination?
> MRS. LIVERIGHT. May I consult with my attorney?
> MR. MORRIS. You may, Mrs. Liveright.
> (The witness conferred with her counsel.)
> MRS. LIVERIGHT. Yes, it does.

By pleading the Fifth, Mrs. Liveright had spared herself a charge of contempt.

But Morris was not yet through. Into the record went a photograph published in the Communist Party's *Daily Worker* for May 10, 1941 (during the last days of the Hitler-Stalin Pact, when American Communists were still passionately *against* U.S. intervention in World War II), captioned: "Betty Liveright of the Yorkville Peace Council addressing meeting Thursday night." Into the record, too, went various nominating petitions for the Communist Party candidate for New York City Council from Queens in 1939, all bearing the signature of "Betty Liveright." But the Mrs. Liveright before us remained uncooperative:

> MR. MORRIS. Mrs. Liveright, I am going to present you with Communist Party nominating petitions, a sequence of them. These Communist Party nominating petitions bear the signature of Betty Liveright, signature of the witness; they were notarized on different dates.
> I ask you if you will identify these documents for the Subcommittee. (Handing documents to the witness.)
> MRS. LIVERIGHT. May I consult with my attorney?
> MR. MORRIS. You may.
> (The witness conferred with her counsel.)
> MR. MORRIS. Will you identify those photostats?
> MRS. LIVERIGHT. I refuse to answer on the grounds of the objection already submitted.

Brief testimony by a handwriting expert, Gilbert Fortier, established, however, that the signatures were hers.

Next on the stand was Junesh Modianos Jenkins, a small woman with a heart-shaped face and sharp brown eyes. Following the now-established pattern, she submitted an elaborate legal memorandum, which Senator Eastland allowed her to insert in the record; but the Fifth Amendment was conspicuous among the objections on which she relied:

MR. MORRIS. Mrs. Jenkins, were you instructed by your Communist Party superiors in Baton Rouge to become associated with the Istoma Baptist Church in Baton Rouge?

MRS. JENKINS. I object on the grounds previously stated.

CHAIRMAN EASTLAND. Did you live in Baton Rouge?

MRS. JENKINS. I did.

CHAIRMAN EASTLAND. When?

MRS. JENKINS. Two years ago, for approximately 2 years.

MR. MORRIS. Did you live in Baton Rouge under the name of Marie Pratt?

MRS. JENKINS. I object on the grounds previously stated.

CHAIRMAN EASTLAND. That is the Fifth Amendment?

MRS. JENKINS. No, I want to claim more than just the Fifth.

CHAIRMAN EASTLAND. All right, but you do claim the Fifth?

MRS. JENKINS. I claim the Fifth, the First, the Tenth, and the Ninth, and any others—

CHAIRMAN EASTLAND. Oh, sure.

MR. MORRIS. Mrs. Jenkins, did you live—

CHAIRMAN EASTLAND. Why did you use an alias at Baton Rouge?

MRS. JENKINS. I object on the grounds previously stated. If you saw that television show last night, you know—a man changes his name five times—

CHAIRMAN EASTLAND. Lady, I am not interested in television shows. I am just interested in facts. And you can help your country.

MR. MORRIS. Mrs. Jenkins, did you—and your husband, Grady Jenkins —live at 1017 N Street, Baton Rouge, under the aliases Louis and Marie Pratt, specifically up to 1954?

MRS. JENKINS. I object on the grounds previously stated.

MR. MORRIS. Have you been the organizing secretary and member of the Louisiana State Committee of the Communist Party?

MRS. JENKINS. I object on the grounds previously stated.

MR. MORRIS. Have you used the alias Judy Green?

MRS. JENKINS. I object on the grounds previously stated.

MR. MORRIS. Have you used the alias Mrs. J. W. Green?

MRS. JENKINS. I object on the grounds previously stated.

A trio of witnesses from Baton Rouge thereupon testified that they had known Mrs. Jenkins and her husband under various aliases, and on that note the day's session adjourned, near 1 p.m.

When the Subcommittee reconvened shortly after 10 the next morning (April 6), the first principal order of business was a report on an amazing cache of Communist documents discovered by the New Orleans police when they searched the living quarters of Hunter Pitts O'Dell, a young Negro who had been employed as a bus boy in the Holsum Cafeteria in downtown New Orleans. The Subcommittee had issued a subpoena for O'Dell, but he had evidently been warned in the nick of time; as the process server entered the front door of the cafeteria, O'Dell vanished out the back. The police, hurrying to his rented room, found no O'Dell, but did discover an astonishing series of documents. Hunter O'Dell, these made clear, was nothing less than the district organizer of the Communist Party in New Orleans, and also the leader of the professional unit or cell (otherwise entirely white) which the Subcommittee had unearthed. Ben Mandel, our Research Director, took the stand and reported that among the documents found in O'Dell's room were:

a list of weekly newspapers and broadcasting stations in Louisiana
a list of Methodist ministers
a list of Louisiana libraries
a list of Louisiana daily newspapers
a list of labor unions
a list of women's organizations in Baton Rouge (La.)
2 Social Security cards, made out respectively to Ben Jones and John Vesey (both aliases used by O'Dell)
handwritten notes on a Montgomery (Ala.) bus strike
a list of newspapers, together with what Mandel took to be code names of O'Dell's contacts on those papers: e.g., "Irv—*La. Weekly*; Walt— *Chi. Defender*; Elaine—*Pitts. Courier*; Monica—*Cath. Action of the S.*" etc., etc.
375 copies of an undated issue of the *Worker*, setting forth "The Southern People's Common Program for Democracy, Progress, Peace"
a document dated November 4, 1955, from the National Organization Commission of the Communist Party "To all districts," on distribution of the *Daily Worker*
an undated document headed "Proposals on Southern Party Organization—1955–56" containing *inter alia* the instructions: "Join organizations that these workers are in, wherever possible—churches, Democratic Party, NAACP, etc."
a vast array of Communist literature from Britain, Belgium, Czechoslovakia, India, China, the Soviet Union, Hungary, Poland and Rumania
an equally large quantity of American Communist literature

publications of numerous organizations cited as Communist fronts by
the Attorney General, HCUA, or the ISSC

Altogether, 175 exhibits found in O'Dell's living quarters were received in evidence by the Subcommittee. Understandably, we were eager
to question O'Dell himself, but he had vanished. Across the United
States, federal marshals were given his description and instructed to
search for him; but, for the moment at least, his whereabouts were
known only to his Communist superiors.

The final major witness before the Subcommittee in New Orleans
furnished a certain amount of unconscious comic relief. Calhoun Phifer,
a rotund, shrill-voiced little man, had decided to plead the Fifth Amendment, but had whipped himself into an authentic frenzy which he obviously hoped would not only obscure his plea of the Fifth but serve as a
denunciation of the Subcommittee in general and of Senator Eastland in
particular. I marveled at the patience of Bob Morris and the senators as
they struggled with this shrieking little Southerner:

MR. MORRIS. Mr. Phifer, have you ever been known by any other name
than Calhoun Williamson Phifer?
MR. PHIFER. I decline to answer on the statement previously read [another memorandum of law], including everything in that statement,
including all of the amendments to the Constitution that might apply,
and article 39 of the Magna Carta, if it does apply, sir.

But Senator Eastland was not to be distracted, even by King John's
charter:

CHAIRMAN EASTLAND. Does that include the Fifth Amendment?
MR. PHIFER. I don't suppose you know what it is.
CHAIRMAN EASTLAND. I overrule your objection, and order and direct you
to answer the question.
MR. PHIFER. Sir, I have no respect for your opinion of the law, and you
have no respect for the Supreme Court.
CHAIRMAN EASTLAND. And I have none for you.
MR. PHIFER. That is for me to say.
CHAIRMAN EASTLAND. And none from you.
MR. PHIFER. A person who has made the statement you made about the
Supreme Court has no right to talk about it.
CHAIRMAN EASTLAND. Wait just a minute. We have seen Reds attempt to
take over hearings.
MR. PHIFER. You better watch what you are saying.
CHAIRMAN EASTLAND. Yes.

MR. PHIFER. You better had; you can't be protected by that thing up there.

Eastland, however, was the soul of aplomb as he brushed aside Phifer's diversions:

CHAIRMAN EASTLAND. I am not going to let you take over this hearing. I overrule this objection, and order and direct you to answer the question.

MR. PHIFER. It doesn't mean anything, sir. Your contempt for the Constitution is pretty well known, especially the Fourteenth Amendment.

CHAIRMAN EASTLAND. You are ordered and directed to answer the question.

MR. PHIFER. I decline to answer, sir, on the same thing. If you want me to read the Magna Carta, I will, sir. Would you like for me to start there? That is 1215. I will start on down.

CHAIRMAN EASTLAND. I order you to answer under—

MR. PHIFER. You deliberately are maligning me by bringing me before this committee, by your own words it is detrimental.

MR. MORRIS. Mr. Chairman, may I at this point—

CHAIRMAN EASTLAND. Just a moment.

MR. MORRIS. May I point out this witness has been called here today because we have received evidence that in 1954 he was a non-dues-paying member of the professional group of the Communist Party in New Orleans.

The committee subpoenaed him, asked him if he would give us, give this committee, evidence of the activity of the professional group of the Communist Party in New Orleans.

Now I would like to ask Mr. Phifer, in view of that, were you in 1954 a non-dues-paying member of the professional group of the Communist Party?

MR. PHIFER. Sir, you can bring up all the questions you asked in closed session. I am not afraid of them. You can read the whole record.

MR. MORRIS. What is your answer?

MR. PHIFER. Everything I gave you the other day, sir. Read the entire record. If you are afraid of it, don't read it. Now, somebody has got to stand up to this thing.

MR. MORRIS. I ask that the witness be directed to answer the question at this time.

CHAIRMAN EASTLAND. I order you to answer the question, under penalty of contempt of the United States Senate, sir.

MR. PHIFER. Sir, I have stated all the grounds that can possibly be given. If you think you are going to frighten me by Fifth Amendment foolishness, I have rights under the Fifth Amendment, and I don't mind taking any rights I have, and you won't take them away from me.

Here Phifer seemed at last to be verging on an explicit plea of the Fifth. Eastland pressed:

CHAIRMAN EASTLAND. All right. Have you availed yourself of the Fifth Amendment?

MR. PHIFER. Sir, I have availed myself of every amendment.

CHAIRMAN EASTLAND. Including the Fifth Amendment?

MR. PHIFER. You won't bother me. I would rather take the Fifth Amendment than be a fifth-rate politician. I mean that.

CHAIRMAN EASTLAND. Including the Fifth Amendment?

MR. PHIFER. You hound me about the Fifth Amendment. Just go ahead. I know who is American and who is not, and who preaches sedition. Don't hound me about that. Just go on with it.

CHAIRMAN EASTLAND. Do you avail yourself—

MR. PHIFER. I don't have to plead the Fifth Amendment or the First Amendment. I will do what I want to, if I have rights within the law. I don't preach against the law.

CHAIRMAN EASTLAND. All right.

MR. PHIFER. All right.

CHAIRMAN EASTLAND. So you do not avail yourself of the Fifth Amendment. I order and direct you to answer the question.
    Read him the question.

(The question referred to was read by the reporter.)

MR. PHIFER. I take all the amendments that I have previously stated, and any others that I know of.

MR. MORRIS. Does that include the Fifth Amendment?

MR. PHIFER. It includes any amendment. Don't you know the Constitution—

MR. MORRIS. Does it include the Fifth Amendment?

MR. PHIFER. I don't care what it includes; you can't scare me by any foolishness.

SENATOR JENNER. You mean, Mr. Witness, you decline to answer the question?

MR. PHIFER. Sir, don't give me a lecture on patriotism, like I saw you did yesterday. I don't need a lecture from you.

SENATOR JENNER. I am not giving you a lecture.

MR. PHIFER. You sat up here and hounded somebody to death over Americanism. I am a better American than you ever will be a person.

SENATOR JENNER. Please, sir—

MR. PHIFER. "Please sir." Thank you.

SENATOR JENNER. I am asking you if you decline to answer the question—

MR. PHIFER. I have made it very clear, sir.

SENATOR JENNER. —because of your privilege under the immunity of the Fifth Amendment.

MR. PHIFER. Under all amendments, not just the Fifth; under all of them.

If you had any respect for the Constitution, you would accept the First Amendment; and if I had the money to fight you and had a Senatorial expense account, I would fight you just on the First.

Since I can't, I will have to take them all.

SENATOR JENNER. Will you answer the question?

MR. PHIFER. I told you. I made it clear. If you want to, you can ask me how many times you want to. This can go on all morning. It is degrading you, not me. Go ahead. Keep it up as long as you want.

MR. MORRIS. Well, the committee would like to know, Mr. Phifer, if you have been a non-dues-paying member of the professional group of the Communist Party in New Orleans in the year 1954.

MR. PHIFER. Sir, I don't want to get monotonous by saying the same thing. I am not going to reduce my rights simply to the Fifth Amendment. They are all amendments, including the Fifth—

There, at last, was the clear-cut plea of the Fifth upon which the Subcommittee had been insisting, and which Phifer had resisted so strenuously.

MR. MORRIS. All right.

MR. PHIFER. If you are low enough to keep hounding somebody about the Fifth. It was good enough for Jefferson, and good enough for me, and good enough for you if you are a good American. I doubt that you are.

MR. MORRIS. Senator, I think the witness has answered the question. He is invoking all other amendments, including the Fifth Amendment, and I suggest we accept that answer.

And that is how Calhoun Phifer, Tulane graduate, achieved the distinction of being (as far as I know) the only witness before a Congressional investigating committee who ever pleaded the 39th article of Magna Carta as a ground for his refusal to answer questions. But it was his plea of the Fifth that counted.

Thus ended the hearings in New Orleans—a considerable jolt to the good people of that city, who understandably liked to think of domestic Communism as somebody else's problem: New York's perhaps, or Chicago's, but not theirs.

But there was to be an epilogue.

All across the United States, law enforcement authorities had been asked to keep an eye out for the missing cafeteria bus boy and Communist Party district organizer, Hunter Pitts O'Dell. The Communist Party is pretty good at hiding its members when it wants to; but evidently the heat must have become fairly severe, because the Party soon made a conscious decision to surface O'Dell and get his testimony over with. One day shortly after the New Orleans hearings ended, the phone rang on Bob Morris' desk. It was a long-distance call from New York, and the caller was an amiable, soft-spoken attorney who had frequently represented Communists in appearances before the Subcommittee. He was as languid as ever:

"I understand you're looking for Hunter O'Dell."

"That's right," Bob grinned, knowing the search was over.

"Well—he's a client of mine, and he'll be glad to come down to Washington to testify."

"Fine! How about next Thursday, April 12?"

"We'll be there."

I was interested to see what this remarkable young man would be like. On the morning appointed, I met him at last at an executive session in Senator Eastland's office. Although carefully shepherded by his attorney, O'Dell was plainly scared, as hostile witnesses often were when at last placed under oath and questioned closely about their Communist activities. But he firmly and repeatedly invoked the Fifth, and we soon adjourned for a public hearing in the Senate Caucus Room. Here O'Dell underwent an almost magical transformation. The frightened bus boy suddenly blossomed forth for reporters and photographers as an impassioned spokesman for Negro rights, who professed to be outraged at the segregationist views of Senator Eastland. He swiftly produced a mimeographed statement blasting Eastland from stem to stern for his attitude on civil rights (which, however unreconstructed, was certainly not relevant to that morning's business). But O'Dell's answers under oath were more relevant and, in their way, more revealing:

> MR. MORRIS. Now, under what name did you work at the Holsum Cafeteria?
>
> MR. O'DELL. Before we proceed with the question, I would like to read this statement.
>
> CHAIRMAN EASTLAND. Now, wait just a minute. You are to answer the questions. This is an investigation.
>
> MR. O'DELL. Well, I understand that it is an investigation, and that is precisely why I have prepared a statement for this investigation. Will I be allowed to read it?
>
> CHAIRMAN EASTLAND. Now, answer the questions, and I will just consider the statement when Judge Morris* concludes his question.

* Morris was frequently addressed by the courtesy title of "Judge," in consequence of his service as a Justice of the Municipal Court in New York City in the early 1950's.

MR. MORRIS. Now, Mr. Chairman, our information is—and we received this on the scene—that this witness, Hunter Pitts O'Dell, was working in the Holsum Cafeteria as Ben Jones, and because he was operating there under the name of Ben Jones, he was able to deceive the process server, and we were not able to effect service.

Now, were you working at the Holsum Cafeteria under the name of Ben Jones?

MR. O'DELL. If I understand correctly, you have already placed that question to me [in executive session], and I declined to answer it under the provisions of the Fifth Amendment.

MR. MORRIS. Now, did you also move about under the name of John Vesey?

MR. O'DELL. I decline to answer that question under the Fifth Amendment.

MR. MORRIS. Mr. Chairman, one of the reasons that we have had difficulty serving this witness has been that we have now learned that he has been operating under three separate identities. We have found a Social Security card that was presumably his, made out to John Vesey, and another one made out to Ben Jones, and as we know now, his name is Hunter Pitts O'Dell.

MR. O'DELL. I would like to know—

MR. MORRIS. Just a minute, please.

MR. O'DELL. Yes.

MR. MORRIS. I would like to offer you two Social Security cards—each one bears a separate number—and ask you if in fact these are your Social Security cards.

(Two Social Security cards were handed to the witness.)

MR. O'DELL. First of all, I want to ask, where did this come from?

MR. MORRIS. Well is it your Social Security—

MR. O'DELL. I would like to know where it came from.

CHAIRMAN EASTLAND. Answer his question.

MR. MORRIS. They were found on the premises that you abandoned, at which you have testified that you no longer live. They were found there by the New Orleans police and they were turned over to the Subcommittee.

MR. O'DELL. I decline to answer this. I mean, you say they were found? I am not sure they were found. Maybe they were placed there, because it seems to me that you are trying to—

CHAIRMAN EASTLAND. Answer his question.

MR. O'DELL. (continuing)—to build up a case here.

CHAIRMAN EASTLAND. Answer his question.

MR. O'DELL. And I am answering the question, Senator Eastland.

CHAIRMAN EASTLAND. If they were placed there, say whether or not they were yours.

MR. O'DELL. I decline to answer that under the Fifth Amendment.

On the direct question of Communist Party membership and activity, O'Dell was equally uncooperative:

MR. MORRIS. Are you now the district Communist Party organizer in New Orleans?

MR. O'DELL. That question was asked previously and answered previously [in executive session].

MR. MORRIS. I ask you that question again.

MR. O'DELL. I decline to answer that question.

MR. MORRIS. Have you been the Communist Marine organizer on the Gulf coast?

MR. O'DELL. I decline to answer that question under the Fifth Amendment.

MR. MORRIS. Now, on September 24, 1954, did you attend the Southern Regional Convention of the Communist Party in New York City?

MR. O'DELL. State that question again.

MR. MORRIS. On September 24, 1954, did you attend the Southern Regional Convention of the Communist Party in New York City?

MR. O'DELL. I decline to answer that question under the Fifth Amendment.

MR. MORRIS. Now, in the year 1950, did you attend the New York Communist Party leadership school, which was under the direction of a gentleman named Al Lannon?

MR. O'DELL. I decline to answer that question.

MR. MORRIS. Do you know Al Lannon?

MR. O'DELL. Why are you interested in who I know? Now, what is this? An inquisition? Do you want me to sit down and list everybody that I know?

MR. MORRIS. Do you know Al Lannon?

MR. O'DELL. I don't think that that is pertinent to anything. What are you trying to do? Ask me, do I know personal friends or something?

MR. MORRIS. Mr. Chairman—

CHAIRMAN EASTLAND. I order and direct you to answer the question. It is very pertinent.

MR. O'DELL. I think I should read this statement here—

CHAIRMAN EASTLAND. Answer his question, please.

MR. O'DELL. (continuing)—before further questions—

CHAIRMAN EASTLAND. Answer his question, please.

MR. O'DELL. I mean, I have no intention of stating who I know and who I don't know. I don't see that that is pertinent to this hearing at all. That is a violation of the—

MR. MORRIS. What is your answer?

MR. O'DELL. I beg your pardon?

MR. MORRIS. What is your answer?

MR. O'DELL. My answer is that I decline under the Fifth Amendment to answer that question.

And O'Dell was also not going to say anything about the apparent code names found on a list in his New Orleans room:

MR. MORRIS. Now, one of these is entitled "Newspapers," and you have the expression "Irv-*La. Weekly*."
   Will you tell us who "Irv" was on the *La. Weekly* paper?
MR. O'DELL. So again you are asking me who I know, and so forth.
MR. MORRIS. Remember, our evidence is that you are the district organizer. We have here what appears to be contacts of yours under code names, or some kind of cryptic names, and this subcommittee is trying to determine the relationship of these people with you, who are the district organizer of the party.
MR. O'DELL. Under the First, Fourth and Fifth Amendments of the Constitution, I decline to answer that question.

Morris went straight through the list of code names—and it was a formidable list.

MR. MORRIS. Who is "Walt" on the *Chi. Defender*?
MR. O'DELL. The same thing.
MR. MORRIS. Who is "Elaine" on the *Pitts. Courier*?
MR. O'DELL. My answer is the same.
MR. MORRIS. Who is "Monica" on the *Cath. Action of the S* at 523 Natchez Street?
MR. O'DELL. My answer is the same.
MR. MORRIS. Who is "Arabella"-*Courier*?
MR. O'DELL. My answer is the same.
MR. MORRIS. And who is "JU"-*Advocate* and *Ethyl News*?
MR. O'DELL. My answer is the same.

So that—and more of the same—was that. The New Orleans hearings ended, as they had begun, in Washington; and in between the Subcommittee had unraveled the tangled thread that led from WDSU-TV's leonine Program Director to his Communist Party superior, the young Negro bus boy.

What came of it all? Was it worth it?
I have begun with the story of our New Orleans hearings, not because they were of great significance intrinsically but because they were the first major hearings in which I participated, because they so clearly illustrate the normal operations of the Subcommittee, and above all because they plainly demonstrated that domestic Communisn, in April 1956, was not yet by any means a paper tiger. In somnolent old New Orleans, far from the bustling centers of the North and East, a profes-

sional unit of the Communist Party, containing some of the city's most prominent citizens, had been in active operation up to the very day our subpoenas were served. If that was true in New Orleans, there was no reason to suppose it couldn't be true elsewhere—anywhere. And that, surely, was a datum worth having, in the post-McCarthy year 1956.

As one result of our hearings, that particular cell was thoroughly exposed and permanently put out of commission. Its members (those who pleaded the Fifth) drifted away, to lose old identities or assume new ones, and perhaps to continue elsewhere their dedicated efforts on behalf of world Communism. Where are they now? I do not know, and certainly the Subcommittee had no investigative facilities to keep tabs on them, even assuming it had a legitimate legislative reason for doing so. One hopes that, wherever they went, the FBI went with them, so to speak.

One member of the cell did turn up, finally, in 1962—and under circumstances that dramatically suggest some of the Communist Party's recent preoccupations. Late that year the *St. Louis Globe-Democrat* reported that the Southeastern Director of Rev. Martin Luther King's Southern Christian Leadership Conference (SCLC) was none other than Hunter Pitts O'Dell, the erstwhile bus boy and precocious leader of the New Orleans cell. In December 1962, Dr. King announced that O'Dell had resigned his post with the SCLC "pending an investigation" of the charges. It must have been a long drawn-out affair, and perhaps not without its moments of near-success for O'Dell, for it was only on July 27, 1963, that the *New York Times* quoted Dr. King in a press conference as saying that O'Dell had left the SCLC on June 26 for a second time, " 'by mutual agreement,' because of concern that his affiliation with the integration movement would be used by 'segregationists and racebaiters.' "

And—just perhaps—by the Communist Party too?

3

The Early Years
of Harry Gold

Spring was coming to Washington. I often wonder whether those of us who live in the northeastern quadrant of the United States fully appreciate the feast that nature spreads for us every year. In only three temperate regions of the globe—western Europe, eastern North America, and East Asia—do great deciduous forests dominate the landscape. Only there, between the tundra and evergreens of the northlands and the rank, riotous foliage of the tropics, between the featureless salt infinities of the World Ocean and the equally barren deserts of the continental interiors, do the broad-leaved trees, including the flowering perennials, hold sway. Working and living for most of my adult life in the concrete canyons of Manhattan, I have always thirsted for this beauty; in fact, only once in the past quarter-century (in 1944, when I was serving in the Air Force in India) have I missed making an *ad liminal* pilgrimage to my old college, Princeton, to slake my soul in the loveliness of the spring season there.

But nowhere, I think, does spring reveal itself more ravishingly than in Washington. This strange, ambiguous city—half world capital, half little Southern town—endures the winter in a gray, slushy monotony, with only the stately grace of the mighty Capitol dome and the Grecian perfection of the Lincoln Memorial to remind men of the ideal of visual beauty. Then, in early April, while cold sharp winds still whistle across the Tidal Basin, the Japanese cherry trees along its borders burst into rapturous bloom, a profusion of pink and white blossoms that simply refuse to admit it's still cold. Finally, as the old globe's northern hemisphere tilts ever further toward the sun, the airs of the Potomac valley soften and warm; every tree, it seems, is budding, bulging with new life. At last, overnight, in the wake of some mild evening, the new season arrives: young greenery, almost yellow in the sunlight, blinks on every limb . . . and the flowers bloom. Yellow flowers, white flowers, red flowers, pink flowers; small, shy petals in maidenly pastels, and great, creamy petals of magnolia-white. The whole city, from the majestic grounds of the Capitol to the tiniest grass patch in Georgetown, is transformed into one vast garden. The buttery yellow of forsythia challenges the eye at every corner; dogwood, magnolia, and azalea vie for attention; and lilacs still bloom in many a dooryard.

From the window of our office, looking across the Capitol grounds toward the imperious dome, Morris and I marked the progress of the season. The park which surrounds the Capitol is itself a major botanical garden, the home of a huge variety of trees and shrubs from every corner of the globe. That April we watched them all turn green, each at its own pace and in its own way, with exotic blossoms on many a twisted limb—a growing chorus of thickening greenery that slowly blotted the vast bulk of the Capitol from our sight, until only the statue of Peace and Freedom could be seen above the treetops, serene against the blue of the sky.

One of the finest qualities of my immediate boss was his restless imagination. Poring over the dusty annals of American Communism, he was able to sense as few could where fresh and valuable insights might be found. And it was one day during that greening April of 1956 that he hit upon a most fruitful line of inquiry.

Few names in the annals of espionage will ever be better known, let alone rank higher, than that of Harry Gold. In 1945, when American science had solved the problem of producing an atomic bomb, it was mousy unobtrusive little Harry Gold who had stolen the basic secret information from our scientific installation at Alamagordo, New Mexico, and delivered it to agents of the Soviet Union. For their participation in that theft, Ethel and Julius Rosenberg had died in the electric chair at Sing Sing in June 1953. Gold, and Ethel Rosenberg's younger brother David Greenglass, had saved their own lives by turning state's evidence, and both were now serving long terms (Gold 30 years, Greenglass 15) in the federal penitentiary at Lewisburg, Pennsylvania.

Both Gold and Greenglass had been fully cooperative witnesses at the trial of the Rosenbergs, and there was nothing the Subcommittee could add to the story of atomic espionage by questioning them further on that score. But as Morris shrewdly recognized, one does not become Harry

Gold, Atomic Master Spy, overnight. There must have been a beginning to the Harry Gold story—a long apprenticeship in Communism and espionage—before he had been assigned to the Big Case. What was that story? Whatever it was, it had not been relevant to the guilt of the Rosenbergs, and hence had remained untold at their trial. But surely it was relevant to one of our Subcommittee's principal lines of inquiry: "Scope of Soviet Activity in the United States." Morris decided to question Gold afresh—and Greenglass too, for good measure—and for that purpose Ben Mandel and I were dispatched forthwith to Lewisburg for a preliminary interview.

Early on the morning of Thursday, April 19, Ben and I set out from Washington in Ben's car: through Maryland's blue Catoctin Mountains, across the neat Pennsylvania farmlands around Gettysburg, bright with forsythia, yellow-green willows and flowering trees, and then up the west bank of the winding Susquehanna to Lewisburg. On the outskirts of the town, we rolled to a stop under the forbidding walls of the federal penitentiary.

I had never seen a major prison before, and I can affirm that the sight is depressing, even on a blue-gold day in early spring. At intervals along the high, bare walls, and at the corners where they met, ugly but highly functional towers could be seen, where uniformed men with submachine guns watched every move below. We were expected, of course, and when we had introduced ourselves at the main gate we were duly admitted—first across a sort of dry moat, then through another high wall with a steel door that unlocked by remote control, then locked again behind us with a dismayingly solid thud. At last we reached the office of the warden, who greeted us cordially and discussed the interview to come. He personally would be present at all times, and he made it clear that no harassment of the prisoners would be permitted (not, Lord knows, that we intended any). We could ask them questions concerning their past activities, and they could answer if they chose to do so. Since both men had already cooperated fully with the government during the trial of the Rosenbergs, and were eager to improve their chances for parole by further cooperation, we expected that they would be glad to tell us whatever they could.

The warden gave a brief order, and a few minutes later Harry Gold entered the small, drab conference room where we were waiting. I looked at him curiously. Well below medium height and correspondingly slight of build, dressed in blue prison denim and old sneakers, he seemed the very antithesis of a master espionage agent. Or was that very fact the man's secret? Balding, unimposing, slightly stoop-shouldered, with a moderately dark complexion and sad brown eyes, this man of forty-three could pass unremarked through any crowd—or, as it had developed, through the high walls of U.S. security into the most secret places of our atomic science.

We shook hands and began to chat. As we had anticipated, Gold was perfectly willing to talk frankly about his fantastic life story. As a matter of fact, it soon became apparent that he positively enjoyed doing so. Like many ex-Communists, Gold had become, as it were, a connoisseur of his own past. Highly intelligent, and now completely done with Communism, he had come to appreciate, as a sort of retrospective spectator, the high drama and low ironies of his espionage career. He told us that he had put the whole story down in writing when he turned state's evidence in 1950, so he had already fully reviewed the ground we were there to explore for the Senate and the public. And here the first bit of irony came to light. In his work as a spy, Gold had honed his naturally fine memory to razor sharpness. The mind that had learned over many years to retain complex instructions, and the dates and places of secret meetings, and code names and code numbers, now was able to summon up in wholly convincing detail the substance of conversations and actions that had taken place as much as a quarter of a century earlier. We let him take his time and tell us about it in his own way. Since what he told us in that first interview did not vary from or contradict, in any important particular, his later public testimony before the Subcommittee in Washington, I will consolidate and paraphrase both narratives here. Quotations from the transcript of the public hearing are taken from Part 20 of "Scope of Soviet Activity in the United States" (April 26, 1956); quotations not appearing there are based on my recollections of our first interview (or, in a few cases, on Gold's 1950 written statement, which is annexed to the transcript as an exhibit).

Harry Gold was born in Berne, Switzerland, on December 12, 1912, came to America with his parents in 1914, and was naturalized on his father's papers in or about 1922. The family settled in South Philadelphia, where Harry attended a public grammar school and high school, then studied chemistry and chemical engineering at the University of Pennsylvania. When the depression struck, the Golds were hard hit; after about two years in college, Harry was forced to drop out in March 1932 for lack of money. He found temporary work with the Pennsylvania Sugar Company but was laid off in December. It is hard, in these times of boom and affluence, to recapture the desperation of those days at the bottom of the Great Depression. Sam Gold, Harry's father, was out of work too, and it must have been nearly impossible for him to feed his wife, his two sons, and himself. "One day," Harry told us, "my father brought home some money—a few coins—that he had obviously begged, and offered them to my mother. But she was a fiercely proud woman, and she slapped them from his hand. 'We won't take charity,' she said. 'If we run out of money to buy food, I'll hang a herring from the ceiling on a string and we'll lick it. And if the time ever comes when we can't afford that . . . I'll take steps.' And I honestly believe," Gold added, "that she meant she would kill us all."

It was in this crisis of the family's affairs, after five or six desperate weeks, that Gold early in 1933 landed another job. A fellow chemist at the Pennsylvania Sugar Company by the name of Ferdinand (Fred) Heller, had a friend in the Holbrook Manufacturing Company in Jersey City. This friend, who was known as Tom Black (though his literarily inclined father had actually named him Tasso, after the Renaissance poet), was leaving his job for a better-paying one, and with Black's help Heller contrived to get Gold hired as Black's successor at Holbrook. "I can still remember the night I went up to Jersey City to take that job," Gold reminisced. "I was wearing a borrowed coat and carried my personal belongings in an old cardboard suitcase."

Up to that moment, Gold seems not to have been deeply involved in politics, though he shared the general socialistic sentiments, and above all the bitter resentment at the locally prevalent anti-Semitism, that characterized most immigrant Jewish families of the time. Heller, who was far more deeply committed, had evidently briefed Black:

> MR. GOLD. The very first thing that Black told me that morning—I got there about 1 o'clock in the morning—the very first thing he told me, he said, "You are a Socialist. Fred Heller has told me that. I am a Communist, and I am going to make a Communist out of you." . . . And he tried for a period of some months, up to September, from January to September of 1933, to get me to join the Communist Party. I attended several meetings of the Communist Party of New York—in Jersey City —and he tried to propagandize me in a variety of ways, but I just kept stalling. I had no interest in the matter whatsoever.

As a matter of fact, Gold never did develop any "interest in the matter." One of the greatest ironies in the whole story of Harry Gold lay precisely in that: this long-time Soviet spy never actually joined the Communist Party at all!

More recently we have seen instances—Harry Dexter White comes to mind, and there are others—of Americans who served the Soviet Union without joining the Communist Party, because they sincerely, if egotistically, felt that such subordination was beneath their dignity. With more than a trace of megalomania, such men believed—and were cynically encouraged by their Communist manipulators to go on believing—that they and Stalin were more or less joint venturers of equal standing, engaged in a common enterprise. But Harry Gold's reservations about joining the Communist Party were simpler, if not fundamentally more modest. He explained them to the Subcommittee with something approaching relish:

> MR. GOLD. I do think that this one point, however, should be brought out, and that was the matter that I was actually repelled by the people that I saw who belonged to the Communist Party.
>
> There was a man by the name of Joe MacKenzie [for example]. He was a seaman, and he used to get into fights with these big policemen in Jersey City, and he always lost. He had practically no teeth. There was a Reap Farga who one evening—the whole thing got rather dreary; it got to be around 4 o'clock in the morning, and they were talking about Marxian dialectics, and they had completely lost me—he got tired of it, too, and he jumped up and he said, "To heck with this. Give me six good men and I will take Journal Square by storm."
>
> These people appeared so unreliable, so completely foreign to me. I came from a poor neighborhood, but the people there were respectable. We could hold our heads up. These were a pretty seedy, shabby, and frowsy lot of characters. I had no respect for them, and I didn't want to be associated—frankly, I would have been ashamed of being seen with people like that. That was my reaction. So I didn't join the Communist Party.

In September 1933 the Pennsylvania Sugar Company offered Gold his old job again, and Harry accepted it and returned to Philadelphia. But he kept in touch with Black, and frequently went to New York City with him to visit a divorcée girl friend of Black's who shall be known here as Dora Gray. Dora had a flat on Ninth Street in Greenwich Village, which a circle of young Communists and sympathizers seem to have used as a sort of informal headquarters. There was always coffee on the stove, and usually a hospitable pot of mulligan stew. Gold recalls that Black, in those days, had a habit of searching the official reports of patents granted for descriptions of new processes that might be of use to the Workers' Paradise. Many of the patented processes were available from the U.S. Patent Office for the cost of a postcard requesting a copy, and Black would simply order them and pass the information along to certain contacts of his in New York, for transmittal to the Soviet Union.

One can almost glimpse, across a third of a century, the scene in that little Village flat: Dora playing the proletarian hostess, Black fiercely scanning the patent reports and pressing the reluctant Harry Gold to join the Party. About April 1934, however, Black suddenly changed his tune. As Gold described it:

MR. GOLD. Black came to me in Philadelphia and he said very frankly, "Harry," he said, "you have been stalling me. You have been trying to get out of joining the Communist Party. And possibly I don't blame you. You know, we are scientific men, and maybe we don't belong in. But," he said, "there is something you can do. There is something that would be very helpful to the Soviet Union and something in which you can take pride. The Pennsylvania Sugar Co. has processes, processes on industrial solvents. These are materials of the type which are used in various finishes and lacquers." And he said, "The people of the Soviet Union need these processes."

He said, "If you will obtain as many of them as you can in complete detail and give them to me, I will see to it that those processes are turned over to the Soviet Union and that they will be utilized."

And that is how I began it. It is a bald statement. I know that. As I said, you are trying to compress 17 years. But I got started. I have examined the reasons why I got started, and I believe that I got started for four basic reasons.

MR. MORRIS. Please tell us those.

MR. GOLD. First of all I owed Black a debt of gratitude. That job was not just a job. It was a job that kept our family off relief, and we had a very strong pride. The one thing we did not want and have never wanted was charity.

MR. MORRIS. Now, who made up your family at the time?

MR. GOLD. My father, my mother and my brother. My mother, in particular, was tremendously opposed to anything having to do with charity. And he saved us from that. That $30 a week that I made in Jersey City—I brought $20 of it home, and we not only lived on that, but we actually paid off debts; $30 went a long way in those days.

So I owed this debt of gratitude to Black for this job he had obtained for me.

Secondly, I got out of the very disagreeable prospect of some time having to join the Communist Party, also as payment for that debt of gratitude. I paid it now by what I was going to do.

The third thing is, I had a genuine sympathy for the people of the Soviet Union.

The fourth matter—and I think that this is important—is that somewhere in me, through the years—I don't know where I got it—but I got a basic disrespect, not so much disrespect, but I got so that I could ignore authority if I thought I was right. I was cocksure. I find that this is—I have seen it repeated in other people, particularly those who are in scientific fields. They get to know their own particular field. We get to know our own job, and most of us get to know it fairly well. And so we think that, "Well, if we are right in this, we are right in all our other decisions."

And so it seemed to me that I had the perfect right to take this authority into my hands to give information which the Soviet Union had no right to. I simply arrogated this right to myself.

Gold's forthright account of his "cocksure" attitude as a scientist, his readiness to break mere national laws in the interests of what he personally deemed a higher good, is of tremendous importance to an appreciation of modern security problems. It helps us, as perhaps nothing else could, to understand the motivation of those other scientists who, years later, were to betray the atomic secrets of the West to Gold and his fellow Soviet spies. The supranational character of the world scientific community, and its indifference to political barriers of all sorts, present a special and subtle problem to officials charged with the maintenance of national security.

In any case, every couple of months thereafter from April 1934 to November 1935, Gold turned over to Black detailed accounts of the secret industrial processes of the Pennsylvania Sugar Company and its subsidiaries: methods of manufacturing paper-sizing materials, vitamin D concentrates, sulfonated oils (synthetic detergents) for textiles, industrial solvents used in lacquers and varnishes (ethyl acetate, butyl alcohol, butyl propionate, amyl acetate, etc.), ethyl chloride (for local anesthesia), absolute (100%) alcohol, and other products.

As the flow of information, much of it in the form of blueprints, increased, a serious problem arose as to how Gold and Black could get it duplicated promptly, for speedy return to the file cabinets of the Pennsylvania Sugar Company. For a time Dora Gray, who worked for a law firm, was able to get the job done commercially by a company in the Wall Street area; but at last this began to prove a serious drain on the trio's slender financial resources. Black consulted his Soviet contact about the problem and promptly came up with a solution:

MR. GOLD. In November of 1935, Black came to me very jubilantly. "Harry," he said, "all our troubles are over. Now we can get all the information we want copied. I've got a wonderful setup. Furthermore," he said, "we have got some very good news about some of the processes you sent to the Soviet Union. They feel they are very happy with them. They've got them in operation. They're very pleased with them," he said, "and there is a Russian who works for Amtorg who is going to arrange"—

SENATOR WELKER. Is Amtorg, A-m-t-o-r-g?

MR. GOLD. A-m-t-o-r-g, the Amtorg Trading Corp. in New York City.

MR. MORRIS. That was controlled by the Soviet Government, was it not?

MR. GOLD. Yes.

He said, "There is a man who works for Amtorg who is very anxious to meet you. He is also the person who is going to arrange for photocopying any amount of material you want. And he can photocopy it and return it to you very quickly." And so I met my first Russian.

Gold's introduction to his first Russian "handler" was in the classic tradition. He met his friend Black one evening near Pennsylvania Station in Manhattan, and together they began walking down the west side of Seventh Avenue, away from the station. A stocky blond with an oval face and flaring nostrils fell in step beside them, and Black said to Harry, "This is Paul Smith."

> MR. GOLD. We walked along together without anything being said, and then the man motioned very peremptorily to Black—he just sort of shoved him off with his hand and said something to the effect that Black could leave now, and Black did leave.

"Paul Smith" gave Gold his basic instructions that same evening. His very first order was that Gold was to have no further contact with Black whatever, unless specifically instructed to do so. Then Smith described further information he wanted Gold to steal from the Pennsylvania Sugar Company—manufacturing processes, plant specifications, etc. Gold had only to bring the data to New York; Smith would arrange to have it copied promptly and returned to Gold. Next Smith demanded and received a complete account not only of Gold's life history, but also of those of his parents. Finally he ordered Gold to commit to memory an elaborate series of arrangements for their future meetings: not only a specific time and place in a given city, but (if either failed to appear) another time and place roughly one week later in another city; a third rendezvous if nothing happened at the second; and finally an "emergency setup," a back-up rendezvous, set a full month or more in advance, in case all else failed.

And so, in November 1935, almost a full decade before his theft of America's atom secrets, Harry Gold was fully launched on his career as a Soviet spy.

It was to be a busy decade for him. For a number of years he continued to be employed by Pennsylvania Sugar, and until midsummer of 1936 Paul Smith remained his Soviet contact. Then Gold was turned over to another Russian, identified only by the pseudonym "Steve Schwartz."

MR. GOLD. Where Smith was of medium height, this man was very large. He weighed maybe 220 pounds and was possibly 6 foot 2 or 3. He was very well built and very handsome, and a little bit of a dude. He even wore spats, but he was too big for anyone to tell him about it. And I continued with him, in giving him information that the Pennsylvania Sugar Co. had, but after a while we began to run out of information. Pennsylvania Sugar only had so much, and I had been very diligent, as I said, and we had looted them pretty completely.

Late in 1937, Schwartz in turn passed Gold along to yet another Amtorg man, introduced to Gold only as "Fred"—a small man with dark eyes and a mustache.

MR. GOLD. He insisted that I leave the Pennsylvania Sugar Co. and get another job, and he told me where to get the job or where to try. He wanted the Philadelphia Navy Yard or the Baldwin Locomotive Works or any firm, any organization, which manufactured military material.

MR. MORRIS. In other words, he was giving you the direction toward what job to take, but you were to take the initiative yourself and get the job?

MR. GOLD. Yes. I had to get the job. He couldn't get it for me. But he was giving me very direct orders. These weren't suggestions.

When Gold failed to follow through by landing one of the suggested jobs, however, Fred assigned him instead to the investigation of various Trotskyites concerning whom his remorseless master in the Kremlin desired certain information. In April 1940 Fred turned Gold over to his fourth Russian handler—introduced to Gold as "Sam," and later identified by him (from photographs supplied by the FBI) as Semen Semenov, who had the double advantage of being not only "the most American-appearing of all the Russians" but a graduate of MIT as well. Under Sam's direction, Gold during the next three and one-half years turned over a truly staggering array of quasi-military industrial secrets to the Soviet Union: information on the manufacture and developing of Kodachrome film, and its use in aerial photography; on nylon, from the DuPont plant at Belle, West Virginia; on highly nitrated explosives, from Holsten Ordnance Works; on the production of Buna-S synthetic rubber; etc., etc. Far in the past, now, were those pleasant evenings with Tom Black and Dora Gray in the cozy flat on Ninth Street. By 1944, Gold was deemed ready for his biggest assignment—the one which led, by slow, agonizing degrees, to that little conference room behind the high, bare walls of Lewisburg.

In retrospect, as Gold later told the Subcommittee, he could see and almost admire the way in which he had been manipulated:

MR. GOLD. We started off in a very innocuous fashion. What, after all, are chemical solvents? We started off in a very innocuous fashion, a very innocent fashion. But then, step by step, they advanced the tempo, they advanced the level on which we worked, or rather, they degraded the level on which we worked, because it is not a matter of going up or down. And you got used to it. It got to be a way of life with me.

It was a dreary, monotonous drudgery. If anyone has any idea that there is anything glamorous or exciting about this, let them be disabused of it right now. It is nothing but dreary drudgery. You work for years trying to get information. Sometimes you are unsuccessful. You spend long hours waiting on street corners. The success, the amount of success actually in the work is very small in proportion to the effort you put into it. And what became even more important, I was gradually losing my identity and my desire to be an individual. I was becoming someone who could be told what to do and who would do it.

There is, of course, much more to the history of Harry Gold, and anyone interested in pursuing it will find it set forth in the transcript of his hearing before the Subcommittee, and of course in the record of his own trial and of that of the Rosenbergs. There one can find the long, absorbing story of his introduction to Klaus Fuchs; of Gold's 1945 trip to Albuquerque; of his meeting there with David Greenglass, who was employed at nearby Los Alamos; of the Jello box top by whose torn halves they identified each other; of the crucial information on the design of America's first atom bomb conveyed to him by Greenglass, and by Gold to his Soviet masters. The Subcommittee's main purpose, however, had been to trace the less familiar steps by which Gold was first led into a career of espionage; and from that standpoint we may leave him now—with a final recollection of his appearance before the Subcommittee on April 26, 1956, a week after our first encounter in the prison.

He arrived from Lewisburg in the custody of two hulking deputy marshals. Looming on either side of him, they made him seem even smaller than I remembered him. When he was brought into our little office, Bob Morris, noticing the physical incongruity, chuckled and said jokingly: "Harry, they certainly aren't taking any chances on letting you get away!" And little Harry Gold, who undoubtedly wanted to cooperate but must have had small relish for this one-day foray amid the microphones and the flashbulbs, shook his head and replied ruefully: "Man, you could put a postage stamp on me and mail me back to Lewisburg."

As often happened in our investigations of Communist activity, our interrogation of Harry Gold suggested further lines of inquiry. What, for example, had become of Tom Black? How had *he* come to join the

Party? Who, exactly, were those Soviet contacts of his? Had he later wandered away from Communism, or remained a loyal agent of the Kremlin? Where, exactly, was he now? By 1956 he would be nearing fifty years of age. If we were to complete our study of Harry Gold's introduction to Soviet espionage, it was vitally necessary to find and talk to Tom Black. And in due course our investigators found him—still employed as a chemist, and working in obscurity in Newark, New Jersey, not far from Jersey City, where Harry Gold had first met him almost a quarter of a century earlier.

Black had been traced and found by the FBI in 1950, in the course of backtracking on the story of Harry Gold, and had cooperated fully with the Bureau at that time. He was equally ready to speak frankly to the Subcommittee, but he was genuinely terrified of testifying publicly. His colleagues in the plant where he was now employed naturally knew nothing about his Communist history, and his talks with the FBI in 1950 had been entirely confidential. Testifying before our Subcommittee in executive session was one thing; doing so in public would be quite another. Black was gloomily positive that his fellow workers would force their employer to fire him, in sheer distaste at working beside a former Communist and spy.

It was a serious dilemma, and not by any means unprecedented in the experience of the Subcommittee. Ordinarily, in such a case, the Subcommittee would be content to hear the witness in executive session and use his testimony only for background purposes, without disclosing his identity. But Black's private talks with us were rich in details that shed further light on the espionage operations of Amtorg in the New York area in the early 1930's. More important still in some ways, the name Thomas Black had already featured largely in Gold's own public testimony, and anyone reading the latter would be bound to wonder what had finally become of Black. All in all, it seemed impossible to close this particular line of inquiry without taking Black's testimony in public. Nor could Black force us to change our minds by threatening to plead the Fifth Amendment or refusing cooperation in some other way. He was already under subpoena and would in any case be identified just as soon as he took the stand. To plead the Fifth or refuse cooperation thereafter would merely make matters worse from his own standpoint.

Morris talked the whole problem over with Black frankly and sympathetically, and at last won his agreement to testify in open session in return for the Subcommittee's promise to commend him publicly for what was, after all, a belated but still valuable service to the Senate and to his country. On Thursday, May 17, Black courageously appeared before the Subcommittee in public session.

His story confirmed Gold's in every important particular and added some highly illuminating sidelights. Black had joined the Communist Party in New York City in 1931, enrolling in "section 2, unit 2-B," on the lower East Side. During the next two years he was transferred first to a Communist Party unit in Jersey City and then to one in Newark. The latter part of this period coincided with that in which Black met Gold and made those strenuous but unsuccessful efforts to recruit him for Party membership. But perhaps Gold's reluctance had more effect on Black than Black's pressure had on Gold, for at last Black went to the Communist organizer in Newark, Rebecca Grecht, and confided to her that his own deepest desire was to emigrate to the Soviet Union and find work there. Much to his disappointment, she told him that the Soviet Union was the one country in the world to which he, being already an American Communist, could never be assigned. Black reacted, not illogically, by quietly dropping out of the Communist Party. A few months later, with that disability now safely behind him, he walked boldly into the office of the Amtorg Trading Corporation in New York City and asked for a job in the Soviet Union.

The man Black spoke to at Amtorg introduced himself—correctly, for a wonder—as Gaik Ovakimian, and that name now occupies a prominent niche in the early history of Soviet espionage in America. To Black, a mere twenty-six-year-old Communist enthusiast, aflame to give his all for the Workers' Paradise, Ovakimian, of course, seemed just what he purported to be—a Soviet trading official, who might be able and willing to obtain for Black the visa he so passionately desired. To the practised eye of Ovakimian, on the other hand, Black must have seemed ripe with all sorts of interesting possibilities; not for work in Russia, of course—Ovakimian doubtless never considered that for a moment—but for gathering valuable information in the United States. Cynically but adroitly, therefore, Ovakimian lured the younger man on:

MR. BLACK. He told me that if he were to recommend me for employment in the Soviet Union, I would have to produce evidence of usefulness. Otherwise he could not personally make a recommendation.

MR. MORRIS. I see. What did he ask you to do?

MR. BLACK. He asked me to give him some information of a technical nature, which would tend to indicate my usefulness to the Soviet technology.

MR. MORRIS. Did you, conforming with his request, begin to supply him with information of a technical nature?

MR. BLACK. I did.

MR. MORRIS. Will you tell us for the record what material you gave him?

MR. BLACK. I gave him information concerning the processes for producing textile auxiliaries and tanning materials; other products of that nature, with which I was familiar. I wrote the processes up for producing these things, and included information on their uses and applications.

MR. MORRIS. Now, on how many occasions did you meet Mr. Ovakimian and give him the information you have just described?

MR. BLACK. Possibly three occasions.

MR. MORRIS. Where did you meet him on these occasions?

MR. BLACK. In New York City. We met in restaurants.

MR. MORRIS. Can you tell us with particularity in what restaurants you met him?

MR. BLACK. I don't recall what restaurants we met in, but they were rather good restaurants. In the Times Square area.

It must be from this period that we can date Harry Gold's recollection of Black poring over patent reports as the two friends sat around Dora Gray's flat in the Village. Rather soon, however, early in 1934, Ovakimian turned Black over to another Soviet handler:

MR. BLACK. Ovakimian told me that he was very busy and that he wanted me to meet a friend of his who would meet with me occasionally.

He said that he had too many other tasks to take care of, and that this fellow would see me and he assured me that the person I was to be introduced to was a friend of his, and I could speak freely with him.

MR. MORRIS. Who was this friend of his?

MR. BLACK. He was introduced to me as Paul Peterson.

MR. MORRIS. Was that his true name?

MR. BLACK. I am sure that it was not, although I have no way of knowing.

MR. MORRIS. How long did you deal with the man known to you as Paul Peterson?

MR. BLACK. I would say up until about 1938.

This "Paul Peterson" was, of course, the same man whom Black subsequently introduced to Gold in November 1935 as "Paul Smith." In the intervening period of perhaps a year and a half, from early 1934 to November 1935, Black, operating under the instructions of Peterson, started Gold on his long series of thefts from Pennsylvania Sugar, and methodically turned over the copied data to Peterson; but during this time he never introduced Gold to Peterson, or even described to Gold in any detail the route by which the stolen information was being transmitted to the Soviet Union. When the problem of duplicating the vast quantities of stolen data became too great for Gold, Black, and Gray to handle alone, Black simply reported that fact to Peterson, and it seems to have been this little crisis that persuaded Peterson to take over the handling of Gold himself. It is interesting, in passing, to note that while Gold was handled by Peterson (or, as he knew him, Paul Smith) only from November 1935 to about mid-summer 1936, and was thereafter turned over to "Steve Schwartz," Peterson did not personally vanish from the New York scene but himself continued to handle Black right up to 1938.

Unlike Gold, however, Black by 1936 had begun to develop reservations about his Communist masters which, while not leading for many years to an outright break with the Party, prevented him from ever developing into a true master spy. The Moscow purge trials of 1936, which shook the loyalties of many Old Bolsheviks (and cost the lives of hundreds of thousands), deeply disturbed Black, and he warned Peterson that he was thinking of becoming a Trotskyite. At first Peterson was furious and broke off their contact; but in a few months he arranged to meet Black once more. Now he was friendly again, and this time he actually encouraged Black's interest in joining the Trotskyist movement —though as a secret Stalinist agent, to be sure.

This interest in Trotsky, and the effort to penetrate the Trotskyist movement (which culminated in Trotsky's assassination by a Stalinist in Mexico in August 1940), were plainly a major preoccupation of Stalin's agents in the United States during 1937. As we have seen, Gold was at this same time being used by Fred to acquire information concerning various Trotskyites. Interestingly, Gold—who violated Paul Smith's instructions and saw Black again from time to time in and after 1937— compared notes with his old friend, who broadly hinted that the murder of Trotsky was in the wind. Neither Gold nor Black was very happy about it; but Gold, the automaton, plodded on, while Black, though continuing to cultivate contacts in the Trotskyist movement, edged away. Early in 1938 Peterson at last turned Black over to a new handler, introduced as "George" (and later identified by Black as that same Semen Semenov whom Gold later was to know as "Sam" and work for in the years 1940-44). After a very short time Black was again transferred, this time to the management of a "Dr. Schwartz," a Russian who actually had a medical degree and as Dr. Gregor Rabinowitz operated in the United States under cover of the Soviet Red Cross.

It was Dr. Schwartz who bluntly urged Black to go to Coyoacan, Mexico (where Trotsky was living), join Trotsky's household, make contact with other Stalinist agents there whose identity would be revealed to him when the time came, and "arrange for the assassination of

Trotsky." Black begged off on a thin excuse, and Dr. Schwartz did not press the point; but the subsequent murder of Trotsky at Coyoacan in August 1940, and the Communist "execution" of Carlo Tresca on a New York street in 1943 (after his trial and conviction for various alleged crimes *in absentia* in Moscow), struck terror in the heart of Tom Black. In 1940, in 1943, and again in 1945 or 1946, another Soviet agent (known to Black as "Jack Katz") made contact with him; but, while never refusing cooperation, Black managed to avoid resuming an active espionage career. His account of his last Soviet contact, in 1950, is worth setting forth here as he described it to the Subcommittee:

MR. BLACK. I received a telephone call from a Miss Watkins. That was the code word that indicated that I was to meet a Soviet agent—

MR. MORRIS. When was this worked out?

MR. BLACK. In 1946.

MR. MORRIS. In 1946 you worked it out with whom?

MR. BLACK. With Katz.

MR. MORRIS. With Katz you worked out a prearranged meeting whereby a phone call would come in to you and a party would announce herself as Miss Watkins?

MR. BLACK. That is right.

MR. MORRIS. And you didn't receive that phone call until 1950?

MR. BLACK. That is right.

MR. MORRIS. Four years later, and the call came in?

MR. BLACK. That is right.

MR. MORRIS. What were the other prearrangements about that?

MR. BLACK. When I got a phone call from Miss Watkins, I was supposed to go on the Tuesday following the phone call to the Trans-Lux Theater and wait under the marquee for 3 minutes, from 7:15 until 7:18, I believe, and identify myself by the color of my necktie and the current issue of some magazine, I have forgotten which.

MR. MORRIS. This had all been worked out 4 years earlier?

MR. BLACK. That is right.

MR. MORRIS. And you remembered the directions?

MR. BLACK. Pretty well; yes.

MR. MORRIS. That had to be quite precise, to wait 3 minutes from 7:15 to 7:18 under a theater marquee.

MR. BLACK. That is right.

MR. MORRIS. And you remembered that?

MR. BLACK. That is right.

MR. MORRIS. When this call came through, did you comply with the call?

MR. BLACK. No, sir.

MR. MORRIS. By failing to take the call, you broke off your relations with

the Soviet agents?
MR. BLACK. That is right.
MR. MORRIS. Have you received any contact from that time?
MR. BLACK. No, sir.

Black's testimony before the Subcommittee was legitimate news and was widely reported in the press, especially in New Jersey, where he lived. The very next day, the storm he had dreaded broke over his head; his fellow employees rebelled, and his employer curtly told him he was fired. Now it was plainly up to Morris to reverse that decision if it was humanly possible to do so. If the Subcommittee was to function at all, it was obviously of the first importance to protect the jobs, and in general the interests, of former Communists who cooperated with it. Morris promptly flew to Newark to address Black's co-workers and try to persuade them to change their minds. He pointed out that, whatever Black had done, he had done it years ago and now wholeheartedly regretted his actions. The crimes of a former decade could not be erased; on the other hand, under the statute of limitations they could not even be prosecuted. There was, however, one thing Black could do, which would in some small degree mitigate his offenses: he could testify, fully and frankly, before a duly constituted Congressional committee, so that the country he had once betrayed might better defend itself against similar betrayals in the future. This Black had agreed to do, fully realizing the penalties attendant on the inevitable publicity. If now he were to lose his job as a result, what other former Communist or former spy would ever again consent to tell the truth about his actions? The protection of Communist defectors, Morris emphasized, was in the highest interests of the United States, and to forgive them their past actions was, in the circumstances, an act of patriotism.

The workers listened attentively to Morris, and saw the cogency of his arguments. It was all very well for loyal Americans to get huffy about working in the same plant with a one-time Communist spy, but this was 1956; there was a cold war on, and there were higher considerations that must be borne in mind. To their credit (and to Bob's vast relief), Black's fellow workers agreed to accept him once more; and—after a private chat with Morris and, I believe, a phone conversation with Chairman Eastland—his employer also relented. Tom Black melted again into the anonymity of the New Jersey hinterland, a burly, graying figure with some astonishing memories.

But we were not quite through, even yet, with our investigation of the early career of Harry Gold. Across the intervening years, one could glimpse only dimly the form of Dora Gray, the Ninth Street hostess who had been Black's girl friend, and who had (according to Gold) joined Black in urging him to become a Communist. What had become of her, in the roughly twenty years since she disappeared from the lives of Harry Gold and Tom Black? Had she drifted away from her Communist friends, or was she now a disciplined agent of international Communism, such as Gold had become and had remained until his exposure in the late 1940's? Once more we sent our investigators down the past's labyrinthine corridors, and once again they found the person for whom we were searching. Dora Gray was subpoenaed and instructed to appear at our Subcommittee's office on a certain day in that spring of 1956. When she appeared without a lawyer (almost always a sign that the witness intends to cooperate), I was dispatched to talk to her and report back to Morris.

I have no idea what I expected her to look like. Gold, in his 1950 memorandum, had described her appearance in 1933, when she was about thirty, as follows: ". . . very graceful, of medium height and build, with straight black hair framing an oval face, an attractive smile (almost a grin), and a pleasant and direct manner." I turned from the hallway into the office where she was waiting, and introduced myself to Dora Gray. The years had been only moderately kind to her. At fifty-three or thereabouts, she was distinctly on the motherly side, and the hair that still framed her face was gray. As for a smile, it must have seemed to her that there was little to smile (let alone grin) about that morning. Over dark clothing she wore some sort of black shawl at which she clutched. She was clearly nervous and unsure of what was to come, and I did my best to put her at ease. I explained that the Subcommittee was investigating the early activities of Harry Gold and Tom Black in the Communist Party and in espionage, and that (as she was sure to know) both had publicly testified to knowing her socially in or about 1933 and for a time thereafter. I emphasized that the Subcommittee had no desire to exploit her association with these men, let alone punish her for it, or even, if it could be avoided, to compel her to testify in public. What we did want was her own account of her friendship with Gold and Black, and especially a frank description of her experiences with Communism, both in connection with the two men and independently of them.

My prologue reassured her; slowly she seemed to relax and indicated she was quite willing to speak freely. Senator Welker heard her in executive session. Since her testimony was taken in private, I cannot quote it here. But it is surely proper to say that it was not inconsistent with the story told by Gold and Black. It seemed clear, however, that Dora Gray herself had never actually been a Communist; as for the

Party activities of her friend Tom Black, and Gold's involvement in them, her memory was dim. It would have been easy to interpret this forgetfulness as evidence of a deliberate intent to deceive; but it would also, at least possibly, have been wrong. After all, twenty-three years had passed since these events, and for most of those years Dora Gray had undoubtedly been trying to forget them. Moreover, the sensational arrest of Harry Gold in 1950, on a charge of atomic espionage that carried the death penalty, must have shocked her profoundly, and multiplied many times the force of her impulse to drive her own recollections of the man into a far corner of her mind. As I listened to her talk—earnestly, softly, hesitantly—I could not bring myself to believe that she was deliberately lying.

Asking her to wait for my return, I hurried upstairs and reported fully to Bob. Dora Gray's testimony, insofar as it shed any light at all on the subject of our inquiry, was merely cumulative; every significant detail was already on the public record in the sworn testimony of Gold, Black, or both. It seemed pointlessly cruel to compel her to repeat under oath, in full view of the press, information we already had, and whose repetition by her could only cause unnecessary pain. After a brief discussion, Bob authorized me to tell her she was free to go; there would be no hearing. It was seldom enough, in the course of my work for the Subcommittee, that I was privileged to be the bearer of such happy tidings. I found Dora Gray where I had left her—sitting in a corner of our staff office on the ground floor of the Senate Office Building, watching the file clerks and typists at their work. I gave her the good news, then shook her hand in farewell. She paused a moment in the doorway, then with a faint smile turned and said to me:

"You know, Mr. Rusher, while you were away I was watching the young people on your staff here. They look like such *nice* young people —all clean, and handsome, and sort of . . . patriotic. And when I think of the work that they, and you, are doing for our country—well . . . I'm just very, very grateful." And then, to my utter astonishment, she picked up my hand, kissed it quickly, and hurried off—a grayhaired woman in shapeless black, shuffling down the long marble hallway.

The testimony of Harry Gold, supplemented by that of Thomas Black and further corroborated in various details by Dora Gray, constituted a single line of inquiry which shed important new light on a thoroughly murky subject, Soviet espionage in the United States during the decade of the 1930's. We had adduced fresh information concerning one major center for Soviet intelligence operations against the United States in those years—Amtorg, an organization which was ostensibly only a legitimate trading corporation, acting for the Soviet Union in this country. We had pinpointed the role of Gaik Ovakimian, and his successful use of Gold and Black to steal the secrets of industrial processes in the early years of the decade. Then—after a period in 1937 during which Moscow's orders were evidently to concentrate on penetration of the Trotskyist movement—we could see the emphasis shift from purely industrial espionage to the theft of paramilitary information as World War II drew near. The whole complicated rigmarole of Soviet espionage —successive "handlers" with bland pseudonyms; fantastically detailed plans for meetings, and alternative meetings, and emergency meetings; the gradual bending of the secret agent's will to new and even higher demands, until he was ready to kill, if need be, on a single crisp order— all of this we were able to piece together from aspects of Harry Gold's long spy career that had not been relevant to the spectacular atomic espionage trials.

Despite Gold's readiness to cooperate with the federal prosecutors, he received an extraordinarily severe sentence, thirty years in prison. No doubt the sentencing judge felt that, in the atomic era, espionage involving the theft of such deadly secrets was simply too ghastly a crime to be mitigated even by full cooperation; and perhaps the judge was right. But surely the parole board, which knew of Gold's unfailing cooperation with the U.S. authorities, and which further knew that he was not only a model prisoner but, as a technician in the prison hospital, was making important advances in the science of blood chemistry, could have moved more promptly than it did. In May 1966, more than fifteen years after the gates of Lewisburg closed behind him, they at last swung open again for Harry Gold. Blinking in the sunlight, smiling a little at the reporters, he climbed into his brother's car and drove off with him to their South Philadelphia home.

He is only in his mid-fifties now and may yet reasonably expect some years of health and comparative happiness. Unless I miss my guess, he is not only through with Communism but, in the larger sense, through with politics. At heart he is, and always was, an intellectual, stimulated by a mental challenge and still capable of responding to one. In any event, you can be sure that if his old Russian superiors were ever to contact him again, you could put a postage stamp on Harry Gold and mail him back to the comparative safety of Lewisburg.

4

The Termites
in the Treasury

Ordinary citizens who become concerned at the degree of Communist penetration of our society, and especially of our government, often mistakenly suppose that every concealed Communist is busily engaged in "policy perversion," i.e., in twisting or slanting our national policies and actions in ways favorable to the Communist cause. Once this assumption has taken root, moreover, it seems perfectly proper to reason backward, inductively, from the number of things that "go wrong" to the number of hidden Communists who must be manipulating things so that they *do* go wrong. And since, in this imperfect world, things are forever going wrong, it soon becomes necessary to posit the existence of a perfectly appalling number of Communists busily at work to bring about these results.

Actually, on the evidence of the investigations conducted by HCUA and the ISSC over the years, policy perversion does not seem to have played the principal role in the Communist program for this country. Public *pressures* on American policy by Communists and their fellow travelers have been numerous, and espionage has been frequent, but actual policy perversion has been less common.

If one thinks about it, it is not hard to see why. Let us turn the tables, and imagine that the CIA has an agent in the Kremlin, a middle-rank official in the Foreign Ministry, say, or a well-placed officer in the high command of the Soviet armed forces. (Col. Oleg Penkovsky, remember, was just such a man; possibly, even probably, there are others.) What, do you suppose, are the standing instructions of this American agent? To demand a détente with the United States at every meeting of the Politburo? To use his official position to engineer as many diplomatic setbacks for the Soviet Union as possible? I doubt it very much. Rather, I should suppose that his instructions are to protect himself, profess orthodox Communist views, attract as little attention as possible—and transmit information when asked to do so. That is the real prize in the game of subversion: *information*—for knowledge is power.

Still, it is a sober fact that during the 1930's and 1940's, when as a nation we were still largely unaware of the existence of a Communist problem, certain American Communists in government agencies did brazenly pervert or sabotage various United States policies in the interests of the Kremlin. One especially well-documented instance of this sort of thing was the deliberate ruin by Communist agents in the U.S Treasury Department of our attempt to support the currency of Nationalist China in 1944-45. It was the subject of a remarkable staff study by the ISSC in 1956.

Most of the Subcommittee's investigations, as we have seen, are conducted by the tried-and-true method of interrogating, under oath, persons believed to possess relevant information. Not infrequently, however, the Subcommittee launches a "staff investigation," usually of documentary materials not involving witnesses. One such investigation was conducted by Subcommittee researchers into the famous "Morgenthau diaries," and a preliminary report was published by the Subcommittee on July 13, 1956, as Part 35 of its inquiry into "Scope of Soviet Activity in the United States." It deserves mention here, not only because it illustrates an important and often overlooked aspect of the Subcommittee's activities, but because it brilliantly pinpoints a classic case of Communist perversion of American foreign policy.

Henry Morgenthau Jr., Franklin Roosevelt's Treasury Secretary, had a lively sense of history. With future historians (and perhaps also contemporary critics) in mind, he kept a voluminous diary, containing not only file copies of all letters and interoffice memoranda but verbatim accounts of literally hundreds of conferences with his subordinates in the Treasury Department and with others. When these diaries, totalling many thousands of pages, were made available to the Subcommittee in 1955, a special task force of researchers was assigned to burrow into them.

In due course the research team emerged with a story that deserves a special niche in the history of the Communization of Asia. Prior to 1943, the Communist policy in the Far East had been to cooperate, at least grudgingly, with the Nationalist government of Chiang Kai-shek in resisting the Japanese assault on China. In 1943, however, the Communists seem to have concluded (correctly) that the ultimate defeat of Japan was only a matter of time, and that the relevant quarrel in China was therefore now between the Communists and the Nationalist Chinese. In America, the Institute of Pacific Relations—a notorious megaphone of pro-Communist propaganda in Far Eastern affairs—swung into action, denouncing Chiang as a corrupt war lord and hailing the Chinese Communists as mere "agrarian reformers." The whole tremendous apparatus of world Communism was turned against Nationalist China, to clear the way for Communism when peace returned at last to that huge country.

In Washington, in the Treasury Department, one particular clique of highly placed American Communists and Communist sympathizers saw a golden—and in this case not only figuratively but literally golden—opportunity to strike a blow for the Communist cause. The Treasury clique was led by Assistant Secretary Harry Dexter White, one of the few persons to have the distinction of being named under oath by *both* Whittaker Chambers and Elizabeth Bentley as a Communist espionage agent. As I have already explained in another connection (Chapter 3, p. 65), White never technically joined the Communist Party, preferring to regard such doctrinaire formalism as beneath his dignity. But he was a dedicated Soviet agent over the whole period of the late 1930's and early 1940's, rising ever higher in the Treasury Department and all the while passing valuable information to such Communist couriers as Chambers and (later) Elizabeth Bentley. In 1948, called at last before the House Committee on Un-American Activities, he denied their allegations under oath—and swiftly died of a heart attack.

When White stepped out as Director of the Treasury's Division of Monetary Research to accept a higher job in the Department, he was succeeded in that post by V. Frank Coe, who subsequently invoked the Fifth whenever asked about Communist Party membership—and who now resides, oddly enough, in Red China. Others in key positions at the Treasury in the early 1940's included Victor Perlo (holder of subversion's Triple Crown, having been identified under oath as a Communist by Chambers, Bentley, *and* Nathaniel Weyl), Harold Glasser, Irving Kaplan, Abraham G. Silverman, and William Ludwig Ullman—all of whom have relentlessly pleaded the Fifth Amendment in response to repeated questions about Communist activities. All in all, it was quite a Treasury Department that turned its attention to the fiscal plight of Nationalist China in the early 1940's.

By 1942 the Chinese Nationalist currency, which had held up fairly well during the 1930's, was sagging under the inflationary pressures of the Japanese war. On March 21 of that year, as an aid measure, the United States granted a credit of $500 million to China and agreed that the funds would be transferred "in such amounts and at such times as the Government of the Republic of China shall request." Please note and remember the words just quoted.

In February 1943 the Chinese Government asked for the appropriation of $20 million of this credit of $500 million to buy gold for shipment to China and sale there, as a means of reducing inflationary pressures. (For the benefit of those, and I am one, to whom such things are not obvious, the sale of this gold in China would tend to support the Chinese paper currency because payment for the gold would be offered, and accepted by the Chinese Government, in such currency. In effect, this would "prove" that the currency was as good as a specified quantity of gold.) The Treasury agreed promptly, though the first actual shipment was not made until September, apparently because of minor technical problems.

In July, meanwhile, Chinese Finance Minister H. H. Kung, noting the rapid growth of inflation in China, made a formal request for the allocation of $200 million of the credit to be used for the purchase of gold for shipment to China. On July 27 Secretary Morgenthau agreed to this request. He stipulated, however, that the funds would be transferred only as fast as the existing transportation facilities could handle shipment of the gold:

> The Treasury agrees to the request of the Government of China transmitted to me by Ambassador Wei Tao-ming that $200 million be made available immediately from the credit on the books of the Treasury in the name of the Government of the Republic of China for the purchase of gold.
>
> In order to avoid unnecessary raising of funds by the United States Treasury, it is suggested that transfers from the credit of the Chinese Government for the purchase of gold be made at such time and in such amounts as are allowed by existing facilities for the transportation to China of the equivalent amount of gold.

Morgenthau's suggestion sounds superficially reasonable, and one may even commend his attempt to economize by shipping the gold only in "existing facilities," as distinguished, presumably, from giving the shipments some sort of costly emergency handling. But China's fiscal plight was severe and growing worse, and there were forces at work in Mr. Morgenthau's Treasury that were not merely intent on frugality.

In any event the Chinese government thereupon, during the latter half of 1943 and the year 1944, began to sell gold in China, first from the small stocks on hand, and then from the driblets that at last began to arrive from the United States. For a time the supply was adequate to cover the demand; but by midsummer 1944 the Chinese gold stocks were dangerously low. Dipping into the Morgenthau diaries, it is not hard to see why. For example, on September 22, 1943, we find Assistant Secretary Harry Dexter White writing to Secretary Morgenthau:

> China has asked us for $50 million worth of gold [i.e., out of the $200 million] in accordance with your promise to make the gold available. I have taken the position that the gold is available as rapidly as they can ship it. We have arranged to ship from one to two tons a month by Army Air transport.

Like the Morgenthau letter of July 27, already quoted, this sounds reasonably brisk; but once again there is that obscure proviso about shipping facilities. Since a ton of gold was worth only about a million dollars, it can be seen that at the pace proposed by White even the $50 million would take from two to four years to reach China.

Just one week later (on September 29) White summarized a discussion with Secretary Morgenthau as follows:

> I then raised the question of satisfying Kung's cabled request that we earmark $200 million of gold out of the amount remaining from the $500 million . . . I said that I thought we ought to be tough with the Chinese on the question of earmarking $200 million of gold for gold sales which they could not make before the gold could be shipped to them. The Secretary agreed. He said that he thinks that we should be tough in this matter and he told me to go ahead and let them have the gold only as rapidly as it could be shipped and sold in China.

Precisely why Secretary Morgenthau (assuming White paraphrased him correctly) was so eager to "be tough in this matter" is not immediately apparent, since he was not by any means personally pro-Communist. White's motive, on the other hand, is painfully clear. In all likelihood it was Morgenthau's Communist subordinates, and notably White, who were responsible for the mood of toughness, and also for the negative tone of a Morgenthau memorandum to President Roosevelt dated December 19, 1943, recommending against a proposed fresh loan to China:

> China has tried two similar monetary remedies for alleviating inflation without marked success.

1. The Chinese Government issued and sold dollar securities for yuan, setting aside $200 million of the aid granted by this country for the redemption of the securities. (These securities were sold at exorbitant profit to the buyers. For instance, a person holding $100 in United States currency could have quadrupled his money in less than two years by selling the currency for yuan on the open market and buying the dollar securities issued by the Chinese Government.) I believe that the program made no significant contribution to the control of inflation.

2. The Chinese Government has recently been selling gold at a price in yuan equivalent to $550 an ounce, about fifteen times the official rate. We have shipped to China more than $10 million of gold and they have sold about $2 million of gold for yuan. This program has not been tried sufficiently to warrant any definite conclusion as to its possible effect.

China now has $460 million of unpledged funds in the United States and is getting about $20 million a month as a result of our expenditures. China could use these funds in selling gold or dollar assets for yuan, although in my opinion such schemes in the past have had little effect except to give additional profits to insiders, speculators and hoarders and dissipate foreign exchange resources that could be better used by China for reconstruction.

Under the circumstances, a loan to China for these purposes could not be justified by the results that have been obtained. It is my opinion that a loan is unnecessary at this time and would be undesirable from the point of view of China and the United States. Large expenditures on ineffective measures for controlling inflation in China would be an unwise use of her borrowing capacity which should be reserved for productive uses in other ways. On reconstruction, it is too soon for us to know the best use or the best form of the aid we might give to China.

The above memorandum introduces two themes that were to become increasingly popular with Morgenthau's Communist subordinates: vague, undocumented charges about "profit to insiders, speculators and hoarders" in Nationalist China, and equally vague proposals to reserve China's assets for "productive uses," especially during "reconstruction" (i.e., after the war). A capital as worldly-wise as Washington found the charges of corruption all too easy to believe, and the idealists who still abounded in the Roosevelt administration were of course fetched by the notion of saving money for purposes of postwar reconstruction. That without a stable currency there might be no free China to reconstruct does not seem to have occurred to anyone—except, of course, the Communists.

Through 1944, the official Treasury attitude toward China's fiscal problems remained stern. Of the $200 million promised, only $12 million had actually reached China by July, a year after it was promised.

On July 12 the Central Bank of China urgently requested air shipments. The U.S. Treasury, instead, languidly dispatched $3 million by sea, and only in September did it finally get around to sending a further $1.5 million by air. On October 2, Chinese representatives presented to White, and other Treasury officials, a further communication from the Central Bank of China, pleading:

> As Federal Reserve Bank of New York advised having shipped balance by plane thus exhausting our $20 million and as sales still extremely heavy and recent arrivals far from being adequate to meet outstanding contracts, please request U.S. Treasury immediately transfer U.S. $20 million or if possible more out of $200 million and ship by plane.

This communication lays stress upon a new factor in China's increasingly unfavorable monetary equation. After October 1944 the gold that had been sold in China exceeded the amounts actually on hand in the country. In other words, the Chinese government was now selling gold that had not yet actually arrived. There was nothing in the least improper, let alone dishonest, about this; the Chinese government had been promised no less than $200,000,000 in gold, and was merely selling a small fraction of this amount in advance of its physical arrival in China. What the Chinese did not reckon on was the successful foot-dragging of the Communists in the U.S. Treasury. Harry Dexter White objected to China's whole policy of selling gold, once more arguing that the gold would be a valuable asset after the war and that its sale would "not substantially retard rising prices or the basic economic situation which was due to acute scarcity of goods." He further contended—not forgetting the other Communist theme—that much of the gold would disappear into hoards. As Dr. Arthur Young, an American financial advisor to the Chinese Government from 1929 to 1946, told the Subcommittee:

> This argument was not sound. Gold was well calculated to check inflation because its official price of C$21,000 [21,000 Chinese yuan] per ounce was equivalent to C$600 per dollar, whereas the black market rate for American currency was about C$250 per dollar. In other words, gold in China was worth 2.4 times as much as American currency, i.e., equivalent to $84 per ounce compared with the legal American price of $35, and at this time the free market price was about C$24,000 or about 14 percent above the official price. As to scarcity of goods, of course many individual items were very scarce because of the war. But most of the goods consumed in China were produced there and despite the war, production of foodstuffs and many local items was pretty well sustained. The price of rice, for example, rose along with other items. Clearly the

main cause of the price rise was the printing and issue of paper money. As to hoarding, it was far better to hoard gold paid for by turning in money that could be reissued, than for that money to remain in circulation and be used in part to buy and hoard scarce goods.

White stuck to his guns, however, and his view prevailed. On December 9, 1944, he boldly told Morgenthau in a memorandum:

> The Chinese are now pressing to ship gold via commercial vessel. Hitherto we have insisted on military transportation. They are pressing very hard to get as much gold exported to China as quickly as possible. We have stalled as much as we have dared and have succeeded in limiting gold shipments to $26 million during the past year. We think it would be a serious mistake to permit further large shipments at this time. We would like to discuss the matter with you.

This amazing memorandum shows just how successful the Treasury Department's Communists had been in their stealthy war against Nationalist China. By insisting on shipment in military vessels, and by similar subterfuges, they had held shipments of gold to a mere $26 million in 1944. Even more important, they had induced Secretary Morgenthau to forget that he had agreed in writing, on July 27, 1943, "that $200 million be made available immediately," and, by vague references to profiteering and the supposed needs of postwar reconstruction, had actually enlisted the good-hearted Secretary in their campaign to stall further shipments.

White next drew up a memorandum dated December 23, 1944, designed for Morgenthau to submit to President Roosevelt. This remarkable document renewed the now familiar charge that China was selling gold "in such a way as to be of benefit principally to hoarders and speculators," and alleged that much of it was finding its way to Japanese-occupied areas. It added that the sales were having "practically no helpful effect on the inflationary situation," and that they provided revenue only "by the sacrifice of valuable national assets at inexcusably low prices." It concluded by suggesting that Roosevelt use future shipments of gold as a "bargaining weapon," to force the Nationalist government "to accept your China program," i.e., to accept the proposals then being formulated (by Ambassador Pat Hurley) for a coalition government with the Chinese Communists. To quote Dr. Young again:

> Commenting on the objections raised, it should have been clear that the sale of gold was deisgned to attract purchase by persons who otherwise would engage in hoarding rice or other important goods and speculate in

them—in other words, so that they would be diverted from this harmful activity, thus adding to the supply of goods available in the market. It was true that some of the gold found its way to occupied areas, but the buyers there were largely Chinese and in any event, the Government got value in local currency withdrawn from circulation for the gold that it sold. As to the effect on the inflation, receipts from gold reduced substantially the deficit covered by the printing press. . . . As to the sacrifice of assets needed for postwar at "inexcusably low prices," in wartime all kinds of valuable assets, including lives, have to be sacrificed. As to the prices, the absence of stocks of gold made it impossible to control the market or to realize the much greater value that would have been possible from selling spot rather than forward [i.e., gold on hand rather than gold merely on order]. Furthermore, measured by the black market prices for American currency, which is admittedly a not wholly satisfactory measure, because of the narrowness of the market, gold [i.e., sales of gold] produced for China in this period sums equivalent to well over $35 per ounce.

To his credit, Secretary Morgenthau did not forward White's December 23 memorandum to President Roosevelt. But the policy it expressed continued to prevail in the Treasury Department; only some $13 million of gold reached China between September 12, 1944, and January 26, 1945, as against sales of over $33 million in the same period. Thereafter not an ounce of gold left the United States for China until April 14, 1945, and even this went by sea, arriving June 14.

Meanwhile Dr. Kung, who had been stationed by his government in Washington, made repeated efforts during the winter months to persuade the Treasury to change its mind. On January 3, 1945, he appealed to Secretary Morgenthau in behalf of Finance Minister O. K. Yui:

As the situation in China requires the immediate arrival of more gold shipments, Mr. Yui has sent another urgent wire requesting me to approach you to facilitate such shipments. During the past decade I have enjoyed your valuable friendship and untiring cooperation and assistance in matters which were of mutual interest to our two countries. Therefore, I am sending you a copy of Mr. Yui's latest telegram and hoping you will give this matter your prompt and favorable attention.

On this document appears the handwritten note, "White—Prepare an answer." On January 5, a bland acknowledgment was signed by Morgenthau:

My Dear Dr. Kung: I have received your letter of January 3, 1945, enclosing copy of cable from Mr. O. K. Yui, Minister of Finance, regarding shipments of gold to China.

I am giving this matter my close attention and hope to be able to give you my decision in the near future. You may be assured that in making my decision I will give fullest consideration to the best interests of China.

As New Yorkers say, that—plus a token—will get you a ride on the subway.

Needless to say, nothing happened (perhaps that was deemed "in the best interests of China"), and on February 26 Dr. Kung tried again, in a long and rather desperate letter written from New York, where he was undergoing medical treatment:

Dear Mr. Secretary: You will recall that on several occasions we have discussed the provision of gold for China, and that you kindly undertook to expedite this matter. Since shipments to China have been considerably slower than we feel necessary, I wish now to present the situation for urgent attention.

The chief present financial problem of the Chinese Government, as you know, is to finance its large and growing deficit. The Government must handle this deficit in such a way that the inflation does not get out of hand—since if this took place, it would cause most serious consequences to the war effort of China and would be very hurtful to the conduct of American operations against Japan in and from China. Moreover, if inflation should seriously accelerate, this condition would undermine China's economic structure, impair internal stability, make it much harder for China to reoccupy and restore the areas now in enemy hands, gravely hamper China's reconstruction and progress in the next few years, and make it much harder for China to play the part in stabilization and peace maintenance in the Far East which its Government and people wish to play and which is desired by the American Government and people.

It is of vital importance, therefore, to reduce in every possible way the deficit financed through increase of note issue. For a little over a year, the Government has been selling gold to realize Chinese currency. . . . The sale of gold has been most helpful, and has definitely prevented the inflation from attaining a higher level which otherwise would have been reached. It helps to check increase of the general price level by diverting to purchase of gold funds which otherwise would be used to buy commodities to be held for higher prices.

The American Government, in order to help China, made available US $200 million of gold out of the US $500 million credit. Of this gold, the first installment was US $20 million. Unfortunately, deliveries of gold to China out of this US $20 million have totaled only US $7,276,066.00. . . . Thus, shipments have fallen far short of what is needed. As a result, the Central Bank was obliged to substitute forward sales for spot sales [i.e., to sell gold that had not yet arrived, instead of gold actually on hand]. A black market for spot gold developed, which the Government could not control owing to lack of ready supplies. . . .

In view of the urgent need for gold in China, we are most anxious to send forward at once by air the balance of US $12,723,933.28 (say 364,000 ounces) of the US $20 million, which is required at the earliest possible moment to meet near deliveries and to make spot sales. We would, therefore, appreciate your good offices in arranging with the American Army Air Transport Command for such shipment. Also we would like to have a further amount of say 500,000 ounces (US $17,500,000) go forward as soon as practicable by air to enable the Central Bank of China to meet further near deliveries and to make spot sales. In addition, we would like to ship at once 500,000 ounces (US $17,500,000) by sea to meet later deliveries. Thereafter, shipments should be adapted to needs in order to avoid again running short of gold in China. . . .

I shall much appreciate favorable action on these matters as soon as possible.

This time Secretary Morgenthau seems to have called upon V. Frank Coe to draft a reply. On March 2, Coe forwarded a draft, together with the following comments, which calmly assume that the foot-dragging policy is still in effect:

To: Secretary Morgenthau.
From: Mr. Coe
Subject: Export of gold to China.

1. Dr. Kung, in letter of February 26, 1945, attached hereto together with suggested reply, requests that the equivalent of $47,500,000 of gold be exported to China . . .

2. Since the situation in China has remained fundamentally the same and no change has taken place in the gold sales program, you will probably wish to continue the policy of permitting only small shipments of gold to China. It will be recalled that Ambassador Hurley agreed with you on the desirability of holding down gold shipments to approximately the same magnitude as in the past.

3. It is therefore suggested that arrangements be made with the Army to export to China during the next three months about $7 million of gold now on earmark in the Federal Reserve Bank of New York, one-half of which would be gold acquired in payment of tin exports from China to the United States. Foreign Economic Administration has informed us that the export of gold acquired as payment for tin exports is essential to maintain tin production in China.

4. The suggested reply to Dr. Kung does not make any definite commitments but, as soon as possible, we would inform his representatives

orally that we have succeeded in making arrangements with the Army for the export of about $7 million of gold during the next three months.

Morgenthau apparently approved the draft, for the very next day (March 3) we find him writing to Dr. Kung as follows:

Dear Dr. Kung: I am glad to receive your letter of February 26, 1945, regarding exports of gold to China. I am very sorry to learn that you are in the hospital receiving medical treatment and do hope that you will recover quickly.

I am sure that you appreciate the many difficulties involved in making arrangements for the export of gold to China. As in every other phase of our activities these days, military necessity takes precedence over everything else.

I have, however, instructed my men to raise again with the military authorities the possibilities of shipping gold to China during the next few months. They will inform your representatives of their findings on this matter.

Any doubts Morgenthau may have had about the correctness of the Treasury's "go slow" policy must certainly have been stilled by a savage dispatch that now arrived from Solomon Adler, who at this crucial moment was serving as the Treasury Department's own representative in Chungking, the capital of Nationalist China. (After denying Communist Party membership to HCUA, Adler departed for his native England in 1950 and forfeited his American citizenship in 1953.) On March 11, 1945, he cabled Morgenthau:

The reckless [Chinese] Government conduct of its gold sales policy can only be described as "frenzied finance."

(A) It has been and is selling gold at an absurdly uneconomic price. The official pretext that price cannot be raised without an adequate supply on hand does not hold water. While official price of gold has been maintained, black-market price has risen to CN dollars 39,500 per ounce; also witness the heavy purchase of six month gold deposits at end of February due to rumor that official price was to be raised at beginning of March. Official claim that raising price of gold would push up general prices still further cannot be taken seriously at a time when prices are skyrocketing in any case.

(B) It is dissipating China's foreign exchange assets, which she will badly need at war's end, at current rate of United States $150,000,000 per annum without significantly affecting economic situation. In fact, since inflation has now entered snowball phase, future sales of gold at current rate will have even smaller effects as brake on inflation.

(C) Part of the gold is finding its way into occupied China.

On April 23, 1945, Finance Minister Yui warned by cable that the delay in gold shipments was reflecting on the credit of China, and added, "I feel much concerned and distressed." On April 28, its garbled syntax betraying its agitation, the Central Bank of China telegraphed: "We cannot overemphasize the serious effect in consequence Doctor White's default in meeting its obligations."

As late as April 27, however, Frank Coe submitted yet another memorandum to Secretary Morgenthau, coolly proposing to tighten the screws. Note that he rings all the old changes, from the innuendoes about "insiders" to the usual threnody about "reconstruction," and treats the perfectly legitimate Chinese policy of selling the promised gold in advance of its actual arrival as some sort of horrendous crime:

To: Secretary Morgenthau.
From: Mr. Coe.
For information.
Subject: Chinese Gold:

For your information these are our tentative views on the subject of gold for China . . .

1. The Treasury should continue to oppose all except minimum shipments of gold, where these endanger American lives or use scarce transport. This policy should continue to apply to China.

2. We cannot now agree to promise the $50 million of gold shipments which the Chinese want in the next few months in order to meet the gold certificates which fall due; the Chinese did not consult us about these forward sales of gold, which are obviously imprudent in the circumstances and were designed to act as a pistol at our heads.

State has not indicated that they are afraid of the political consequences of this refusal. I suppose, however, that if in later months a great fuss is made and if State tells us that they are afraid of grave political consequences, we would agree to step up gold shipments in order to clear up these arrears.

3. Without condoning the past program, we should tell the Chinese that we expect them to stop all forms of forward sales of gold immediately.

4. In any case, all further gold sent to China should be out of their own funds, and not out of the $500 million loan. Your own responsibility for the uses to which this loan is put is the basis for this recommendation. The program of forward sales of gold, like the predecessor programs of $200 million United States savings certificates and bonds, has been used as a device for enriching a few insiders and has had negligible effects upon the Chinese inflation.

5. After consideration of the whole history of the $500 million loan, and the uses to which it has been put, we think that you should tell the

Chinese that you wish them to put aside the remaining $240 million of the loan, and an additional sum of their own United States dollar exchange, of perhaps $260 million, as a fund to be used for stabilization and reconstruction purposes, in accordance with an agreed program, to go into effect at an agreed date. The program should include the fiscal, economic, and administrative measures necessary to stabilize the currency, and the date should be the earliest time when we and the Chinese agree that they can go forward on such a program.

If the Chinese are not willing to accept this proposal, we think it wise policy to allow no further depletion of the loan. (In addition to this $240 million the Chinese now have some $700 million of United States dollar exchange.)

We have prepared charts and analyses to show that the acquisition by China of additional foreign exchange and the sale of gold or any other form of foreign exchange by China have had no discernible effect in halting the inflation.

Observe that Coe in this memorandum introduces, for the first time, a brand-new proposal: to force the Chinese to put the entire balance of the $500 million credit, plus other funds, into a postwar stabilization fund. The idea had at least the merit of consistency; it was the next logical step in the financial strangulation of China.

But help, though belated—fatally belated—was at last on its way. Dr. T. V. Soong, Foreign Minister and Acting President of Nationalist China and the brother of Madame Chiang Kai-shek, had been in San Francisco during April, attending the founding meeting of the United Nations. From San Francisco he proceeded to Washington, where he laid the whole matter of China's financial plight, and in particular the question of the gold shipments, directly before President Truman.

Mr. Truman had been President less than a month, but one senses a fresh impetus at work in Washington. At a minimum, the second and third echelons of the Roosevelt bureaucracy seem to have been nervously uncertain as to what the new President might want or do, and top-ranking officials of the *ancien régime* like Secretary Morgenthau were understandably eager to please him. On May 1, at Truman's request, Morgenthau and various other Treasury officials (including Coe and Adler) conferred on the gold problem with representatives of the State and War Departments. Their discussion was recorded by a stenographer and appears in full in the Morgenthau diaries. Morgenthau may have had a twinge or two, but he was obviously not really uncomfortable as he addressed General Somervell and State's Will Clayton and casually tried to implicate their Departments, retrospectively, in the Treasury policy of delaying gold shipments:

H.M., JR. Well, General, as you know, the President gave me this task of dealing with T. V. Soong on his request for more gold shipments, and as you know, we have been in consultation with State and War as to how fast we should feed this thing out, and we've made it just as difficult for the Chinese to get it as possible, that being a sort of joint policy. Now, I'd like to have some advice from the State Department and War Department whether they want to change this policy.

Clayton was cautious, but plainly reluctant to be critical of the Treasury policy:

MR. CLAYTON. Well, from what I know of it it seems to me that you've been handling it very well, and I have no reason to believe [doubt?] that your idea that the sale of this gold and the way in which they've been handling it is really not a very effective anti-inflationary weapon. It seems to me your arguments on that are pretty good, and I would think that from what I know of the way in which you've been handling it, that it's very intelligent and all right. I'm not too well posted, but from what I know of it, it seems all right to me.

General Somervell, being no economist, had no complaint to make either, and conversation soon shifted to the possibility of shipping consumer goods, especially textiles, into China. It was agreed to take up the whole subject with Dr. Soong jointly, "so he won't be trading one of us off against the other," as Morgenthau put it.

On the morning of May 8, Morgenthau convened a meeting of his Treasury team to go over the draft of a memorandum he was planning to read that very afternoon to T. V. Soong. It mentioned that consideration was being given to the shipment of textiles and trucks to China, and recommended Coe's new idea of a stabilization fund that would absorb (and incidentally freeze) the balance of China's $500 million credit. On the subject of gold, and especially forward sales of gold, the memorandum was stern:

As you know, the United States Treasury was not consulted when this program was initiated. In view of the difficulties of shipping gold, the limited effects of sales upon price rises in China, the public criticism of such sales and the desirability of using foreign exchange resources to achieve maximum effects, this program is ill-advised.

The Treasury will endeavor, as in the past, to make available limited quantities of gold for shipment to China during the next few months, having due regard to the need for restricting gold shipments where these endanger lives or use scarce transport facilities. However . . . it is believed that further shipments should be financed out of foreign exchange assets other than those proposed to be earmarked for currency stabilization.

All in all, Secretary Morgenthau was well pleased with the memorandum. As he remarked to his staff, with an irony far greater than he knew:

> I think we should give them something in writing because he'll tell me six months from now he didn't understand what I said and I think the only way you can deal with the Chinese is to give them something in writing and then there's no argument about it.

That afternoon was to prove one of the most unsettling of Henry Morgenthau's life. For Dr. Soong, when the memorandum had been read to him, promptly turned the tables and gave Morgenthau "something in writing"; he simply produced a copy of Morgenthau's letter of July 27, 1943, to H. H. Kung, flatly stating that the Treasury "agrees to the request . . . that $200 million be made available immediately . . . for the purchase of gold."

Whatever else Henry Morgenthau was—and there is considerable evidence that he was a gullible fool—he was an honest man. He had, quite simply, forgotten his 1943 promise to China; he had been lulled over the years into thinking—mistakenly—that it applied only to the first $20 million of the whole $500 million. He felt, and rightly, that his aides should have called the letter to his attention. He didn't know that several of them were Communists, bent on the cold-blooded destruction of America's ally. Thus the conference that took place at the Treasury the next morning (May 9, 1945) belongs on the credit side of Henry Morgenthau's ledger. Coe was there, but not White. Others present were Adler (apparently back from Chungking on a visit), Daniel W. Bell and a couple of lesser lights named Mr. Friedman and Mrs. Klotz. They all got the Riot Act:

> H.M., JR. Look, you people, I think you should be severely criticized for letting me go into court and try my case before T. V. Soong, and the letter of July 27, 1943, where I gave the Chinese Government a firm commitment on two hundred million dollars worth of gold—I think it's inexcusable. After all, you were so worried about saving face, what about my face? I have given, in writing, the Chinese Government a firm commitment that they can have two hundred million dollars worth of gold and you—I don't remember it, I can't remember it. I do ten things a day. Bell comes in here and in three minutes we settle ten billion dollars worth of financing, and it's impossible for me to remember, and

you put me in an absolutely dishonorable position, and I think it's inexcusable. I think it's absolutely inexcusable to have me bargaining and chattering around when right here in writing is this thing.

Coe moved in to stanch the hemorrhage:

MR. COE. Mr. Secretary, in this proposal to the Chinese we did not say that we would not give them the gold.

But Morgenthau was through, at last, with sophistry:

H.M., JR. That has nothing to do with it. I am facing the Acting President of China, and here I am put in the position that I am bargaining with him about something that I gave my commitment he could have. Now, in this world, and certainly Government to Government, a person's word, and particularly his written word, means something. One of you three should have said, "Now, remember, Mr. Secretary, on July 27th, 1943, you told them they could have it. Now, do you want to bargain with them about it?" You are so worried about his face. What about my face? What about the honor of this Government? I think it's inexcusable . . .

Morgenthau now turned his wrath on various others present:

H.M., JR. Why, in God's name, didn't you bring this letter to my attention, Sol? [Adler] You knew this existed!
MR. ADLER. I wasn't aware of it explicitly. I had seen it in the file but—
H.M., JR. You didn't know about it?
MR. ADLER. I knew—
H.M. JR. You should have—what about you? [addressing Friedman]
MR. FRIEDMAN. Well, Mr. Secretary, if I may say, on this specific thing, you will recall that at the time of the 1943 letter, when you signed the letter, you and Mr. White discussed it with P. W. Quo and Mr. Hsi Temou and the Chinese at the time the question of two hundred million dollars of gold came up. You expressed to them that you were considerably doubtful as to this whole idea, and they said to you that the President said to Madame Chiang that they could buy the gold, and you told them and Mr. White told them that you could make the commitment to buy the gold for anti-inflation and for anti-hoarding purposes. Then we very deliberately at the time put into that document all this reference to anti-inflation and anti-hoarding purposes, because you were afraid at the time that they might use the gold for other purposes, and you didn't feel that that would be a justifiable use of the two hundred million dollars. And we have all along in conversations after that with

Mr. Quo and Mr. Chi, who were designated by Dr. Kung, stressed it that the gold was being sent for anti-inflationary and anti-hoarding purposes.

To which gobbledygook Morgenthau coldly replied:

H.M., JR. That's all very nice, but in cold print there it's "You can have the two hundred million dollars of this money for gold."

Once more Coe tried to smooth matters over; but once again Morgenthau rebuffed him:

MR. COE. And, Mr. Secretary, your proposal as given to Mr. Soong yesterday does not at any rate in cold print dishonor your letter in 1943. What you said to him in that proposal was (1) we would like the Chinese Government to segregate one sum of money and another sum of money. Obviously, if they decide to segregate for a stabilization fund the remainder of this sum, you cannot give them the same sum over again for gold.

H.M., JR. Did you know about the letter of July 27th?

MR. COE. Yes, sir.

H.M., JR. Well, I certainly think somebody would have said before I went into this conference, "Here's this letter. Here's what you said, Mr. Morgenthau."

MR. COE. The whole basis, as I understood it, of the Treasury giving them limited sums of gold over a longer period had been the original statement that we would, and month by month they were told there is so much transport available.

H. M., JR. But White told me we were running out of excuses.

MR. COE. The only excuse I ever heard—I have picked this stuff up—the only excuse I have ever heard of has been transportation, and we all think that transportation is a thin excuse.

H.M., JR. Well, I made my statement. I think, before I went into that meeting yesterday morning, I should have been shown this document so that I knew that there was a written commitment that they could have two hundred million dollars worth of gold.

The next day Morgenthau was in a better mood, but not much. Among those present on this occasion (May 10) was Harry Dexter White. He had lost none of his cool. The "go slow" policy, he admitted, had always been technically indefensible, but he still insisted that it had been morally correct:

MR. WHITE. I understand you were troubled about the letter of the two hundred million. Mr. Secretary, we have always taken the position we had absolutely no legal grounds for withholding the gold; that what we were doing was skating on thin ice and offering excuses and we were getting away with it as long as we could, and remember because I said we are getting away with it that you better get the President's backing when they begin putting on the heat. It's because I said we have no basis for it. We have been successful over two years in keeping them down to twenty-seven million and we never understood why the Chinese didn't take it in there and do what they are now doing. The whole history is we had no basis for it.

H.M., JR. I can't remember things that happened, and when he flashed that letter on me it caught me sort of off guard and I didn't remember it. . . . I don't know how far I'll go, but I certainly want to loosen up, and I think this is a psychological time for the Treasury to demonstrate we can be a friend to China, when they really need it, with their own money.

Morgenthau was obviously determined, and White at last gave in— with a display of solicitude for the historical record:

MR. WHITE. That isn't the same way I'd do it. [But?] I'll drop that. I do think you need to have now for your own record—and this is wholly for your own record—you need now an exchange of letters from you to the President indicating that this money is being badly used. It will not help inflation and cannot be justified on economic grounds, and that the only basis for it must be that they feel it is militarily necessary to satisfy his demands. Because, Mr. Secretary, this record—we have advised them against the use of this. It has been badly used and all the rest.

On May 15, however, at another conference with Morgenthau, the Treasury's Communist clique made a last concerted stand:

MR. WHITE. We have a memorandum prepared, and we thought that it would be preferable to get State Department concurrence in it, but we didn't have a chance to clear it with you, so what we did is send over a carbon copy saying you hadn't finally approved it yet, so if you want to change it, we can without commitment. On the other hand, they'll have a chance to see it this afternoon. (Mr. Coe reads "Memorandum for the President; Subject: China.")

In accordance with your instructions, I have been discussing the Chinese request for about $200 million of gold with the other government agencies concerned and with Mr. T. V. Soong. It was agreed by all the agencies concerned that—

(a) we are anxious to give full support to an anti-inflationary program for China;

(b) the gold sales policy, which was initiated against Treasury advice, is not an effective anti-inflationary device;

(c) the history of the Chinese uses of the $240 million which they have so far received from the 1942 $500 million loan threatens to become a scandal in the United States as well as in China;

(d) the exhaustion of the $500 million loan would invite requests for additional financial aid probably on a larger scale.

Therefore, I gave Dr. Soong a memorandum endorsed by the State and War Departments and the Foreign Economic Administration in which we proposed to Dr. Soong—

(a) the establishment of a $500 million Fund for combating inflation and stabilizing Chinese currency, to be constituted from the outstanding $240 million of the 1942 $500 million loan and from China's very substantial dollar balances, and

(b) the termination of the present gold sales program and the continuation of only limited shipments of gold to China to be financed out of her dollar balances.

Dr. Soong, in reply, insisted that China must have the nearly $200 million of gold out of the remaining $240 million of the 1942 loan. He cited commitments made in July 1943 by Mr. Roosevelt and myself under the $500 million financial aid agreement. By so doing, he was, in effect, turning down our proposal for a $500 million Fund for combating inflation and stabilizing China's currency. He stated that he was referring the question of the Fund to the Generalissimo, but if we accede to his request for the gold immediately, such a reference would be purely formal.

The present Chinese gold sales policy has culminated in a public scandal in China. To make large shipments of gold to China at this time, particularly without making every effort within our commitment to induce the Chinese to withhold their request, would make the Administration vulnerable to criticism at home.

It was implicit in all our arrangements with the Chinese that effective use be made of the funds made available to them from the $500 million financial aid. Dr. Soong advanced no new argument for us to revise our judgment that the sale of gold is not an effective anti-inflationary weapon and that it represents a dissipation of China's foreign exchange assets which she will desperately need to restore economic stability.

The State Department has concurred in the suggestion that I therefore inform Dr. Soong that:

(a) You feel that the Chinese should give most serious consideration to our recommendation for the establishment of a $500 million Fund, and . . .

(b) You agree that it is in the best interests of Chinese-American relations that China withdraw for the time being her request for immediate heavy shipments of gold. . . .

But the Communists in the Treasury had lost much of their influence with Henry Morgenthau:

H.M., JR. The first thing I want, please call up whoever has a copy at the State Department. I want them immediately withdrawn, immediately. I'm not going to follow this position. It's ridiculous. Will you please, wherever they are, get them right back.

(Mr. Friedman leaves conference temporarily.)

H.M., JR. I mean, you just keep going over the same ground, the same ground, the whole time. This doesn't make it plain to the President of the United States that these people own this gold, that I, over my signature, told them they could have two hundred million dollars worth of gold.

MR. WHITE. That's where I disagree.

H.M., JR. I know you do.

After further discussion, Morgenthau summed up his fuzzy but unmistakably honest personal view of the situation:

H.M., JR. Let me just make a little speech before Mr. Harry White becomes the devil or the devil's advocate. Here is the situation, the way I see it. I think that the Treasury, up to this time, has been correct. And I certainly am part and parcel of this policy of slowing down the shipment of gold just as much as we could, because it wasn't good for them, and looking forward to the day they really need the money. And it's there. If they get it now, we'll have to give them more later on, so we're giving it twice. . . . Now, I was going along with these fellows [i.e., his Treasury subordinates] up to a point, and I suddenly made up my mind this was all wrong, and I'm just going to turn a somersault on this thing, and I want to do it; and, particularly when I see that my written word and the promise of Franklin Roosevelt is at stake. Now, I haven't got a leg to stand on. Never mind what I told the Congress. Never mind what I say they told me. They get very vague about it, but unfortunately we have nothing in writing. But there is my written word you can have two hundred million dollars worth of gold. Then, for some reason or other, Kung was very dumb on this thing. He didn't force it. We always thought he would. You couldn't understand why he didn't.

MR. WHITE. That's right.

H.M., JR. And this fellow [Dr. Soong] is smart. He comes along and first thing he says is: "Mr. Morgenthau, what are you going to do about it? Is your written word good or not?" And the only answer is "it is." Now, even though I didn't have my written word—that influences me greatly, having given that, and he has gone over and told that to President Truman—as between governments, I don't think we have a leg to stand on. Even if the Chinese weren't fighting with a letter over my signature that they could have this, I think I'd be inclined to say it's yours. Now, I'm through.

Even now, White made a final desperate effort to prevent the $200 million from being used to support Nationalist China:

MR. WHITE. Mr. Secretary, it's entirely true. You wrote that letter, and I think there's a way of wriggling out. The wriggling out is justified on the grounds that they are not using this money wisely, and what you're saying, in your responsibility to assume that they are going to use this money well, is that they are not using these funds effectively, and that was the supposed purpose of the grant. . . . I think where we part company is on two things, one that it would seem to me that the mere fact of having written a two hundred million dollar letter should not commit you to a policy of the rate of speed, because you're going to give it to the Chinese Government. It's not like you were trying to withhold it from the Government. The question is to use it most effectively, and I think you should very definitely state in writing that this money is not being used wisely but badly. . . . Now, what I'm saying is I don't know why you should take the responsibility for making a decision that China needs, Chiang Kai-shek needs the two hundred million dollars, or he won't fight. We don't know if that's true. . . .

H.M., JR. The thing I'm objecting to is this memo to the President. Maybe I can get out of Will Clayton a letter from him and the Secretary of War saying "for political or military necessity, let this gold go."

MR. WHITE. If you say at the same time that on economic grounds, it's not justified.

H.M., JR. I'll say that verbally. I don't have to say it in writing. If they write me a letter saying, "For political and military reasons we advise this gold go out," that's good enough for me. We're fighting a war.

MR. WHITE. Well, of course, you made an assumption which has put us on very weak ground. You assume the two hundred million dollars they're getting is going to make Chiang Kai-shek fight, and they are fighting, both of which I question.

H.M., JR. I think you're wrong. I don't know. How long since you've been there, Adler?

MR. ADLER. I left Chungking on April 7, sir, a little over four weeks ago.

H.M., JR. Do you feel they're fighting now?

MR. ADLER. Very little. You take these stories about Foochow. Everybody in Chungking knew the Japanese occupied it with two hundred men last year.

Nevertheless, Morgenthau had now, at ruinously long last, made up his mind to reverse the Treasury policy and aid Nationalist China. Five substantial shipments of gold were dispatched in May 1945, and ten in June. Beginning June 16, shipments were made by air.

Alas, it was too late. During the spring and summer of 1945, inflation of the Chinese Nationalist currency grew apace, and while it moderated for a time after Japan's surrender in August, fatal damage had been done. The fiscal weakness of the Nationalist government in the ensuing four years is directly attributable to the sapping operation carried on in the U.S. Treasury Department by White and Coe in the crucial years 1943-45. As Dr. Young put it in his memorandum to the Subcommittee, with characteristic understatement:

> It is hard to understand how the Treasury could have stressed its favorite arguments of lack of transportation facilities and the need to conserve the dollar resources for postwar. As to transport, when the Army wished to expedite the construction of the Chengtu airfields, it agreed without hesitation to help to fly in Chinese bank notes needed to pay for the work. Data as to the weight of these notes are not at hand but it may be estimated that it was of the order of several hundred tons. During 1944 nearly 2,000 tons of banknotes and banknote paper were flown to China over the Hump by the China National Aviation Corporation using planes and pilots provided from the U.S. It is absurd to think that means could not have been found to fly in gold as needed. A million dollars in gold weighs about a ton. The sale of a million dollars worth of gold, at say C$20,000 per ounce, would have provided about C$500 million. But a ton of C$20 banknotes would only amount to about C$20 million.
>
> As to conservation and postwar, there was no more reason to hold back gold on that account than to have held back troops in wartime because the men would be needed after the war. Certainly gold should have been deemed to be expendable to minimize the ever-present risk that China's acute inflation would gradually pass to the stage of hyperinflation and financial collapse.

Economics being the inexact science it is, there will probably always be non-Communist economists willing to argue with Dr. Young and to insist that the financial collapse of Nationalist China was inevitable in any case. Nevertheless, thanks to Henry Morgenthau's voluminous diaries, the ruin of the Chinese Nationalist currency through the machinations of Harry Dexter White and V. Frank Coe in the Treasury Department is probably the best documented case of policy perversion in the history of that depressing subject.* Unfortunately, with White dead, and Coe in Red China, prosecution seems out of the question even if a statute could be found squarely covering the subject.

In the case of Harry Dexter White, however, who followed Alger Hiss in denying Chambers' allegations under oath (and who, like Hiss, was

---

* Those wishing to pursue the matter further are referred to the massive excerpts from the Morganthau diaries which the ISSC began publishing in February 1965. For a comprehensive overview of the entire subject of America's tragically wrongheaded China policy in the 1940's, see Dr. Anthony Kubek's *How the Far East Was Lost* (Chicago: Henry Regnery Co., 1963).

obviously gambling that no corroborating witness or document could be produced that would provide evidentiary support for a perjury charge), it seems clear that only his sudden death in 1948 prevented him from following Hiss the rest of the way: to the federal penitentiary at Lewisburg. For the famous "pumpkin papers," subsequently produced by Chambers in response to the demand of the Hiss lawyers, contained documents furnished to Chambers (in his capacity as a Soviet courier) not only by Hiss, but by White. Following Hiss' conviction, these were introduced into the *Congressional Record* by Congressman Richard Nixon on January 26, 1950. Replete with secret information of great value, set forth in White's own handwriting, they proved beyond a doubt that White was consciously spying for the Soviet Union as early as January 1938.

Certainly it is possible to overstate the role that Communists in government have played in perverting America's policy during the past thirty-five or forty years, but it simply will not do to argue that they have played none at all. Every American soldier who died in Korea, or who has died or will die in Vietnam, or who must yet die elsewhere before Communist China is tamed at last, is in one sense a victim of the high-ranking Americans who served the cause of Communism in the Treasury Department in the years 1943–45.

5

The Elusive
Jacob Javits

In fulfilling its assignment to survey the delicate field of internal security, the ISSC inevitably trod on some very influential toes. In the 1930's and 1940's many Americans—some out of conviction, and some no doubt out of mere opportunism—had become involved, to a greater or less degree, in the far-reaching activities of the Communist Party. As the Cold War developed in the late 1940's and domestic Communists became intensely unpopular, many such people quietly severed such contacts and continued their careers without a backward glance. Early in my service with the ISSC I became aware that one such individual might be the then Attorney General of New York, Jacob K. Javits.

Javits was a New York City attorney who, during the 1930's, had built up a successful practice with his older brother Ben, representing minority stockholders in suits against vulnerable corporations. During World War II he had served as a field-grade officer in the Chemical Warfare Service. Then in 1946, out of the Army and back in New York City, he had run successfully for Congress as a Republican (with Liberal Party endorsement) on the West Side, defeating his Democratic opponent in what had theretofore been a safely Democratic district. In 1948, 1950, and 1952 he had won reelection to Congress, and in 1954 had run for Attorney General of New York on the Republican ticket. Once again Javits was victorious; indeed, he was the only statewide Republican candidate to survive the Democratic sweep that year, which put Averell Harriman in the Executive Mansion in Albany. Always a crusading liberal, Javits had cheerfully been forgiven his leftist leanings by a GOP hungry for winners. Jaunty, aggressive, articulate, he was plainly a Man to Watch.

Over a period of months in 1955 and the first half of 1956, however, information reached the Subcommittee which, unless all of it was perjured (and it came from several sources), made it highly probable that some ten years earlier, when Javits was embarking on his political career after the war, he had sought and received Communist aid. It would be hard to imagine a state of affairs that could have presented the Subcommittee with a stickier problem. On the one hand there were the facts themselves, which Javits had naturally never revealed. On the other was a fact of another sort: the political fact of life that Javits was now (1956) a very powerful man indeed, with many allies in the press and elsewhere ready to denounce, and if possible to destroy, anyone who dared to block his upward path. It was already widely rumored that he would seek the Republican senatorial nomination that autumn, and it seemed likely that if he received it he would be elected—would become, in short, a member of the very body whose Internal Security Subcommittee possessed the facts concerning his earlier dealings with the Communists.

For a time this dilemma rolled indigestibly around in the belly of the Subcommittee, while its leading members and staff attorneys mused on their duty—and on the manifest perils of doing it. Then, fortunately, the decision was taken out of our hands. During the spring of 1956, some of those possessing the damning information—persons who had already talked privately to the Subcommittee—began to speak more openly of what they knew. Such word travels fast in political circles. One radio commentator made a veiled allusion to the whole affair. Thereupon, we learned, Javits was bluntly warned by high Republican officials that he must either confront and satisfactorily refute the rumors, preferably in an appearance before the Subcommittee, or be denied the Republican senatorial nomination. Fascinated, Bob Morris and I waited to see what Javits would do. Obviously, the last thing on earth he wanted was to raise the whole subject in midsummer 1956, with the Republican State Committee of New York scheduled to pick a senatorial candidate in September. Just as obviously, however, he was going to be denied the nomination unless he did so.

Javits' first move was cautious, and characteristically shrewd. Late on Thursday afternoon, July 26, he phoned Morris. The air in our little office promptly turned electric when the operator advised Bob that Attorney General Javits was calling from Albany. The Attorney General couldn't have been nicer. How was Bob? Fine? Gee, that was swell! On rambled the familiar, razor-sharp tenor voice, discussing a trivial matter then before the Subcommittee in which New York's Attorney General might plausibly have a professional interest. It was soon clear, however, that Javits was hoping Bob would raise the touchy subject that lurked just below the surface—and thereby give Javits a chance to contend that *we* had asked for information, which *he* would then grandly consent to give. But Bob was not so easily trapped. He stayed away from the hot potato, and the phone call ended without reference to it.

Still, Javits was plainly now committed to further action. It was not long in coming. About a week later he reached Morris by phone again, this time at Bob's home in Point Pleasant, New Jersey. And now Javits came straight to the point: he acknowledged that there were "certain rumors" floating around about him, and he wanted a meeting with Bob and Senator Eastland "to clear them up." Bob promised he would consult Eastland. It was by no means clear that Javits was asking for an official Subcommittee session, let alone a public one; all he had proposed was a "meeting." But Eastland and Morris were cautiously determined not to humor Javits by granting him an altogether exceptional private and unofficial absolution of some sort. The Democratic National Convention was scheduled to take place in Chicago during the week beginning Monday, August 13, and was expected to be over by Thursday the 16th. Bob was instructed to advise Javits that he could be heard by Senator Eastland in executive session in Washington immediately thereafter, on Friday or Saturday, August 17 or 18.

Javits objected that he would have to leave for the Republican National Convention in San Francisco on the 16th (it was scheduled to start on the 20th); nor was he much inclined to postpone the hearing until after San Francisco (i.e., until the week of August 26), because, as he explained candidly, the question of the New York Republican senatorial nomination might be settled out in San Francisco, and he wanted the matter cleared up before then. Eastland thereupon offered to hear Javits in an executive session *during* the Democratic convention, if Javits would visit Chicago secretly on August 13 or 14. Javits, however, declined this offer too, and there the matter was left, unresolved, while the two major parties held their national conventions.

I attended the Republican convention in San Francisco (as I had attended the Republican conventions of 1948 and 1952) simply as an observer, though certainly an interested one, in view of my years of activity in Young Republican and regular Republican circles. The convention itself was a torpid affair; Eisenhower's renomination was of course a foregone conclusion, and only Harold Stassen's grotesque attempt to wrest the Vice Presidential nomination from Nixon provided an element of comic relief. So I was free to visit with my many Republican and Young Republican friends, sample the charms of San Francisco —incomparably the most agreeable of American cities—and (not least) watch with interest the goings-on in the neighborhood of the New York delegation during convention sessions in the cavernous Cow Palace. The chivalry of the New York GOP was assembled there: former Governor Thomas E. Dewey, State Senate Majority Leader Walter Mahoney, Republican State Chairman Judson Morhouse, Attorney General Javits and many others. Among them, earnest and industrious, strode two newer but already influential figures, both also delegates: Nelson Rockefeller and John Hay ("Jock") Whitney. And what was it that these two men were urging on their elders and superiors? Why, the nomination of Jacob Javits for the Senate, of course. (In recent years, as various fissures between Governor Rockefeller and Senator Javits have appeared and widened, I have wondered what both men must think as they savor the irony of Rockefeller's formidable work for Javits in San Francisco in August 1956.)

The week, however, was not to pass without one further development which profoundly affected the proposed Javits hearing. On Tuesday, August 21, Jay Sourwine—the former administrative assistant to the late Senator Pat McCarran, who had served as chief counsel to the ISSC between Bob Morris' two hitches, and who had resigned that post early in 1956 to run for the Democratic senatorial nomination in Nevada—issued a statement blasting the Republican Party for countenancing a man (meaning Javits) who had knowingly trafficked with Communists. Admirers of our theoretically untrammeled press will be interested to know that for almost 48 hours no paper in America (at least, so far as I have been able to discover) carried this arresting story. Then on Thursday the 23rd the *Buffalo Courier-Express* reported it. That tore it; without further ado, Javits renewed his request to the Subcommittee, and an executive session was scheduled for Wednesday morning, September 5. The Republican State Committee was scheduled to meet in Albany on Monday the 10th to pick a senatorial nominee. It was to be a heart-gripping fortnight for all concerned.*

* Readers are invited to compare the foregoing detailed description of Senator Javits' elaborate maneuvers in August 1956 with his bland description of the same episode on a CBS broadcast entitled "Washington Conversation" on May 13, 1962. CBS interviewer Paul Niven asked Javits:

> Senator, in 1956, before you—shortly before you first ran for the Senate, you appeared before the Senate Internal [Security] Subcommittee which had allegations that you had had Communist associations; the hearings which came to nothing. But I wonder, was somebody trying to get you and why?

During the last days of August rumors of the forthcoming hearing swept journalistic circles, but hovered just below the level of actual publication in the press. At last, on Thursday, August 30, Javits himself broke the uneasy silence: he was, he declared, being smeared by vicious rumors, and *might* have to request a formal hearing to deny them. The press descended forthwith upon our embattled little office, where I alone was left to tell the tale, Morris having already departed to spend the upcoming Labor Day weekend in Point Pleasant. I simply referred all journalistic inquiries to Point Pleasant, where Bob in turn steadfastly refused any comment whatever.

The truth was that we were all beginning to wonder whether Eastland would go through with the hearing after all. Despite his reputation as a tenacious investigator (or hounder of innocent people, depending on one's point of view), Eastland was actually an extremely cautious and not overly courageous chairman of the ISSC. He had now begun to growl to Morris about the desirability of having other members of the Subcommittee present on the 5th, to share whatever brickbats Fate might have in store for him; and since few (if any) of his colleagues would relish such a role, it seemed entirely possible that Eastland would cave in and refuse to have any hearing whatever, even at Javits' express request. Such were the calculations being weighed, as Labor Day approached, in the inner councils of the Subcommittee that, according to its critics, loved nothing better than smearing people. Finally Eastland's nerve held, and on Saturday, September 1, the ISSC publicly confirmed that, at the express request of Attorney General Javits, it would hear him in executive session on the morning of September 5.

I traveled to Point Pleasant to spend the long Labor Day weekend

---

Senator Javits replied calmly:

> I will never know, Paul. That was really one of the strangest things that's ever happened in my life, because as you say it not only came to nothing, it was nothing. What happened was that some chap who had worked for the Internal Security Committee was running for, in the primary, I think it was for Senator from Nevada and he suddenly out of a clear blue sky, when I was at the Republican Convention in San Francisco in 1956, announced that— made these charges against me to which you have just referred, and the first I heard about it was when the, one of the press associations called me and told me about it and asked if I had any comment, and I was just thunder-struck. So that I subsequently found that these were completely uninvestigated matters which were contained in the files of the Senate Internal Security Committee which this fellow had picked up. Subsequently, incidentally, he ran last in a field of five or six in his primary race in Nevada. But in any case, I insisted on a hearing to Senator Eastland, the Chairman of the Committee, and to Bob Morris, who is now president of a college down in Texas and who was then Counsel for the Committee.

with the Morrises. On the sunny, sloping beach, watching the Morris children play, or at night in the old frame house, listening to the crickets and sniffing the sea fog, Washington and Jacob Javits and the whole long, sick story of domestic Communism seemed incredibly far away. And yet we knew that we were about to pass through a desperately dangerous period, when the slightest misstep might spell not only the ruin of our individual careers—for whatever they were worth—but the destruction of the ISSC itself. For make no mistake: Javits' friends were powerful, and frightened, and furious. The *New York Times* all but bit itself in two editorially, in its rage over the coming hearing and its frustration at the shielding fact that Javits himself had requested it. In an editorial entitled "Mr. Javits Speaks Out," the *Times* left no doubt where its sympathies lay:

> The victim of vague and defamatory innuendo, Attorney General Jacob K. Javits has put himself on the witness stand to make clear to all who will listen his loyalty to our democratic institutions. "Let me say categorically for now and all time that I am not and never have been associated in any way in any Communist activities or organization or knowingly sought the help or aid in public or private life of any person or organization engaged in such activities," he has written to the Republican State Chairman. "Innuendos and rumors to the contrary are just false and my whole life, career and public record give the lie to any such contentions. I have deep convictions about United States world leadership for free institutions, civil liberties in our country and the system of the private economy as being, together with the Constitution, the surest guarantee of our freedom." Mr. Javits . . . is scheduled to appear before the Senate Internal Security Subcommittee in Washington. The degree of justice he receives at the hands of this subcommittee will have an important bearing on the immediate future of Mr. Javits, who is a leading candidate for the nomination for United States Senator, a nomination to be decided by the Republican State Committee meeting next Monday in Albany.
>
> The circumstances in which the flimsy rumors about Mr. Javits have been given circulation require scrupulous political fairness by the subcommittee, which is dominated by Democrats. There should either be complete exoneration of Mr. Javits—in whom we have complete confidence—or the fullest disclosure of any derogatory facts, charges and adverse witnesses so that the public can judge for itself what weight or credibility they deserve.

By Tuesday the 4th we were back in Washington again, and that evening conferred till the wee hours with Ben Mandel, shaping the questions that Bob would put to the supple Mr. Javits. At last we were ready.

The press, of course, was ablaze with curiosity about the hearing—which, be it remembered, was to be held in executive session. Neither Javits nor we had promised that a public hearing would follow the secret one; both the witness and the Subcommittee wanted to appraise the results of the executive session before deciding how to handle that crucial question.

To avoid a crush of reporters at the door, therefore, the executive hearing was set for 10 a.m. Wednesday morning in Bob Morris' little flat in Schott's Alley, a scant half block from the Senate Office Building. Present for the Subcommittee were Senator Eastland, Morris, Mandel, a stenographer, and I. Attorney General Javits arrived punctually, beaming with delight (presumably to be among such old friends again) and accompanied, to our surprise, by Republican Senator J. Glenn Beall of Maryland. Why Javits chose to bring Beall, and why Beall (who, though a liberal Republican, was not really famous for it—or indeed for much of anything else) agreed to come, were and remain mysteries to me. Understandably, Javits may have wanted a friendly witness of senatorial rank. In any case, while Beall was not a member of the ISSC, or even of its parent Judiciary Committee, both common and senatorial courtesy under these rather exceptional circumstances dictated that he be permitted to stay and watch. Which he proceeded to do, without interposing any interruption or interference whatever.

The executive session lasted an hour or more, and naturally cannot be discussed in any detail here. But it did not differ in its broad outlines from the public session which followed at noon in the crowded Caucus Room of the Senate Office Building, before the eyes of a fascinated world. Javits' strategy in both cases was the same: not to offer, at any key point, a *direct* denial of *any* evidence he suspected was in the possession of the Subcommittee. Concede where necessary; forget where possible; minimize at all costs—but *deny*, never. This of course left great chunks of damaging testimony uncontroverted on the record; but Javits evidently counted on his powerful friends, especially in the press, to drown out or at least dilute the obvious implications of such testimony. The great thing, he knew, was to avoid like the plague a flat contradiction of any witness already heard by the Subcommittee, a contradiction that would enable observers to say, "Someone is lying." By the time the executive session was over, Javits knew what testimony was in the Subcommittee's possession and seemed to feel that he could cope with it in public. At any rate, he promptly asked for a public session, and his request was as promptly granted.

Watch, as we quote from the record of the ensuing public session, the masterly broken-field running of this accomplished lawyer-politician.* Senator Eastland began by stressing the point that was his chief shield and buckler:

CHAIRMAN EASTLAND. Mr. Javits, I want the record to show that this hearing is at your request. This is correct, is it not?

MR. JAVITS. That is correct, Senator. May I express to the committee my greatest appreciation for the courtesy and cooperation that is shown in affording me the hearing which it has this morning, in this public hearing, at the direction of the chairman.

MR. MORRIS. I think, Mr. Chairman, since this issue has been raised that I would like the record to show the fact that the initial request by Mr. Javits for this hearing was communicated to me as counsel for the committee on August 3. At that time I was not able to reach Senator Eastland—he was fishing off the coast of Florida at that time—until August 6, at which time Senator Eastland expeditiously tried to make this hearing as early as possible.

I think, General** Javits, you will recall that between the 16th and the 26th August it was impossible for you, and up until the 16th of August it was impossible for the Senator, unless you would agree to a very quiet hearing in Chicago—the fact being that there was a political affair on then.

But the point is that Senator Eastland has tried in every way to have this hearing earlier than today.

MR. JAVITS. Judge Morris—

MR. MORRIS. Because of the political fact, the overtones of this political affair on then. [Morris is referring to the two conventions just concluded.]

MR. JAVITS. I am completely satisfied that the committee has done its utmost to cooperate. They could have said, "We are not calling you—we won't be bothered." On the contrary, it put itself out to answer my request and I am very grateful. And if the chairman will allow me, I would like to say that in all my years in the Congress I tried very hard to get to the point where people would not be ashamed to deal with matters of this kind specifically and on the facts. And I must say that in my case this has come to pass today, and I am very appreciative.

CHAIRMAN EASTLAND. Proceed.

---

* I have taken the precaution of quoting in full the public interrogation of Jacob Javits, as set forth in Part 43 of the Subcommittee's 1956 investigation into "Scope of Soviet Activities in the United States."

** This is the rather misleading courtesy title of an Attorney General.

Morris wasted no time putting on the record a summary of Bella Dodd's crucial testimony:

> MR. MORRIS. Mr. Chairman. General Javits, on the 14th of June 1956 we received in executive session testimony from Dr. Bella Dodd, who had earlier been a member of the National Committee of the Communist Party, a member of the State Committee of the Communist Party, and the person in charge of [its] legislative activities in New York State.
>
> She had testified that some time, as she put it, in 1945 or 1946, she had been told by persons in the Communist Party that a Jacob K. Javits had just come from the west coast, where [i.e., after] he had seen service in Europe, in the European theater and in the Pacific theater; and that, as she put it, "some of our people"—meaning the Communist people, at that time—"were very much interested in Mr. Javits' political future."
>
> And they asked her, if she, in her official capacity, as the person in charge of political activity in New York State, advising and analyzing focal points of Communist support, whether she would have a discussion with Jacob K. Javits. She said that Mr. Javits came to her office, 100 West 42nd Street, and they discussed at that time what district in which he might concentrate in carrying out any activities in connection with his political future.
>
> She said they specifically discussed the Washington Heights district, because the Democratic Party was split there. And she said that thereafter the Communists, for whom she was in charge of the State Committee, did support Mr. Javits in connection with that forthcoming 1946 campaign.
>
> Now, I have tried to be as careful as possible, General Javits, to discuss this particular testimony and to state it for you. And as you know, we mentioned this in executive session today, and we would like to ask you if you will now testify, as much as possible, about that particular episode.
>
> MR. JAVITS. I will be glad to, Judge.

Morris was not always the most precise of interrogators, but the garbled syntax of the passages just quoted is to be blamed on the pressure he was under that afternoon. The slightest error—the tiniest misstatement or overstatement—was sure to be leaped on by Javits' friends in the press corps, and in Eastland's edgy mood it was far from certain that he would defend his counsel if called upon to do so.

Still, the facts as alleged were pretty damning. In 1945-46, Bella Dodd had been one of the most prominent public leaders of the Communist Party in New York State. In or about 1949-50 she had broken with the Party, and had subsequently become its bitter foe. And now, in

1956, she had told the Subcommittee under oath in executive session:
(1) that some ten years earlier, certain of her fellow Communists had
expressed great interest in Javits' political future and had asked her to
talk to him; (2) that Javits had in fact come to her office and discussed
his political future with her; and (3) that thereafter the Communists
had, under her direction, quietly assisted Javits' 1946 candidacy for
Congress.

Before hearing Javits on this subject, however, Morris first wanted to
clear up the matter of his presence on the west coast at the time in
question, and introduce certain other evidence concerning it:

> MR. MORRIS. May I begin, General, by asking—as you told us in execu-
> tive session: Had you been on the west coast prior to this alleged
> meeting with Dr. Dodd?
> MR. JAVITS. I was on the west coast, according to my best recollection,
> in 1945, in the period May-June, in round figures, when I was on
> terminal leave as a lieutenant colonel from the Army, in connection with
> a visit I was making to observe the U.N. Organization, because I had
> nothing better to do with my time at that time.
> And the time to which you refer, which is the only call I have ever
> made upon Dr. Dodd—and I will give all of the details of that, of
> course—is, in round figures, 1 year later.
> MR. MORRIS. Well, now, did you, as the committee has learned, arrive
> —as the committee has been told—I do not know whether it is a fact or
> not—I do not make any presumption whatever about the fact—did you
> arrive in San Francisco on April 22, 1945?
> MR. JAVITS. That date would be reasonably correct. I cannot give you
> the exact date. It was in the spring, and in connection with the U.N.
> conference there.
> MR. MORRIS. Did you go to San Francisco by train?
> MR. JAVITS. My best recollection is that I did.
> MR. MORRIS. You did?
> MR. JAVITS. Yes.
> MR. MORRIS. Did the train have as its terminal point, Oakland?
> MR. JAVITS. Yes.
> MR. MORRIS. The Oakland station?
> MR. JAVITS. Yes.
> MR. MORRIS. Did you get off the train at Oakland in the company of
> Frederick V. Field?

Here Morris had reached an extremely important question. Obviously, he had not pulled it out of the air; the Subcommittee plainly had
information to the effect that Javits *had* got off that particular train in
Oakland on April 22, 1945, in the company of Frederick V. Field. What

made this circumstance so intriguing was the fact that Field was a well-known American Communist at the time (he now lives in Mexico, to spare himself the necessity of further pleas of the Fifth Amendment before Congressional committees), and in April 1945 had just been designated by the *Daily Worker* as its UN correspondent. Javits, of course, was perfectly well aware of Field's reputation when Morris brought up the name, and his reaction was to give us a reprise of the rather vague account he had first offered in executive session:

> MR. JAVITS. I think I can say flatly that I did not get off the train in the company of Frederick V. Field. My recollection upon that subject as I have stated to the committee—I will repeat—is that I met a young man on the ferry who said something about the scenery or some ordinary expression of that kind, who was a college-boy-looking type of chap and described himself as Fred Field and said he was going to cover the UN conference for some newspaper work. And we exchanged some pleasantries that made no particular impression on me. And then I may have seen him—this I have no distinct recollection on—but I may have seen him around the conference to say, "Hi" to—that is all I know about Fred Field or anything to do with him.

Pretty gossamer—and yet Javits did not deny that he had met Field. He did, however, seem to be denying that he *got off the train* with him; and Morris sought to nail down this apparent contradiction of the Subcommittee's information:

> MR. MORRIS. But you will deny, will you not, General Javits, that you got off the train with Fred Field?

Instead Javits neatly sideslipped:

> MR. JAVITS. Well, whether I met Fred Field on the train or not, in the same capacity, I really could not tell you, but I am quite sure that I did not, but in any case, I did not leave New York with Fred Field—I had no business with him—he was not my traveling companion, which I understand to be the purport, the point of the questions.

Eastland now intervened to clarify matters—and instead permitted Javits to slither away under the cover of the word "recollection":

> CHAIRMAN EASTLAND. As I understand this voyage on the train, so far as it is concerned, you have no recollection of meeting him on the train?
> MR. JAVITS. That is true.

Morris now resumed the interrogation:

MR. MORRIS. Did you meet Mr. Field subsequently on the Oakland ferry at an early hour of the morning?

Once again it was obvious that Morris was basing his question on explicit information, and once again Javits fudged:

MR. JAVITS. I have no recollection of that whatever, Judge Morris. I do not even remember when I went back to New York or whether I went back by train or by plane.

MR. MORRIS. And you cannot tell us now whether or not—you cannot recall having a subsequent meeting with Field on the Oakland ferry?

MR. JAVITS. Well, to stretch it to the uttermost, if I ran into him, I ran into him, but I have no recollection of it whatever. And as I say, I don't even remember how I went back to New York.

MR. MORRIS. You have no recollection of making several trips on the ferry while Mr. Field was aboard the ferry?

Now, however, Javits sensed that Morris had shifted to mere probing. He had not been confronted with a flat statement that "the committee has been told that you did make several ferry trips with Field," and he accordingly entered a splashy denial:

MR. JAVITS. I not only have no recollection, but the answer is flatly "No"—decidedly "No." I just went about my traveling, whatever it was, without any business with Field or anybody else of that kind that I can in any—not only cannot recall—the answer is flatly "No."

Morris started to turn to fresh subject matter, then had an afterthought about Frederick Field:

MR. MORRIS. Now, we have been told, General Javits, that an individual named Louise Bransten—and Mr. Mandel, I wonder if you have a short outline of who Louise Bransten is. I would like to put this in its proper framework. I might say in connection with Mr. Field, at that time he was entitled "UN editor to the *Daily Worker.*" That was his title at the time.

Mr. Javits again leaped at the chance to say something—anything —"flatly":

MR. JAVITS. I am glad to get that information, Judge, but I can say flatly that that is something I did not know when he encountered me.

Morris then resumed his development of certain facts concerning a woman named Louise Bransten:

> MR. MORRIS. Mr. Mandel, would you put in the record at this time what evidence we have about Louise Bransten, who she was?
>
> MR. MANDEL. In a previous hearing with Louise Bransten, conducted in October 1953, we placed into the record an FBI memorandum which read as follows:
>
>> During the United Nations Conference on International Organization held at San Francisco in the spring of 1945 Louise Bransten entertained at her home Dimitri Manuilski, the principal representative of the Ukraine SSR, who was more widely known as a long-time official and spokesman for the Communist International. Bransten is at the present time [November 1945] in New York City where she has established contact with Pavel Mikhailov, acting Soviet consul general, who has been reported to this Bureau and to the RCMP [Royal Canadian Mounted Police] by Igor Gouzenko, mentioned elsewhere in this memorandum, as the head of the Red Army intelligence espionage activity—
>
> MR. MORRIS. That is all now about Bransten?
>
> MR. MANDEL. Yes. [Continuing]:
>
>> Gregori Makovich Kheifetz, whose cover name was Mr. Brown, was, until his departure from San Francisco for the Soviet Union, July 6, 1944, the vice consul [at the Soviet consulate] at San Francisco. According to the protocol form filed by the Soviet Embassy with the Department of State, Kheifetz was born in Moscow, in 1899. Reportedly, from this protocol form, Kheifetz served as vice president of the Society for Cultural Relations with Foreign Countries—
>
> MR. MORRIS. I think that is enough. [Not quite. Neither Morris nor Mandel got around to adding that in 1949 an FBI agent had sworn that Louise Bransten had met Kheifetz in November 1942 and was subsequently "a constant associate of his in his NKVD activities."]
>
> CHAIRMAN EASTLAND. Proceed.
>
> MR. MORRIS. Is there anything else, Mr. Mandel, that should be in the record by way of characterizing Louise Bransten?
>
> MR. MANDEL. I have here a memorandum from the House Committee on Un-American Activities in its hearings conducted in August and September 1950. May I read a portion of it?
>
> MR. MORRIS. Yes, very briefly.
>
> MR. MANDEL. [Quoting:]
>
>> Louise Berman, formerly Louise Bransten. During the hearings in October 1947 regarding Communist infiltration of the motion picture industry, before the Committee on Un-American Activities, Louise Bransten was identified as a native of Berkeley, Calif. and an heiress to a considerable fortune. The home of Louise Berman, then Bransten,

was described as a meeting place of Communists and Communist sympathizers in the vicinity of San Francisco. Many social affairs were given in her home, also, for the purpose of entertaining and bringing together Communist Party members, including members of Communist espionage rings. She was in contact with several persons who were employed by the Soviet Government, including Vassili Zubelin, of the Soviet Embassy, in Washington, D.C.

MR. MORRIS. Then, it goes on to list more Soviet personnel, does it not?

MR. MANDEL. Yes.

Javits looked progressively less and less comfortable as these statements were being put into the record, and Morris at last undertook to reassure him:

MR. MORRIS. General Javits, that is strictly for the purpose of identifying her.

MR. JAVITS. I understand there is no implication that involves me in that very long and seamy description.

MR. MORRIS. That is right. [To Mandel:] Thank you.

But Morris thereupon proceeded to ask a question that did indeed involve Mr. Javits with Louise Bransten:

MR. MORRIS. We have information and evidence to the effect that you did know Louise Bransten in San Francisco. I was wondering if you would tell us if you met her—when you met her and as many occasions as possible.

Javits took a deep breath and plunged in:

MR. JAVITS. Yes, Judge, I am glad to. And anything I know about her which is of use to the committee is fine with me.

I was introduced to Mrs. Bransten by a friend of mine and a colleague, because he and I represented for many years the same great corporation, the Crown-Zellerbach Corp., of San Francisco. The gentleman is Philips Ehrlich, one of San Francisco's most distinguished lawyers, who told me about Mrs. Bransten, said I ought to meet her. I was a bachelor then on terminal leave as a lieutenant colonel from the Army. Mr. Ehrlich said that he had just settled an estate for her, her mother's estate, which involved the sale of her interest in a company called Rosenberg Bros., and that she had come into a very considerable amount of money, was a very attractive girl, and I ought to meet her. That I remember. And I have refreshed my recollection by talking with Mr. Ehrlich about that.

Now, the only encounter which I recall with Mrs. Bransten, of my own knowledge, is that I met her for cocktails at the Mark Hopkins Hotel, sometime in that period that I was in San Francisco.

You say I got there in April. Then I will assume that it may be the first few days of May, or something like that. I did not stay more than a week or 10 days. I waited for her for about an hour and a half. When I was about to leave, she arrived, which did not make a particularly good impression.

We had a drink. I did not like her particularly, and she did not me. And, from my recollection, that is the last I saw of her until some years ago, 5, 6, 7, when I ran into her in a grocery store on University Place in New York, where I was going to make a phone call, and she was apparently making a purchase.

I said, "Hello." I do not know whether I called her "Louise" or "Mrs. Bransten." "What are you doing here?" She said that she is married, living in that neighborhood.

I said, "Goodby; good luck," or whatever I did, and was on my way.

Now, Mr. Ehrlich, whom I have endeavored to refresh my recollection with, tells me that he arranged a dinner either at his home or at Mrs. Bransten's home—he is not clear which—that is his recollection. It is not my recollection. That is all I know about Louise Bransten.

It may have been "all," but the coincidences were beginning to pile up: the alleged talk with Bella Dodd (which had still to be confirmed or denied); the encounter with Frederick V. Field (which Javits had not quite dared to deny); and now his meeting—indeed, apparently more than one meeting—with Louise Bransten, who just happened to be a good friend of many prominent Soviet Communists, including several spies.

Morris now sought to refresh Javits' recollection concerning a further meeting with Louise Bransten:

MR. MORRIS. Do you recall a meeting at Bransten's home at which you and she were present, and engaged in a serious conversation and there came into the room a gentleman named Dr. Max Yergan?

Once again Javits' memory failed him:

MR. JAVITS. Judge Morris, I do not remember being at Mrs. Bransten's home. I have really searched my recollection and recall only a very minor fact which I asked you about, as you remember, that I was in some home in San Francisco as a visitor, which had paneling, but apparently you could not identify it. So I could not tell you. So that I cannot tell you that I did or did not go to her home, or meet Max Yergan, but I do know a Max Yergan, and I will be glad to tell you what I know about him, to the best of my knowledge.

MR. MORRIS. I think it would be wise for you to do so.

MR. JAVITS. Max Yergan, as I recall, is a fellow I ran into years ago, I cannot tell you where, who was interested in African affairs. I cannot think of any detailed discussions I had with him, but I think it is logical to assume, with the serious interest I have in these matters of foreign policy, that if he was a fellow interested in African affairs, I had some kind of a parlor discussion with him about what he thought and what I thought, but I had no business or association or closeness of contact or intimacy with Max Yergan.

Morris thereupon furnished some interesting additional details:

MR. MORRIS. Dr. Yergan at the time was the director of the Council on African Affairs, which was an organization which was then controlled by the Communists. Dr. Yergan, being at that time a person who was involved with the Communists, has told the committee that on this occasion he joined you and Louise Bransten in a discussion in the home of Louise Bransten; and we asked him particulars about the house. He said a two-story house, which is entered through a front door, through a hallway, off to the left is a living room and a dining room combined, and going through that room you go into a large living room which has a large picture window looking out on San Francisco Bay.

And presumably in that—in the living room, that was where the discussion took place.

Is it your testimony that you do not recall that?

But the Attorney General's memory just wasn't up to it:

MR. JAVITS. I wish I could. I asked you to give me a clue, because the only memory I have is of some house with paneling. Other than that, I just cannot recollect. I would not say "No," and I would not say "Yes," because I cannot recollect, but I have given you the circumstances of my encounter with Mrs. Bransten, and with the refreshment of memory which comes from talking with the man who introduced us.

Morris now sought to probe Javits' memory concerning yet another encounter with Louise Bransten on a different occasion; and this time he introduced the names of some other fish in California's well-stocked Communist pond:

MR. MORRIS. Now, General Javits, can you recall another occasion, again in Bransten's home, at which were present a man named David

Hedley—and Mr. Mandel, I wonder if you would tell us who David Hedley was at that time?

MR. MANDEL. According to the record available to the committee, the following is the information about David Hedley:

David Hedley was subpoenaed and testified before the California Committee on Un-American Activities, in Oakland, on November 5, 1947. He stated that he was the assistant director of the California Labor School. He admitted that he had taught a course at the predecessor of the California Labor School, the Communist Tom Mooney School.

Incidentally, I might add that the California Labor School has been cited as subversive by the Attorney General.

To go on with the California Committee: Although not a citizen, he stated that he believed that: "Any kind of a political affiliation or political activity that I may engage in is my right guaranteed under the Constitution—that it is not proper for the committee to place questions of that kind."

David Hedley was identified as a member of the Communist Party by Louis Rosser, a former member of the party in California. Rosser testified before the House Committee on Un-American Activities on December 1, 1953, pages 3122 and 3123.

MR. MORRIS. The next name at this meeting about which, General, we would like to ask you a few questions is Nancy Pittman, wife of John Pittman, managing editor at the time of the *People's Daily World.*

Mr. Mandel, do you have anything describing either John Pittman or Nancy Pittman?

MR. MANDEL. In testimony before the House Committee on Un-American Activities on July 21, 1947, John Pittman is listed as a committee member of the California district of the Communist Party. In the above testimony he is also listed as a contributor to the *Daily Worker* and the *Daily People's World* and *Political Affairs,* all three Communist publications. John Pittman was a contributor in the issue of August 1950, his article being entitled, "War on Korea, a Point 4 in Action."

This recital moved Javits to protest:

MR. JAVITS. Mr. Chairman, if I may, I would like to make this observation. It is not charged that I had anything to do with these people. And I think that we can assume that those Judge Morris would ask me about have some kind of a Communist record. And yet, in a public hearing it seems to me that as all of this stuff goes in the record, I do not know who might get some impression that I did or did not have anything to do with that. I put that up to the chairman.

CHAIRMAN EASTLAND. I agree with you. Proceed.

But this was pure timidity on Eastland's part. He knew perfectly well that Morris would never have introduced these names and facts into the record if they had not been pertinent to the inquiry at hand. Morris' very next question revealed their pertinence:

MR. MORRIS. The question is, General, did you meet at the home of Louise Bransten in the company of David Hedley, Nancy Pittman, and Louise Bransten sometime during this period?

Javits' reply was a masterpiece of caution:

MR. JAVITS. I have not the remotest recollection of meeting any of these people. If it were not 11 years ago, and that this was not dredged out of the past, I would say flatly, "No." But how can one who encounters thousands of people, goes to hundreds of homes, attends hundreds of meetings—I just would not do it as a lawyer—I would not be that reckless. I have no recollection whatever of these people or, indeed, we might have been, but if so, it was certainly not more than once, because, as I say, Mrs. Bransten and I just did not take to each other. That was that.

It sounds so forthright, doesn't it? And yet, save for a bunch of apologies for his memory, all Javits had really said was, in effect, "I don't remember." Morris tried to prod his recollection with a piece of information about the meeting that sounded ominously specific:

MR. MORRIS. And did you at that particular meeting discuss a luncheon that you had with Max Radin that day or the day earlier?

Once again Javits' reply sounds candid and unequivocal:

MR. JAVITS. Again, I answer in the frame of reference I have mentioned before, "No."

Unfortunately "the frame of reference [he had] mentioned before" was (as already noted) a mass of qualifiers that neatly denatured his "No." He was full of information about Max Radin, however, which Morris had not requested.

MR. JAVITS. But I would like to tell you that I have a recollection of a Max Radin that I have met the man some time since 19—since I got out of the Army, because my life in a sense began again at that time in a social way. And as I recall Max Radin, he is the dean of a law school in

California. Whether I had lunch with him or not—what I ever said to him or he to me—I just do not know—but again, this is a man with whom I have no particular association, business connection or anything else.

Now Morris returned at last to the deadly testimony of Bella Dodd:

MR. MORRIS. Now, General Javits, did you subsequently have a meeting, referred to by Dr. Dodd, with Dr. Dodd?
MR. JAVITS. Yes, if you would be good enough to allow me, I would like to state that in some detail, because I guess that is the main point we are talking about.

Indeed it was. And since Javits' reply was correspondingly lengthy, we will comment on his points as he made them.

MR. JAVITS. [continuing]
In the area of May-June 1946, when I was in the process of being nominated for Congress, it is my recollection that I got—whether I got it myself or the Liberal Party gave it to me or friends gave it to me—a long list of people that I ought to see, to get educated about what is going on in New York. I had been out of things from about 1941 until I came back in 1945. And this included university presidents, ministers of various faiths, newspaper editors, et cetera. And I went the rounds.

So far so good.

MR. JAVITS. [continuing]
When this Bella Dodd question first came up, or excuse me, Dr. Dodd, first came up, I had searched my recollection and, remember this, that in that period I went to see Dr. Dodd, it was my recollection, as one of the people on that list to get educated, about teachers with which I was told—with whom I was told she had some connection as a secretary —I have since refreshed my mind on it—of the teachers' union for many years.

Superficially plausible, if a little disjointed. The aspiring candidate, making the rounds of opinion leaders and similar knowledgeable types, is advised by somebody to call on Bella Dodd, who "had some connection as a secretary . . . of the teachers' union." And indeed Bella Dodd had been for many years the Legislative Representative of the New York Teachers' Union. What Mr. Javits neglected to add was that by 1946 the Teachers' Union had been identified for at least five years as a Communist-controlled organization; that Bella Dodd had stepped down as its Legislative Representative back in 1944; and that she was, at the very moment he called on her, the declared Communist Party candidate for Attorney General of the State of New York.

MR. JAVITS. [continuing]

Now, in an effort to refresh my recollection on this whole situation about Dr. Dodd, I talked with one of the men who was my political mentor in that period, that is, in the 1946 period, who is Alex Rose, the political head in a sense of the Liberal Party. And Alex tells me the following, which may and may not have any connection with my visit to Dr. Dodd, but I am stating it because I want to give everything which I possibly can think of that could have any connection.

He says that I told him in a meeting when we were talking about the Liberal Party designation—and let me emphasize that it was a designation—not a nomination, because the Liberal Party was not even on the ballot—you had to go out and get 3,000 signatures of citizens in the district that were valid to even get on the ballot—and that was some rough job—but I told him that some friends of mine were talking about the fact that I ought to try to get an ALP designation for Congress, because that would help me get elected in a district which was 2 to 1, 3 to 1 Democratic, the 21st Congressional District. And I have the details here. That many Democratic candidates and some Republican candidates had taken the ALP designation, including the assemblyman who was running with me in the principal part of my district, Samuel Roman, who was running in the 15th Assembly District.

That when I told Alex that, he says—now he refreshes me on this, and I accept it and state it as a fact—he said, "Don't you know Jack, that this ALP crowd, we have just broken off from, and they are Commie dominated."

And then I said, "I want no part of them. I would rather lose the election. I will not go in for any deals like that."

And that was that.

MR. MORRIS. Was this in connection with the 1946 campaign?

MR. JAVITS. My first campaign for Congress.

In this wordy anecdote, Javits is trying to demonstrate that he was strenuously opposed to dealings with Communists back in 1946, the very period under discussion. His point, quite simply, is that he had considered seeking the support of the American Labor Party in his race for Congress that year (as other major-party candidates had done), but that he dropped the idea instantly on being advised by Alex Rose, one of the top leaders of the leftish but anti-Communist Liberal Party, that the ALP was Communist-dominated.

This little story is inherently so appealing that it seems almost cruel to note that one of its key points is wildly implausible: namely, the proposition that Javits was unaware that the ALP was Communist-controlled in 1946 until Alex Rose told him so. We were soon to hear—indeed, Javits had already heard in the executive session—a less complimentary version of this episode or a very similar one. Meanwhile, sophisticated observers undoubtedly smiled inwardly at Javits' professed innocence on the subject of the ALP, but noted an important secondary aspect of his account: by invoking the name of Alex Rose in support of his version, Javits was quietly playing a powerful card. In 1956 Rose was not only widely recognized as a long-time anti-Communist, but was a major figure in New York politics. If he was standing by Jack Javits today, this was a fact of great practical importance, whatever Javits might have done or been in the past.

With that point made, Javits relaxed a bit, and treated us to a long and largely irrelevant account of his entry into Republican politics:

> MR. JAVITS. [continuing] I think it might also be helpful, Mr. Chairman, to detail how I got into trying to run for Congress. And if I may, I will do that as briefly as I can.
>
> CHAIRMAN EASTLAND. Proceed.
>
> MR. JAVITS. In 1945, when I came back from San Francisco, the logical thing would have been for me to just go back and practice law, as I did before, but like so many people who had served, I was not too happy about that. I wanted to do something else. My brother, who is the senior partner in my law firm, asked whether I thought I had a chance, at least, and an entry, if I wanted to go to work for Jonah Goldstein, who was the Republican-Liberal-Fusion candidate for Mayor in New York City, who was a good friend of ours, and whom we all knew as "Johnny."
>
> I said that sounded interesting to me. I would go and see him. He was in the Criminal Courts Building. And I said, "I would like to help you, Johnny, if that is agreeable to you."
>
> And he said it was. And a few days later gave me the job of being head of his research division, which I organized and put together.

An interesting *datum*. The New York mayoralty election was held in November 1945, and Javits testified that he had organized and headed the Research Division of the Goldstein campaign—a job requiring a very considerable degree of knowledge about political matters. Yet he managed to discharge it without ever learning that the American Labor Party was Communist-dominated. And just six months later he had walked into the office of Bella Dodd, National Committeewoman of the Communist Party for the State of New York, without—as he would shortly testify—realizing her political affiliation!

Javits continued regaling us with irrelevancies:

MR. JAVITS. [continuing]

In connection with that activity I met the managers of the Goldstein campaign, Arthur Schwartz of New York, and Bill Groat of Queens. I also met a number of the Liberal Party leaders, Alex Rose, Dave Dubinsky, a man named Davidson, who was their secretary, and many other officials of the Liberal Party.

After the campaign was over, Arthur Schwartz or Bill Groat or both, talked with me about whether or not I might like to run for Congress in some district which the Republicans never got anywhere in, anyhow, but which might be interesting to me, if I wanted to break into active political life. I said I would be interested.

They thereupon told me that the opening was, at the moment, in the lower East Side where I was born, where there was a special election. This was, say, December-January, 1945-46. I said I would look into it and let them know.

I went to see Sam Koenig, a very old friend of mine, and a former Republican leader of New York County. And I asked him about running in his district, which was the lower East Side district. Sam said, "You were born there, it is true, but I advise you strongly against it. You would not get anywhere."

So I went back and told Bill Groat and Arthur Schwartz, "This doesn't look like a good thing for me. Maybe we could have another."

They then turned up a couple months later with the idea of possibly doing something on Washington Heights.

Incidentally, when I told them this, they asked where I had lived. (And I say "them" because I do not know whether it was Arthur Schwartz or Bill Groat or both or mixtures of different kinds.) I said I had lived in Brooklyn when I went to Boys High School, and finally lived on Washington Heights, where I had been in the first graduating class of the local high school, George Washington High School.

A couple of months later, Arthur Schwartz or Bill, I think it was Arthur, suggested the possibility of a candidacy on Washington Heights, where also the Republicans never got anywhere and said he knew a leader up there, Sam Leppler, Republican leader—he would introduce me to Sam, and that they would try to work this out.

He thereupon did that. And in a meeting in his office on Broadway, 1440 or 1441, I met Sam Leppler, and Sam said he liked me, thought it was a good idea. From there we went on trying to get the Republican nomination which I will say immediately was not too tough, because their man had been beaten regularly 2 to 1 up there for more years than I am old.

At the same time, I then told them that I would try for the Liberal Party endorsement, which might give me a chance, and I then went to work with Alex Rose, and everything that has happened to me in a political sense has followed that situation.

By this time we had been all around Robin Hood's barn, and Morris moved to bring his loquacious witness back to the point:

MR. MORRIS. General Javits, may we get back to the encounter with Bella Dodd?

MR. JAVITS. Certainly.

MR. MORRIS. At that time, is it your testimony you did not know that she was, you might say, openly and notoriously a member of the national committee of the Communist Party?

MR. JAVITS. I have no recollection of knowing that, Judge Morris. I do not know what the newspapers showed at that time, either. I can only tell you this: That it is inconceivable to me that I would call, for any reason, on a person who was an open and avowed Communist. That is all I can tell you about it.

But I did make the call, and I have explained everything I remember about it, or can find out by talking to other people who might have known.

Now, one may surely be pardoned for considering this an extraordinary piece of testimony, especially in the context of what had gone before. Here was a smart and prosperous New York attorney who "really could not tell" whether he met the *Daily Worker's* UN correspondent on a train in 1945; who "just cannot recollect" whether he was thereafter in the home of a noted lionizer of Communists; who "has not the remotest recollection" of meeting two named individuals with Communist associations in that home (but also won't deny it); who shortly after these alleged events took on the highly responsible job of Research Director for the Republican candidate for Mayor of New York, without learning in the process that the American Labor Party was Communist-dominated; and who then, a few months later still, admittedly called on Dr. Bella Dodd in connection with his own Congressional campaign—yet has "no recollection of knowing" that she was, at that time, a member of the National Committee of the Communist Party.*

Morris swiftly made it clear that Dr. Dodd's Communist affiliations

---

* The irrepressible *National Review*, in its issue dated September 29, 1956, put it this way:

There was a young man named Javits,
Who had the most sociable habits.
    But unlike you or me,
      On duty or spree,
He encountered more Commies than Babbitts.

were hardly a secret. Into the record went a *New York Times* article on the Communist Party's plans, dated August 13, 1945, describing "Bella V. Dodd, national committee member," and a large picture from *Life*'s issue of July 29, 1946, captioned in part: "Communist leaders stand together at a rally in New York's Madison Square Garden. Left to right: Dr. Bella V. Dodd . . ." Javits saw the damaging implication of these documents without any difficulty, and tried to minimize it as best he could:

> MR. JAVITS. I will say, if you will allow me, that I saw Dr. Dodd before that July date. I would think that the nominations, primary, and so forth, were pretty well crystallized along about May-June of 1946.

But, while Javits thus placed his talk with Bella Dodd as having occurred *before* publication of the *Life* article, there was little he could do about the fact that it had occurred some nine months *after* the story in the *Times*. Moreover, as I have noted—and although Morris regrettably did not put the fact in the record—Bella Dodd was already, in the spring of 1946, the declared candidate of the Communist Party for Attorney General of New York (a post that Javits himself, ironically, was holding at the time of our hearing). While the average New Yorker in 1946 might have been forgiven for overlooking the Communist allegiance of such a prominent public personality as Dr. Dodd, it is simply not credible, in view of Javits' history, his interests, and his immediately preceding activities, that he was ignorant of it.

Morris now turned to an area already touched on by Javits. According to information in the Subcommittee's possession, Javits in both 1946 and 1948 had been volubly confident, in talks with political associates, that he could have the American Labor Party nomination for the asking. This, if true, tended to confirm Bella Dodd's testimony, because the ALP in 1946-48 was solidly controlled by the Communist Party through long-time fellow-traveling Congressman Vito Marcantonio. Javits, as we have seen, did not even deny that he could have had the ALP nomination in 1946, but did insist that he had personally vetoed the notion on hearing of the Communists' control of the ALP. On the other hand, the Subcommittee's information suggested that Javits' rejection of the ALP endorsement was due to the bitter opposition of the Liberal Party leaders to the whole idea, rather than to any squeamishness on his own part. (The Liberal Party had split off from the ALP in 1944, in protest against the Communists' control of the latter; and it certainly was not disposed to let any Republican it had endorsed accept the ALP designation as well.)

All of this ground had been covered in the executive session, and Javits was well prepared for it. His one supreme objective, clearly, was not to contradict, in any factual particular, the assertions of any of his Liberal Party associates:

> MR. MORRIS. Did Murray Baron, the chairman of the Liberal Party in New York County, make clear to you on several occasions that you would not be allowed to take the Liberal Party—retain the Liberal Party designation, if you had an ALP designation?
>
> MR. JAVITS. This meeting I referred to with Alex Rose, again in an effort to refresh my recollection, I talked with Mr. Baron, who was very active in the Liberal Party at that time. He tells me he attended that meeting, and remembers that I was so told.
>
> I have no doubt that on that occasion and other occasions the Liberal Party made it very clear to me they were completely at war with the ALP. I would assume, Judge, too, that having run on this ticket four times, they looked me over very carefully with X-ray eyes, and were pretty well convinced that I wouldn't be interested in the ALP.

This comfortable assumption, however, was badly shaken by Morris' next question:

> MR. MORRIS. Did you not tell Murray Baron, in connection with the 1946 election, that you could have either the secret support of the ALP or they would remain neutral, depending on what you wanted? Mr. Baron has told us that.

Whereupon Javits headed for the high timber:

> MR. JAVITS. I wouldn't challenge Murray Baron because I have the highest regard for him.
>
> I have no such recollection, and I would like to point out to you that the ALP candidate, a man named Connolly, tried to win the Democratic Party nomination in an election, so the facts are not consistent with that proposition. They did their utmost to knock me off in 1946 and [again in] 1948, when they ran Paul O'Dwyer, and he almost defeated me.
>
> MR. MORRIS. Wasn't the problem to keep the ALP and the Democrats from endorsing the same person, because they together would be an insurmountable bloc?
>
> MR. JAVITS. This fellow Connolly ran in the Democratic Party primary. You couldn't do any more than that. He tried to capture that.

Javits' point here was that—whatever he had said to Murray Baron, or vice versa—the ALP, instead of volunteering to endorse him in 1946, had run a candidate of its own (Connolly). Javits chose to construe this as evidence of the ALP's opposition to him. Morris, in response, pointed out that the ALP, by running a candidate of its own rather than endorsing the Democratic candidate or sitting the race out, was actually helping Javits, because it thereby drew away leftist votes that would otherwise probably have gone to the Democrat.

But Morris was not through. He next turned to the election of 1948. (Javits, by the way, had in that year been the only Republican member of Congress to vote *against* renewing the appropriation of the House Committee on Un-American Activities.)

MR. MORRIS. Subsequent to 1946, didn't you again tell Murray Baron that you had word from a man named Louis Merrill, who was one of the leaders of one of the Communist-controlled unions, that he would help, if you wanted his assistance, in the forthcoming 1948 campaign?

But Javits had his rule, and he stuck by it grimly:

MR. JAVITS. Again, the last thing in the world I would want to do is challenge Murray Baron, who is a good friend of mine, and who has been swell.

Incidentally, Murray Baron was one of the principal factors in winning the 1948 campaign for me. He campaigned in Inwood, which is a very tough part of my district, as a Liberal Party member. This was almost running a physical risk. I just remember no such conversation.

I am sure I reported to Murray and to Alex Rose every conceivable political fact which came to my attention, because they were the people I looked to to guide and help me.

MR. MORRIS. He has told us that this particular conversation about Merrill took place in a taxicab. You cannot recall that?

MR. JAVITS. I am sorry. I wish I could. I can only give you the frame of reference.

May I just add one further word, which my brother just handed me a note of, and I remember it, and I would like to state it for the record:

Another one of the men who helped me get the Liberal Party nomination and support was Eugene Lyons.

(Evidently the Javits brothers had decided—quite soundly—to put in the record the names of noted anti-Communists who had aided him.) Morris pressed on:

MR. MORRIS. Now, General Javits, in connection with the 1948 campaign, wasn't there a discussion at the time that if the Democrats and the ALP would endorse the same candidate, the combination of the Republican and Liberal votes would be overcome by such a combination, and at that time did you not take up with Baron and with Alex Rose the possibilities of your having ALP support in the 1948 campaign?

Morris was plainly paraphrasing what the Subcommittee had already been told by somebody, and Javits was accordingly most cautious in his reply:

MR. JAVITS. In the 1948 campaign there was unquestionably a conversation about the fact that this was a very tough combination to beat, and that we probably might not be able to beat it, but I recall no discussion about my taking ALP. On the contrary, I am very clear, aside from the muddle I may have been in in the 1946 campaign, when I was new on the job, in a sense, I had no doubts about the ALP thereafter.

By 1948 I had served 2 years in Congress, and I had encountered ALP doctrine in the shape of its Congressmen here.

MR. MORRIS. It is your testimony that you did not ask to have ALP support?

No, it wasn't. Instead:

MR. JAVITS. I have no such recollection, Judge. The only thing one can do, like myself, who does so many things, is to try to get a recollection in the frame of reference, and this, it seems to me, to be absolutely inconsistent with everything I was doing at the time.

I will tell you this: You can explore any number of things with your political confidants, and what recollection they would have about them, and I would have about them, would be very different, and yet one might not necessarily contradict the other. I would not contradict Murray Baron. I know the man and have the highest regard for him.

Regard not unmixed, one suspected, with a certain amount of fear.

Morris then concluded with a small item concerning the astonishing praise heaped by a close Javits associate on Bella Dodd's successor as Legislative Representative of the Communist-controlled Teachers' Union in 1954 (less than two years before our hearing took place).

MR. MORRIS. Did the Liberal Party—Does a man, Sam Roman, work for you?

MR. JAVITS. Sam Roman is the assemblyman of the Fifteenth Assembly District who ran with me four times, the man I referred to before, and he is now one of my executive assistants.

MR. MORRIS. Did the Liberal Party object through you [i.e., to you] to a tribute that Sam Roman paid to Rose Russell, the legislative representative of the Teachers' Union, on November 20, 1954?

MR. JAVITS. Judge, I cannot—

MR. MORRIS. The protest was presumably because he was your executive assistant and that he should not—

MR. JAVITS. November, 1954 he was not my executive assistant. I took office as Attorney General in January, 1955, and in November, 1954, he was a defeated assemblyman.

MR. MORRIS. Was there a protest, did they protest to you that a man who was associated with you should publicly commend Rose Russell? Was there such a protest?

Connoisseurs of the Javits style will have no difficulty, by this time, in predicting the opening words of his reply:

MR. JAVITS. I have no recollection of it, but I do recall that I had to relegate Sam Roman to the Liberal Party to work out his own fortunes on occasions for one reason or another, whatever they might be, but I think it would be very unfair to Mr. Roman for me to say anything about that in this context. I just don't know. I don't have any recollection whatever of any such discussion, but he didn't work for me at the time, as I just made clear.

MR. MORRIS. Well, General Javits, the question was based on the committee evidence and information that we have.

The questioning was over, and—whatever the participants and spectators privately thought—it was bound to end in an exchange of civilities.

MR. MORRIS. As you know, as we made clear from the very beginning, we were having this hearing only to afford you an opportunity to give your version of the committee evidence and information.

MR. JAVITS. Certainly. Thank you, Judge.

MR. MORRIS. There are many things, Senator, that we could go into, that are not particularly important. We cannot trail this thing out to the very end. But what we have presented to you, General Javits, is for the most part the committee information and evidence which has been accumulated in the record of the committee during the course of our current investigation of Communist penetration into the political parties, and in no sense do we present this in any context other than in connection with your request for a hearing today.

MR. JAVITS. It is my duty as Attorney General, as a citizen, as a former Congressman, to come to you and do what I am doing here. I am delighted to see this committee handling matters with such meticulousness and in any way I can contribute information, I want to, and if you feel I have left anything unsaid and you want to question me again, go to it. I will be very pleased to do so.

I would hope that before we are through with the hearings, you will allow me, and I know it is asking a great deal, to introduce into the record something of which I am very proud, my congressional record, which consists of letters and reports entered into the Congressional Record which I wrote twice a year, so that they were not done in preparation for this hearing, to all my constituents, where I stake my political neck, and I think, Mr. Chairman, with all modesty, that it represents an effective anti-Communist struggle, which I put up here as a Congressman and as a member of the Foreign Affairs Committee of which I am very proud, and I would consider it a great privilege from the Chair if the Chair would allow me to do that.

CHAIRMAN EASTLAND. Yes, I will permit you to place that in the record.

MR. JAVITS. Thank you.

It is impossible to read Javits' testimony with a rationally skeptical mind and still believe he was being wholly candid with the Subcommittee. One simply does not, even after eleven years, have a near-total failure of recollection concerning a whole series of encounters like those Javits had with Louise Bransten and her Communist friends in San Francisco in 1945. Nor is it credible that a lawyer-politician with Jacob Javits' experience, sophistication, and sources of information would blunder into Bella Dodd's office in the spring of 1946, in pursuit of her political help, without even knowing that she was, at that very moment, the Communist Party's National Committeewoman from New York and its declared candidate for Attorney General of the State. Finally, there is no reason—certainly Javits provided none—for doubting the assertion of Murray Baron that Javits, in both 1946 and 1948, had told the Liberals that he could have the ALP designation, with all that implied.*

---

* Senator Javits' memory has not improved with the years. Consider the following account of our hearing that he gave CBS interviewer Paul Niven on May 16, 1962:

> I got the hearing and what they apparently had in their files is that when I was an Army—still an Army officer but just about to leave the Army on, I think some kind of—I forget the technical term which is used with respect to it but—(Mr. Niven: "Terminal leave?") Terminal leave, exactly. The last two months of my service—I had been posted by my service out to the United Nations organization in San Francisco in '45 as an observer, and apparently at that time both socially, in a cocktail party or something, and meeting some fellow on a ferry who—the greatest happenstances in the world, I ran into people whom the FBI was following, and naturally the FBI—I

But if we must conclude that Javits was being disingenuous in his testimony, it does not *necessarily* follow that he was, at any time, personally a Communist or even sympathetic to Communist ends. That conclusion is of course possible; but it is equally possible that he was merely the sort of opportunist we have seen before in American (and not only American) politics: an office-seeker who was not fastidious about where he solicited support. In 1945 and early 1946, the public attitude toward the Soviet Union and international Communism was measurably mellower than it later became, and domestic Communists, while widely unpopular, were far more visible and vocal than they are today. Javits may have decided to chance a relatively innocuous romance with the Communists in those years, and then quietly dropped it when the Cold War made such gambits too risky.

On the other hand, if truth is to be of any concern in politics, the bellows of the pro-Javits press immediately after the hearing were unforgivable. The *New York Times,* editorially, took the preposterous position that nothing whatever reflecting on Javits had come out of the hearing:

> We must say that the evidence made public thus far leaves our confidence in Mr. Javits unshaken. Most of it is the tawdry, dreamy stuff so often pulled out of a committee hat to make somebody look a little gray when he cannot be utterly blackened.
>
> Did you get off the train with a certain man? Did you meet a young man on a ferry, not only on a ferry but early in the morning on a ferry? Did you take a "voyage" on a train with somebody? Did you meet somebody in a West Coast living room that was to the left of a hall? . . . No evidence is offered at any point that Mr. Javits had direct or even lefthanded help from Communists or left-wingers in winning public office, unless it held against him that he was sometimes opposed in a Congressional race by an A.L.P. man and this helped divide the Demo-

---

didn't necessarily have any connection with these people of any kind. As a matter of fact one of them was very amusing, it was a girl who a lawyer friend of mine in San Francisco thought it would be a good idea if I married. She happened to be very well placed socially and a person of considerable means but apparently they were following her and this other chap that was concerned whom I met on a ferry, it was just happenstance, admiring the San Francisco skyline. So they had my name in their files in this connection. And also when I was making the rounds in New York in respect of getting the Republican and Liberal Party designations in '46, I called on everybody and his grandfather in order to make myself known and apparently again I ran into somebody who they were keeping close tab on, and of course there again a record was made of it.
Period.

cratic vote. There are some things eight and ten years ago that Mr. Javits cannot remember, or where his recollection differs from that of others. Most of us would have similar trouble. He wasn't too clear back in 1946, when he first ran for Congress, on the coloration of the American Labor Party, whose right wing broke off and formed the Liberal Party in 1944. Liberal party leaders set him right on what A.L.P. meant, and he never ran with the A.L.P. endorsement. The Javits record—and he stands unimpeached in our considered opinion as a good, fair-minded, liberal, loyal American—belies these last-hour efforts to besmirch his good name. If this is all the Eastland committee has to deliver it should say so and offer apology and an honorable discharge to Mr. Javits.

Quite a different view, however, was being taken in the high councils of the New York Republican Party, as I learned later through my own sources in the GOP. On Friday evening, September 7 (the day after the *Times* editorial just quoted), a caucus of New York Republican leaders was held in New York City under the chairmanship of ex-Governor Thomas E. Dewey, to consider Javits' strong bid for the Senatorial nomination. A phone call was placed to U.S. Attorney General Herbert Brownell, Dewey's long-time ally, who had certainly read the transcript of our public hearing and probably had reviewed the Justice Department files as well. Dewey asked Brownell for a frank assessment of the case against Javits. Brownell's reply was not reassuring. Disconsolately, the group in New York reviewed other possible nominees. For various reasons it was considered essential that the candidate be Jewish. The names of N.Y. Attorney General Nathaniel Goldstein and RCA Board Chairman David Sarnoff, among others, were considered and gloomily rejected. Someone suggested phoning Bob Morris for a talk about Javits, but nobody could find his home number. At last the conferees broke up, with no decision reached. Governor Dewey, however, seems to have been determined to find a way to stop the Javits nomination if it was humanly possible to do so.

Saturday morning's *New York Herald Tribune*, however, gave the Javits candidacy another and important boost. In a front-page editorial headed "Javits for Senator," the doyen of Eastern Republican newspapers endorsed his cause. This was a major development, for at least as late as Wednesday afternoon the "Trib's" high command was undecided (and perhaps sharply divided). Evidently Javits' friends had been busy, and successfully so.

Sunday the 9th passed in comparative silence, at least as far as I was aware. That evening Walter Winchell reported, on his regular radio broadcast, that Javits would be nominated by the Republican State

Committee the next day, despite what Winchell identified as Dewey's opposition. According to Winchell, Eisenhower favored the Javits nomination—which confirmed other rumors reaching us. It seems, incredibly enough in retrospect, that Eisenhower, who would be up for reelection that November, was genuinely afraid that Adlai Stevenson might defeat him, and considered that if he blocked Javits' nomination he would enrage Jewish voters in New York and elsewhere, thereby increasing his own peril.

The Republican State Committee was to meet in Albany early on the afternoon of Monday the 10th. Before it did so, Dewey made one last secret, desperate effort to stop the Javits designation. On Monday morning, Republican National Chairman Leonard W. Hall was on Capitol Hill, testifying before the Gore Committee on Election Expenditures. Midway in the hearing he was called away to the telephone. The caller, whose business was evidently urgent, was Alger Chapman, for many years Treasurer of the New York Republican State Committee and widely known as one of the two or three most intimate friends of Thomas Dewey. Choosing his words with care, Chapman stated it to Hall as *his* opinion that Dewey himself would agree to run for the Senate *if publicly asked* to do so by President Eisenhower. Hall got the point, hung up, and promptly called the White House, where he was put through to Presidential Assistant Sherman Adams. He relayed Chapman's message, and added the warning that, if the President was going to act, he'd better act quickly because the Javits nomination was only hours away. Adams thanked Hall noncommittally for his phone call.

One may assume that the next couple of hours were fairly tense—at the White House, in Dewey's New York office, and in Albany, where the State Committee was gathering. But the minutes ticked on and nothing broke the silence at 1600 Pennsylvania Avenue (which some wag, on another occasion, had dubbed "The Tomb of the Well-Known Soldier"). At last the Albany session got under way. The Executive Committee of the State Committee was the first to act: by a vote of seventeen to eight it endorsed Javits. Thereupon, all opposition collapsed. Late in the afternoon, the full Republican State Committee formally and unanimously nominated Jacob Javits for membership in the United States Senate.

For me, as a lifelong and indeed rather impassioned Republican, this action marked a watershed. The Javits hearing was no secret; its transcript had been carried in full in the *Times* and elaborately summarized in every other newspaper in the State of New York. At a very minimum, it strongly suggested that Javits had cynically and opportunistically solicited Communist support in launching his political career just eleven years before. And yet, knowing this, the Republican State Committee of New York, bowing to the pressures that weighed down upon it, had blandly and unanimously nominated this man for the U.S. Senate. I sympathized with one member of the State Committee who, knowing what was about to happen and sickened by it, deliberately missed the meeting. For my own part, I formally transferred my legal residence that fall from New York to Washington, so that I would not have to break a lifelong habit by voting for Javits' Democratic opponent, Robert Wagner.

There remained the question as to what, if anything, the Subcommittee should do further in the Javits case. To be sure, the Javits hearing had been held at his instigation, not ours; and anyway his nomination for the senatorship obviously made it difficult, probably impossible, to proceed without charges that a Democratic subcommittee was merely trying to "smear" him in the midst of his campaign. On the other hand, the ISSC was in possession of sworn testimony (summarized by Morris in his questions to Javits at the public hearing) which, if not squarely contradicted by his adroit replies, certainly was at variance with his innocent explanations. Morris and I favored putting these witnesses on in public session and inviting Javits to contradict them under oath if he dared. The decision, however, rested in the cautious hands of Chairman Eastland, and he preserved a Buddha-like silence on the subject. Throughout the remainder of September we waited, but no indication came from on high. Understandably, Eastland could hardly be very eager to press an investigation of a man who might well become, within four months, a member of the Senate himself. But what about the larger issues involved?

There is some reason to believe that Eastland may have referred the whole sticky question (of whether to continue the Javits investigation) to the Democratic Party, and even to its New York branch. But if so, he received either a negative reply or none at all, for he never gave the signal we awaited so eagerly. Other investigations absorbed our attention; Javits was duly elected to the Senate; and that was that.

And there you have the story—or as much of it as ever seems likely to be told, in these days when the investigation of domestic Communism is under such sharp attack. As for Jacob Javits, you pays your money and takes your choice. It is simply not possible to believe that his Communist contacts in 1945 and 1946 were all totally innocent. But was he a Communist sympathizer, as some of his critics believe? Or was he merely a garden-variety opportunist, as his more candid defenders contend?

6

Subversion in Paradise

Of all the matters competing with *l'affaire Javits* for the attention of the Subcommittee in that autumn of 1956, one of the most intriguing to me personally was the problem of Communist activity in Hawaii. As a boy, listening to the radio with my parents in the 1930's, I had fallen under the spell of "Hawaii Calls," a musical program broadcast from the Hotel Moana at Waikiki, to the accompaniment of the long Pacific breakers pounding on that famous beach. It had been one of my father's ambitions to visit the Hawaiian Islands, but he had died of a heart attack in 1947 with the ambition unfulfilled. Now suddenly it began to seem very likely that I would see Waikiki myself, in line of duty for the ISSC. The trip that ensued was the closest thing to a vacation that I was to get during my seventeen months with the Subcommittee.

For all its mild airs and tropical languors, Hawaii had long been a major target of Communist penetration. It was comparatively small in population and composed of ethnic blocs which could easily be set against one another in economic and political competition. More important still, it had been heavily organized by the International Longshore-men's and Warehousemen's Union, a union solidly dominated by the Communists and led by Harry Bridges, an Australian-born labor leader widely known for his Communist sympathies. Most important of all in the far-seeing eyes of Moscow and its American allies, Hawaii was (and is) the absolutely indispensable bastion of United States military power in the mid-Pacific. In any war with the Soviet Union or Red China, the power to disrupt (for example) the port facilities of Honolulu would be a trump card in Communist hands. Just how vulnerable *was* Hawaii? The members of the Subcommittee indicated they wanted to know.

Fortunately we were not exploring virgin territory. The House Committee on Un-American Activities had held hearings there in 1950, during which thirty-nine witnesses pleaded the Fifth in response to questions concerning Communist activities. In addition, in 1952 the U.S. Department of Justice had launched criminal prosecutions under the Smith Act against seven individuals in the islands, charging them with conspiring to advocate the overthrow of the U.S. government by force and violence. All seven were found guilty, fined, and sentenced to prison terms, but in the latter half of 1956 all were still free on bail, pending the appeal of their convictions.* Finally, the Territorial government itself had not been idle. In 1949, the Territorial Legislature had created a Commission on Subversive Activities, to maintain a regular watch over the Communists in Hawaii. The Chairman of the Commission was William B. Stephenson, whom Bob Morris had met and come to know when both were officers in Naval Intelligence during World War II. It was doubly natural, therefore, that Morris should turn to Stephenson for advice and guidance on the problem of Communism in Hawaii in the autumn of 1956.

The first step was to determine whether developments in Hawaii since the HCUA investigation of 1950 warranted a fresh inquiry into the situation there. For this purpose, Morris flew to Honolulu on Monday, October 1, instructing Frank Schroeder and me to meet him in San Francisco later that week, on his return. Then, if an investigation was recommended by Bob and approved by Eastland and the Subcommittee, Schroeder and I could proceed without loss of precious time to Hawaii to lay the groundwork.

I had already had the various inoculations required of all persons traveling (as Schroeder and I were to do) as guests of the U.S. armed forces, and I ruefully reflected, nursing my sore arm, that it would be hell if I didn't get to Hawaii after all this. On Tuesday, October 2, however, Schroeder and I were aboard a regularly scheduled flight of the Military Air Transport Service, bound nonstop from Washington to Travis Air Force Base, northeast of San Francisco. Save for a

---

* All seven cases were dismissed, and the defendants freed, by the U.S. Court of Appeals for the Ninth Circuit on January 20, 1958, in view of the *Yates* decision handed down by the U.S. Supreme Court in June 1957.

thoroughly exhausting four-stop trip to San Francisco for the Republican convention some six or seven weeks earlier, this was my first westbound flight across the continent, and I watched with fascination as the great map of America unrolled: haughty Chicago, Des Moines amid the prairies, Omaha on the Missouri, the Rockies of southern Wyoming, the parched flats around Great Salt Lake, the barren wastes of Nevada, the pine-clad slopes of the Sierras. At Travis, where we landed near sunset, the Army had provided a little twin-engined LT-23 to take us across San Francisco Bay to a landing strip at the Presidio, its base on the peninsula proper. I will never forget the sheer loveliness of that short flight in the twilight, with the lights of Richmond, Oakland, and San Francisco twinkling on around the bridge-girt Bay: surely one of the most beautiful sights in the world.

The next morning a phone call from Senator Eastland brought us swiftly back to more mundane matters. The chairman was in a gloomy mood about the state of the ISSC's budget, and ill-disposed toward a hearing in Hawaii. He all but said that Morris had exceeded his authority in ordering Schroeder and me to San Francisco. I did my best to mollify him and quickly reported the substance of his remarks by phone to Morris in Hawaii. Bob was noncommittal, but that evening he phoned back and now his mood was different; there were quite definitely developments in the islands that called for an investigation, always provided Eastland would approve. Schroeder and I were to prepare to sail by Army transport to Honolulu on the 6th; he himself would return to San Francisco by plane early that same morning and give us detailed instructions before we sailed, if in fact the Subcommittee flashed the green light.

Schroeder and I spent the 4th and 5th in San Francisco, being processed by the Army authorities and discussing the Communist affiliations of the ILWU and various related subjects with an assortment of west coast experts. On the evening of the 5th, when our tension was building toward dizzy heights, Morris phoned again from Hawaii. He was now passionately convinced that there should be hearings there, but he had been unable to reach Eastland and hence was in no position to authorize us to proceed to Honolulu. He himself, however, would be returning to San Francisco by air early the next morning as scheduled, and we agreed to postpone a decision in the hope that he might have reached Eastland by then—narrow as the margin would be, for our ship was to sail at 11 a.m. (Obtaining new orders, through the Army in San Francisco, for travel to Hawaii by government aircraft might take weeks.) I had the distinct feeling that Bob wanted us to sail with the ship but, lacking Eastland's approval, was unwilling to assume the responsibility of ordering us to do so. A fine dilemma for an eager young special counsel!

Early on the morning of the 6th Schroeder and I were at San Francisco's International Airport. As luck would have it, it was shrouded in the sort of fog that only London and San Francisco ever know: a real "pea souper." As one experienced flyer wisecracked, even the gulls were walking that morning. Somewhere overhead, Bob's plane was circling in the sunshine, watching its fuel and calculating how long it could wait for the sun to burn the deadly cotton off the runways. Meanwhile, the hands on my wristwatch moved inexorably forward toward 11. At 9:30, unable to wait any longer, Schroeder and I decided to take about as long a gamble on Senator Eastland's patience as anyone ever has, and headed for the Army docks. At 11 sharp, in thick, raw weather, the USNS *Fred C. Ainsworth* cast off and sailed under the Golden Gate Bridge onto the broad Pacific, bearing with it two thoroughly edgy members of the staff of the Senate Internal Security Subcommittee.

The Army did its efficient best to make us comfortable, but we were naturally eager to have our status, or more precisely our whereabouts, regularized. So later that day, by radiophone, I spoke with an Army major at the Presidio and asked him to beseech Morris (who, it appeared, had landed at last) to wireless the Subcommittee's decision. The next morning, like a benediction, Morris' reply arrived: Schroeder and I were authorized to stay a week in Hawaii, preparing the groundwork for a hearing in late November. As if to celebrate the news, the sea became calmer; and that night the stars gleamed overhead in the vault of a cloudless sky.

The ocean voyage from San Francisco to Honolulu took five days. As the ship sailed south and west the days grew warmer, and at night one could see phosphorescent patches in the wave created by its prow—the winking lights of innumerable microscopic plankton. The *Ainsworth* was no luxury liner; the great majority of the nonmilitary passengers were the wives and children of military personnel sailing to join their husbands and fathers in Hawaii or the Far East. Schroeder and I shared a cabin containing a double-decker bed, the lower bunk of which Frank claimed by reason of seniority and (tacitly) of avoirdupois. So I developed, perforce, quite a knack for scrambling into the top bunk, even in a pretty fair sea when the ship was yawing sharply.

It was only a day or two before I was overpowered by an all but unutterable languor—composed, I guess, in equal parts of fatigue, the warm salt air, the gentle roll of the ship, and a regime of forced idleness. I would have breakfast, doze a bit, rouse myself for lunch, nap most of the afternoon, join Schroeder for dinner, and then watch the stars wink on over the darkening waters of the Pacific before tottering off to our cabin and making once again that leggy ascent to my sanctuary in the top bunk.

On October 12, having been duly warned the previous evening, I was up and out on deck at dawn. The ship was sailing slowly through Kaiwi Channel, with the island of Molokai low on the eastern horizon and the mountains of Oahu sharply etched against the western sky. As the sun rose we rounded Diamond Head, and at 9 a.m. docked at the Army Port. A military car drove us to our hotel.

We lost no time getting in touch with the two men who were central to our plans for an investigation in Hawaii. About forty years old, blond, heavy-set and cheerful, Bill Stephenson was a prosperous attorney in private practice in Honolulu, as well as Chairman of the Territorial Commission on Subversive Activities. Ted Emanuel, the executive secretary and only full-time employee of the Commission, was a thin, intense figure with deep-set eyes and a chronic cough. Between them, they knew most of what there was to know about the problem of Communism in Hawaii; it was our job to put that knowledge on the record before the Senate and the U.S. public, in the form of expert testimony and relevant witnesses—friendly or otherwise. We conferred with Stephenson and Emanuel all through the afternoon of the 12th, and the next morning paid a brief courtesy call on Governor Samuel Wilder King in frayed but graceful old Iolani Palace, seat of the Territorial government. Then Stephenson turned over to us the Commission's own small office in the basement of the Palace, and we got to work, reviewing the history of previous investigations, examining reports of the recent activities of known Communists and Communist sympathizers, and preparing subpoenas for those whom we decided the Senators should hear.

Our authorized week stretched into ten days, and all of them were busy ones. In addition to the bread-and-butter task I have just described, we made it our business to call on the relevant military authorities, to discuss the measures they had taken to guard against Communist-inspired interruptions of vital public facilities in the event of a crisis involving the Soviet Union or Red China. We also talked informally with a variety of business and political leaders, soliciting their estimates of the degree of Communist influence and penetration in Hawaiian life. Not one of the individuals we spoke to doubted for a moment that the Communist presence was formidable and its menace real. The key Communist-controlled instrumentality in the islands was (as anticipated) the International Longshoremen's and Warehousemen's Union (ILWU), which had long since been expelled from the CIO as Communist-dominated. Headquartered in California and led nationally by Harry Bridges, the ILWU in Hawaii had achieved a degree of political and economic power almost unparalleled by any union, Communist-controlled or otherwise, on the U.S. mainland. Its Hawaiian chief, Jack Hall, was one of the seven individuals who had been prosecuted and convicted under the Smith Act for conspiring to overthrow the U.S. government by force.

But despite the records of these men, the incredible truth was that they were still a recognized and accepted part of the political and economic life of Hawaii. On November 10, less than a month after our arrival and less than three weeks before the hearings themselves actually opened, the Territorial Attorney General, Edward Sylva, appeared at a testimonial dinner in honor of Jack Hall (and was promptly fired by the Governor). The ILWU simply wielded too much political power to be ignored by a prudent politician. As for economic power . . . well, if the ILWU were to strike the docks of Honolulu, or pull off the job the tens of thousands of workers it had organized and controlled, directly or indirectly, in the sugar cane industry and other fields, the Hawaiian economy would, quite simply, grind to a halt.

That was the situation we found, and which we prepared to put before the Senate. Unfortunately, while Hawaii did not lack for brave men in either politics, business, or (least of all) the armed forces, it also had a liberal supply of cowards who were frankly unwilling to buck the ILWU. I remember particularly one prominent Hawaiian politician who had long been allied with the ILWU, but who had recently broken with it, and who was therefore suggested to us as a ripe prospect for cooperative interrogation. We arranged to call on him and were momentarily encouraged by his readiness to meet with us. But when at last we faced him across the table, it developed that all he wanted to do was egg *us* on to investigate his erstwhile friends. When we suggested that he undoubtedly knew a great deal that could aid us in our investigation, a look compounded of sheepishness, caution, and distress crossed his shrewd old face. "Look, fellas," he pleaded. "I'm just a pol. Those guys could *ruin* me. *You're* the investigators—*you* go after 'em."

So after 'em we went. To the U.S. Marshal we handed a first batch of twenty subpoenas, for service on prospectively hostile witnesses. To this number, others were added before we left Honolulu. In addition we secured the cooperation of a large number of business and political figures who were only too glad to help the Subcommittee by appearing before it and giving testimony. At last the job was done. Frank and I, however, having laid the groundwork, were to return to Washington, and would miss the hearings themselves. Murphy, as the saying goes, had had his drink. The hearings were set for late November, and those present for the Subcommittee would be Senators Eastland, Watkins, Johnston, Welker and Butler, plus Bob Morris and Ben Mandel.

We returned to the mainland and Washington on a regularly scheduled flight of the Military Air Transport Service leaving Honolulu on Monday evening, October 22. Bill Stephenson and his fellow Naval Reserve officer Sam P. King, son of the Governor, treated us to a farewell dinner in the Officers' Mess at Hickam Field. There is a tradition in Hawaii that each departing visitor gets a flower *lei,* as a token of friendship and to insure his return. I really did not suppose that our two husky friends were likely to indulge in any such sentimentality over us; but sure enough, as the loudspeaker boomed out the summons to our plane, Sam King rather sheepishly shoved a brown paper bag into my hand—and when Diamond Head had sunk out of sight behind us, I found that it contained two *leis.*

The actual hearings of the ISSC in Honolulu in late November and early December 1956 are set forth as Parts 39, 40 and 41 of the Subcommittee's published reports on "Scope of Soviet Activity in the United States." Here it will only be possible to summarize them. I personally was not present to witness them, being at the time in quite a different part of the globe on another aspect of the Subcommittee's business.

First, on November 16, the Subcommittee, still in Washington, took the testimony of Lt. Gen. John W. O'Daniel, U.S. Army, retired, who had commanded the U.S. Army, Hawaiian Department, from September 1952 to April 1954. General O'Daniel testified that he had found a definite Communist danger in Hawaii during his tour of duty as commanding general; furthermore, that he had visited the islands repeatedly since he commanded there and had learned that "the danger is just as great or greater than it was then." He pointed out the importance of Hawaii as a headquarters and supply depot for all U.S. operations in the western Pacific, and cited the ILWU-led sugar strike in the late 1940's as an example of Communism's economic power in this vital archipelago. He described himself as "delighted to know" that the ISSC was contemplating an investigation of the current influence of the Communist Party there.

Thus it was that five members of the Subcommittee—Senators Eastland, Watkins, Johnston, Welker and Butler—journeyed to Honolulu, and there on Friday morning, November 30, in Iolani Palace, flanked by Bob Morris and Ben Mandel, they opened their hearings in the islands.

The first witness was Governor Samuel Wilder King. The distinguished old gentleman treated the Subcommittee to some recent local history:

GOVERNOR KING. Mr. Chairman and members of the committee. As Governor of Hawaii, I welcome the investigation into the Communist problem here in this Territory which this Senate Subcommittee on Internal Security is now holding.

We know there are Communists in these islands.

We know who some of them are, but we do not know how many others there may be.

During April 10 to 19, 1950, a subcommittee of the United States House of Representatives Un-American Activities Committee conducted an investigation here into the same problem.

Some 39 witnesses called before this committee invoked the protection of the Fifth Amendment of the Constitution to justify their refusal to answer questions put to them by that committee.

Locally these persons are referred to as the "reluctant 39."

They continue to be at large, active in various pursuits, and most of them have made no effort to deny that they have been or are Communists.

More recently, from November 5, 1952 to June 19, 1953, on charges preferred by the United States Government, based on information developed by the FBI, seven members of this community were tried and convicted under the Smith Act for conspiring to teach and advocate the overthrow of the United States Government by force and violence.

The trial was held in the United States District Court for the District of Hawaii before a Federal judge and a local jury. All 7 were found guilty; 6 of this group were sentenced to imprisonment for 5 years and fined $5,000 each; the seventh, a woman, was sentenced to 3 years imprisonment and fined $2,000.

For a period of well over 3 years, since July 1953, all 7 of these persons have continued at liberty on bail, with very little interference with their normal pursuits in this community, pending action on their appeals in the United States Ninth Circuit Court.

The freedom permitted these leaders, even after conviction in Federal court, is a further demonstration to the membership that the charges and the convictions of these Communists were merely a union-busting, anti-labor frameup.

Once the truth of the charge against these Communists is realized by the workers, they will be rejected and replaced by men of unquestioned loyalty. The people of Hawaii are loyal and patriotic Americans. We have a very high percentage of veterans in our population. We maintain an active and highly efficient National Guard, recruited to full strength for which funds have been appropriated.

We have close and friendly relations with the military forces stationed here in large numbers. I cannot for a moment believe that any Communist-led "uprising" against the authority of the United States is possible.

However, strikes, work stoppages, slowdowns, and other phases of economic tactics common to controversies in industry could well be used by these Communist leaders to impair America's military activities. These possibilities point up again the national character of our Communist problem.

The presence of this subcommittee is a logical development of the realization all over the United States that the Federal Government must take the lead in bringing relief from Communist activities to separate communities in our Nation.

Now the Subcommittee moved briskly to question some of Hawaii's most prominent and powerful personalities: Robert McElrath, public relations director of the ILWU in Hawaii and a well-known newspaper editor and radio commentator; Joseph Kealalio, an international representative of the ILWU in Hawaii; Ernest Arena, business agent of the ILWU's Oahu Division; Newton Miyagi, secretary-treasurer of ILWU Local 142. All of them rigorously and monotonously invoked the Fifth Amendment when asked about Communist affiliations and activities. The political complexion of this potent union was grimly clear.

The next cooperative witness was Judge Ingram Stainback, a former (Democratic) Territorial Governor and at the time of the hearing a member of the Supreme Court of the Territory. Opening the hearing on the morning of December 1, he gave a detailed description of his own long battle with the Communists, and was asked in conclusion about their continuing influence:

MR. MORRIS. I wonder if you could tell us whether or not these people whom General Hull told you about [i.e., the Communists], the people you encountered, whether or not they still exercise any influence on the community today?

JUDGE STAINBACK. I am confident that they do, through their control of the labor, the large labor organization. It is very unfortunate that they control. At one time one of the members in Hilo attempted to break away from Communist control, but he was quickly squelched and properly punished, I think. So we are putting up with this Communist control. They are still active in politics, I understand, although I am no longer active in any respect, since I've been on the bench. I note by the *Star Bulletin*, last election, it stated that Hawaii elected 26 out of 28 endorsed by the ILWU, I believe. I noticed 2 years ago, in the county elections here, they are supposed to have endorsed 7 of the supervisors and 6 of them were elected. And one of them that they didn't endorse, who was elected, was a former Communist, a Japanese boy who disavowed them, and came clean, and he was elected in spite of the Communist opposition. I say ILWU, a Communist-controlled union, is more powerful, of course, on the outside islands, than they are in Honolulu, because a larger percentage of the voters are plantation workers. Here we have a large population that are not members of the ILWU. We have a fairly large AFL bunch here in the Territory, carpenters and people of that type workers, and we also have a much larger white-collar population, and their [the ILWU's] influence is not as great on this island as it is on the other islands. But I think they still have considerable influence.

Then, in response to our subpoenas, two more officials of the ILWU were called: Thomas Sukichi Yagi, divisional director of the ILWU on Maui, and Frank Silva, ranking ILWU official on Kauai. Like their colleagues before them, they resolutely pleaded the Fifth in response to all questions.

On Monday, December 3, the first witness was Dr. Lyle G. Phillips, president of the Hawaii Residents Association, an anti-Communist organization of civic-minded citizens known locally as "Imua" (the Polynesan word for "forward"). Dr. Phillips gave the Subcommittee a chilling glimpse of the power still exercised in Hawaii by the Communists in the ILWU. His informed conclusion was blunt:

DR. PHILLIPS. It is my considered conclusion, that I have arrived at slowly and definitely, that nowhere that I know of in the United States have identified Communists gone further in obtaining their primary objectives than in the Territory of Hawaii.

SENATOR BUTLER. You say you will come to it later, but to what extent and in what directions has infiltration taken place?

MR. PHILLIPS. First, may I mention these objectives, which are quite apparent, I think. They are the same objectives that the Communist Party used in gaining control in Guatemala, Czechoslovakia, and presently in Singapore, and many other places. Those objectives are these, in my opinion:

To infiltrate and control a major segment of the community's labor forces. Now, by "a major segment," down here I mean control of the sugar and pineapple industries and the waterfront. Those are so essential to us that control of them by the labor unions and by the Communist leaders of those labor unions amount effectively to the control of our economy.

Also, to a lesser degree, there has been control of governmental and hospital employees.

The second point is this. To use this power derived from that control of labor to control politics, thereby making possible their ultimate aim; the third, to control our Government.

MR. MORRIS. Those are the objectives. Now, all of the objectives haven't been attained, have they, Dr. Phillips?

DR. PHILLIPS. To a considerable degree, as I hope to point out to you, they have been attained.

To illustrate his point, consider this brief excerpt from Dr. Phillips' extensive testimony:

DR. PHILLIPS. There has been attached some significance to an incident that occurred during the legislative session. An item appeared first, I think, in the *People's Daily World,* the Communist newspaper on the mainland, recording that a complimentary gavel had been sent to Harry Bridges, head of the ILWU, then in convention in Los Angeles, by Speaker Charles Kauhane, speaker of the House of Representatives of the Legislature of Hawaii. It is understood—this was reported in the press—that Mr. Kauhane gave this gavel to Newton Miyagi, an identified Communist, and that Mr. Miyagi transmitted this gavel with Mr. Kauhane's compliments to Harry Bridges.

That has been considered of some significance, I believe.

"Of some significance"—that the Speaker of the House of Representatives of the Legislature of Hawaii had asked Newton Miyagi to deliver a complimentary gavel to Harry Bridges, head of the ILWU!

Dr. Phillips had much more to say; but for our present purposes perhaps his most important observation was the following:

DR. PHILLIPS. It has been my observation and is my opinion that, as the power and influence of the Communist apparatus has grown in this community, there is an ever-increasing number of persons who are definitely non-Communist and not Communist sympathizers who, however, have been finding it expedient not to be openly and actively anti-Communist.

SENATOR WATKINS. Just what do you mean by that?

DR. PHILLIPS. I mean this. That as this Communist influence has grown and as people look at their labor relations and their business affairs and their political affairs and so forth, that it is quite apparent that many of them, although they are good American citizens—they are not Communists, they are not Communist sympathizers—do not speak out.

Newton Miyagi was then recalled and given an opportunity to deny (among other things) the story of the gavel; but he had other ideas:

SENATOR WELKER. Now, in the proceedings of the 11th biennial convention of the International Longshoremen's and Warehousemen's Union, at page 77 thereof, Chairman Lawrence is reported, in the official document thereof, of that proceeding, as saying:

Thank you, Reverend Richman, for your most inspiring address. I told you. He's quite a guy when he gets rolling. At this point I understand that Local 142 of Hawaii wants to make a presentation. Newton Miyagi of Local 142, come on up here. Brother Newton Miyagi. [Loud applause.] Delegate Miyagi, Local 142. Brother Chairman, brothers and sisters, fraternal delegates and guests. I have been asked by the Speaker of the House of Representatives of the 28th session of the legislature in the Territory of Hawaii to help them out in presenting a gavel to our great president, Harry Bridges. [Loud applause.]

Now, Mr. Miyagi, did you do that; did you make those remarks?
(The witness consults with his counsel)
MR. MIYAGI. I rely on the fifth amendment.
SENATOR WELKER. Have you ever been at Long Beach, Calif.?
(The witness consults with his counsel)
MR. MIYAGI. Same answer.

There followed more hostile witnesses: David Evans Thompson, educational director (i.e., propaganda chief) of the ILWU; Tadashi Ogawa, director of the Oahu division of the ILWU; and Saburo Fujisaki, an official of both the ILWU and the United Public Workers (UPW), the latter being a union of civil service employees through which the ILWU had penetrated this crucial sector of Hawaiian life. All three men stolidly pleaded the Fifth. Fujisaki's testimony was typical:

MR. MORRIS. Are you presently a Communist, Mr. Fujisaki?
MR. FUJISAKI. Same answer.
MR. MORRIS. Have you been the director of the ILWU defense fund?
MR. FUJISAKI. Same answer.
MR. MORRIS. Have you been a courier for the Communist Party between San Francisco and Hawaii?
MR. FUJISAKI. Same answer.
MR. MORRIS. Have Communist Party meetings been held in your home?
MR. FUJISAKI. Same answer.
SENATOR WELKER. Have you ever been off the mainland or over on the mainland and out of the islands?
MR. FUJISAKI. Same answer.
SENATOR WELKER. Have you ever carried secret Communist documents and materials from the mainland to the islands or from the islands to the mainland?

MR. FUJISAKI. Same answer.

SENATOR WELKER. Did you ever carry oral instructions or information from the islands to the mainland or from the mainland to the islands?

MR. FUJISAKI. Same answer.

Finally Senator Johnston broke briefly through Fujisaki's personal Iron Curtain:

SENATOR JOHNSTON. Let's think about some other things for a minute. You like apples don't you? Do you like to eat apples?

MR. FUJISAKI. No; I don't.

SENATOR JOHNSTON. Don't like to eat apples. Do you—you know what an apple is, don't you?

MR. FUJISAKI. Yes.

SENATOR JOHNSTON. What would you do if you had a barrel of apples and you knew that there were about 6 or 8 in the whole barrel rotten. What would you do with those rotten apples?

MR. FUJISAKI. Throw them away.

SENATOR JOHNSTON. Throw them away. Don't you think the best thing the ILWU could probably do would be to throw some of the rotten apples out of the union and clear it up and then go ahead?

MR. FUJISAKI. Same answer.

That afternoon the Subcommittee began with the testimony of Roland B. Jamieson, a Honolulu attorney, judge and labor conciliator, who recounted conversations he had held with Jack Hall and Louis Goldblatt of the ILWU during a 1951 strike against the Hawaiian Pineapple Company on the island of Lanai. The talks evidently got pretty blunt, and produced one highly interesting piece of information:

MR. JAMIESON. Goldblatt said that one-half of the strike committee (that was the strike committee having the immediate supervision of the Lanai strike) . . . had learned guerrilla warfare with the Huks.

Hall said that the strike was going to continue until Cadagan got fired. That means fired by Hawaiian Pineapple Co.

Goldblatt emphasized that the strike was going to go on to destroy the company on Lanai.

Hall and Goldblatt talked about there being nothing left on Lanai after the strike.

MR. MORRIS. Now, what was that? I don't quite understand. What was that reference to the strikers being trained? May I ask you about that again?

MR. JAMIESON. . . . What he meant by "the Huks" was the Communist army in the Philippines, which was active during World War II and then after the war made war on the Philippine Government. Goldblatt said that half of the strike committee had learned guerrilla warfare with the Huks. And he suggested that if necessary the strikers would be able to, you might say, "take care of themselves" on Lanai in that way. In other words, if there was violence, they had some knowledge as to how to carry it on.

Then, and also the next day (December 4), the Subcommittee turned to various potentially hostile witnesses: Henry B. Epstein, director of the United Public Workers, which had been expelled from the CIO in 1950 as Communist-controlled; Max Roffman and Stephen Murin, UPW organizers; Edward Rohrbaugh, principal stockholder in, and a writer for, the *Honolulu Record*; Yugo Okubo, the *Record*'s second largest stockholder; and Wilfred Oka, who as late as 1950 had served as secretary of the Oahu Democratic County Committee. They too unanimously invoked the Fifth—and thereby made just that much clearer the vast scope of the problem confronting the American people in the Hawaiian archipelago.

On the morning of December 5, Bob Morris began the hearings with a tantalizing statement:

MR. MORRIS. Senator, before beginning the regular session, I would like to report for the public record—one of the ways we have of getting into the record here some of the developments that take place out of the formal hearing—we had issued a subpoena within the last few days to a person who has been identified as a Communist. Now, he called this morning to ask if we would see him outside the Iolani Palace because he was afraid to come to the hearing at the palace grounds.

He acknowledged that he had been a Communist; he told us he had left the party; when he had left the party; gave us some interesting information that we plan to develop; stated that he will testify fully before the committee in executive session. And then we asked him if he would cooperate with the Territorial commission. He acknowledged that he would. And he is standing by, in the event that the Subcommittee may want to see him again.

Thus did the Subcommittee move to protect the name and reputation of a former Communist who was willing to cooperate by testifying freely.

The first public witness that morning was the possessor of a famous Hawaii name: Benjamin F. Dillingham, a Republican member of the Territorial Senate and the son of Walter F. Dillingham, President of the Oahu Railway and Land Company. Senator Dillingham acknowledged that many prominent Hawaiian businessmen (not, however, including himself) had felt compelled to attend testimonial dinners in honor of Jack Hall, despite the latter's conviction for conspiring to advocate overthrow of the government by force. The reason was pathetically simple:

MR. DILLINGHAM. Senator Welker, we, as you know, are primarily an agricultural community and, outside of the basic industries of sugar and pineapple, we are dependent upon service industries to service in effect those two basic industries. Now that is outside of any businesses that are affected by the presence here of our armed services. Because we are an agricultural community, we're particularly vulnerable to plant life, you might say, so that, when pineapples get ripe, they don't wait because there's a strike going on, they have to be picked when they're ripe. The plantings have to go forward in order to meet the cycles, to assure a constant rate of production. They have to be weeded, they have to be fertilized, they have to be sprayed against blight. And, when a strike is called, all of that stops.

In the sugar industry, in addition to those factors, sugar must be watered, and when you don't water the cane it dies, and it died in 1946, I believe it was, when there was a very serious sugar strike here, island-wide. Not a drop of water was put on the cane. It dried up and looked like grass. Acres of it. Gone forever. Two years of effort thrown out of the window for that fact.

Now, a strike in the pineapple industry can wipe out a crop, wipe out several crops. It can wipe out the harvest. The same applies in the sugar industry. And then, once you have—assuming you have got the sugar harvested and in the raw condition, and pineapple in the cans, it is important to get that sugar and pineapple to market, because you don't get paid for that crop unless it is marketed, shipped.

And because of the hold which the ILWU has over the shipping industry, a stoppage there can block you again from getting any of those products out of the Territory and to market.

Likewise, we depend upon shipping for virtually all our basic needs of life here. Outside of airmail and a few commodities that can be brought in by air, we have no trucking service, we have no railroad service to fall back on, to relate us, to tie us to other communities of the United States; we are dependent upon ships. So when the shipping is cut off, we're not only denied access to the mainland for the sale of our products we produce here and depend upon for a livelihood, but we are denied an opportunity to receive our food, our clothing, our necessary supplies.

And when you realize—and as I say, except for the military, which is very substantial to be sure, but it is not by any means our staff of life, you might say—when you realize that the shipping and the pineapple and the sugar industries are subject to the whim, regardless of contract or any kind of obligation, subject to the whim of one man, you will understand the position this community is in every day, every week, every month of every year.

When Senator Dillingham stepped down, the Subcommittee turned its attention to the Communist Party's leading attorneys in Honolulu: Myer C. Symonds and Harriet Bouslog Sawyer, of the firm of Bouslog & Symonds. These two individuals had represented and advised many of the hostile witnesses previously heard, but that was not the reason they had been subpoenaed. On the contrary, in view of their prominence and activities it had been the intention of the Subcommittee to call them as its first witnesses, and it was at their own request that they were permitted to testify only after the last of their clients had been heard. Myer Symonds was sworn, and promply followed, with a lawyer's naturally greater artistry, the tried and true path:

MR. SYMONDS. The Fifth Amendment states, in the language that Senator Welker stated at the first session, that I need not bear testimony or give evidence or testimony against myself.

SENATOR WATKINS. And you want the full protection under all of the grounds of the Fifth Amendment?

MR. SYMONDS. I certainly do, and under the First Amendment.

SENATOR WATKINS. I want to make it clear that you are not just claiming it under one specific ground.

MR. SYMONDS. No, Senator.

MR. MORRIS. Mr. Symonds, did you attend this beginners class of the professional section of the Communist Party from August 17, 1943 up until September 3, 1943?

MR. SYMONDS. I am unable to pinpoint it, as to these dates you are giving about things, and I refuse to answer the question.

MR. MORRIS. For the reasons you have given?

MR. SYMONDS. For the reasons I have already given.

MR. MORRIS. Were meetings of the beginners class of the professional section of the Communist Party held in your home?

MR. SYMONDS. May I have that question again?

MR. MORRIS. Were any classes of the professional—or meetings, rather —of the beginners class of the professional section of the Communist Party ever held in your home?

MR. SYMONDS. Same answer.

MR. MORRIS. Was this beginners class of the professional section of the Communist Party taught by a gentleman named Jules Carson—C-a-r-s-o-n?

MR. SYMONDS. Same answer.

MR. MORRIS. Did you subsequently become membership director of the Lawyers Club of the Communist Party in San Francisco?

MR. SYMONDS. Same answer.

MR. MORRIS. When you joined the Army in 1944, were you a member of the professional section of the Communist Party?

MR. SYMONDS. Same answer.

MR. MORRIS. When you entered the Army, were you placed on military leave from the Communist Party?

MR. SYMONDS. The same answer.

MR. MORRIS. In 1945 did you become—resume your position of membership director of the Lawyers Club of the Communist Party?

MR. SYMONDS. The same answer.

MR. MORRIS. In 1946 did you become a member of the Haymarket branch of the Communist Party?

MR. SYMONDS. May I have that question again, please?

MR. MORRIS. In 1946 were you a member of the Haymarket branch of the Communist Party?

MR. SYMONDS. The same answer.

MR. MORRIS. Now, when you came to Honolulu, did you take an oath before the Supreme Court of the Territory that you had never been a member of the Communist Party?

MR. SYMONDS. I don't recall any such oath.

One might suppose that Symonds must have experienced a bad moment when Morris promptly produced the chief clerk of the Supreme Court of the Territory, who swore that Symonds, on applying for admission to the Hawaii bar in 1948, had answered negatively, and signed, a whole series of questions concerning Communist membership and affiliations. But it soon appeared (as Symonds undoubtedly knew all along) that the questionnaire he had signed had *not* been under oath, and he was positively breezy as he galloped home free:

MR. MORRIS. The first thing is the "No," did you write the "No" in there?

MR. SYMONDS. Yes, I did.

MR. MORRIS. All right. Now, was that answer a truthful answer to the question—the "No?"

MR. SYMONDS. I give the same answer that I have given to the previous question, relying on the First and Fifth Amendments.

MR. MORRIS. All right. Now, I will go to Question 3, which reads:

Have you ever attended any meetings of [a] cell, faction or other unit of either the Communist Party of the United States of America or the Communist Political Association? And did you write the word "N-o" after that question?

MR. SYMONDS. Yes.

MR. MORRIS. You did. Now, was that a truthful answer, that you gave at that time?

MR. SYMONDS. I give the same answer, for the same reasons that I spelled out in my first answer to the question which I refused to answer.

MR. MORRIS. Again, in the interest of time, Mr. Chairman, I would like to ask the witness if he signed the statement, as his signature appears to be at the bottom of page 2, January 12, 1948. Did you sign that statement?

MR. SYMONDS. Yes, I did.

MR. MORRIS. Were the answers given on pages 1 and 2, in other words, points 1 to 8, were they accurate when you wrote "No" to those 8 questions?

MR. SYMONDS. I decline to answer those questions, that question, for the same reasons that I have heretofore given.

SENATOR WELKER. Mr. Chairman. Not only were they accurate; were they true answers, when you wrote the word "no" after the questions? Were they truthful answers, Counsellor?

MR. SYMONDS. Is that a question to me?

SENATOR WELKER. Sir?

MR. SYMONDS. Was that a question directed to me?

SENATOR WELKER. Yes, sir.

MR. SYMONDS. My answer is the same.

SENATOR WELKER. That is, that you take advantage of the protection afforded you by the First and Fifth amendments?

MR. SYMONDS. I don't "take advantage of the Fifth Amendment," sir.

SENATOR WELKER. Well, what are you doing, then?

MR. SYMONDS. I rely on it.

His partner Harriet Bouslog was no more cooperative. In her case, however, the Subcommittee had the assistance of testimony previously given in New York City by a certain Dorothy K. Funn (later Mrs. Edward A. Swan), who had herself been a member of the Communist Party for a number of years before breaking away.

MR. MORRIS. Did you know a woman named Dorothy K. Funn, Mrs. Bouslog?

MRS. BOUSLOG. I would like to consult with my counsel.

(The witness consults with her counsel.)

MRS. BOUSLOG. I am going to rely on my rights under the First and Fifth Amendments. And in this respect, I would like to adopt the statements made by Mr. Symonds as to the reasons why I rely on the First and the Fifth Amendments.

MR. MORRIS. Now, she [i.e., Dorothy Funn, in her testimony] goes on to tell us "I met Harriet regularly at Communist Party cell meetings of the legislative branch of the various Communist Party unions, namely, the UE, the AEA, the Mine, Mill, United Public Workers, United Office and Professional Workers of America, United Auto Workers, and Federation for Constitutional Liberties, et cetera."

Now, did Mrs. Swan, now, formerly known as Mrs. Funn, Dorothy K. Funn, regularly meet you at Communist Party cell meetings of the legislative branch of the various Communist Party unions that I read?

MRS. BOUSLOG. May I consult with my counsel?

(The witness consults with her counsel.)

MRS. BOUSLOG. I give the same answer I have given before, on the First and the Fifth Amendments.

Finally Morris got down to more recent times—with the same result:

MR. MORRIS. You would not care to deny any of those things that Mrs. Swan has told us? Is that right, Mrs. Bouslog?

(The witness consults with her counsel.)

MRS. BOUSLOG. Same answer.

MR. MORRIS. Now, since you have been in Honolulu, in Hawaii, have you been a member of the Communist Party?

MRS. BOUSLOG. Just a moment, please.

(The witness confers with her counsel.)

MRS. BOUSLOG. The same answer.

MR. MORRIS. Are you a Communist now, Mrs. Bouslog?

MRS. BOUSLOG. The same answer.

The final major witness before the Subcommittee was the man who probably deserved the rather desperate honor of being called Communism's chief enemy in Hawaii: our friend and colleague William B. Stephenson, Chairman of the Territorial Commission on Subversive Activities. He took the stand on Thursday morning, December 6. It was, in the framework of the hearings, his function to summarize the major problems, and to discuss the question of possible additional legislation to deal with them. After dwelling at length on the apparent connection, or coordination, between certain strikes in Hawaii and Communist-inspired strikes in England, Australia, and elsewhere, he confirmed previous testimony concerning the weak-kneed attitude of many Hawaiian businessmen:

MR. MORRIS. Now, Mr. Stephenson, yesterday Senator Dillingham told us that industry has not taken a firm stand against the Communist leadership of the ILWU. Now, in view of the paralysis that you have stated they have been able to effect here on the islands, do you feel that industry has taken a firm stand against the force that can bring about such paralysis for political considerations?

MR. STEPHENSON. I think they have not.

MR. MORRIS. Will you develop that?

MR. STEPHENSON. I base this not only on community observation (and this is my statement purely in a personal capacity because most of the information antedates my connection with the Subversive Activities Commission)—I base it not only on open observation and reading newspapers but talking to some rather important men in industry. I can recall three specific conversations in which I was told directly that they resented my anti-Communist efforts, that of myself and others in the community.

SENATOR JOHNSTON. Did they use those words "anti-Communist?"

MR. STEPHENSON. They said "People who are too strongly anti-Communist stir up trouble," and I remember the term: "muddy the waters of labor and industrial relations." Several of those meetings were during the 1949 strike.

MR. MORRIS. And you say those sentiments were expressed by representatives of industry and management?

MR. STEPHENSON. Yes.

MR. MORRIS. Certain ones, of course, not all of them?

MR. STEPHENSON. That is correct.

MR. MORRIS. Were there any exceptions to that general outlook that you encountered?

MR. STEPHENSON. I think—oh, yes, individually. After all, bargaining was on a centralized basis. And the industry position in general out here has been to say that you can't talk about Communism because it is irrelevant to the issue of this particular bargaining session on wages, hours, or working conditions, or mechanization, or something else, and you can't talk about the Communist issue any more than you can talk about the other bargainer's religion, or his political party. I don't happen to accept that premise, but that has been the premise of industry.

The 1951, 1953, 1954 and 1955 Reports of the Territorial Commission on Subversive Activity were then made a part of the record of the Subcommittee. With that important formality out of the way, Morris asked a final question of his old friend:

MR. MORRIS. Mr. Stephenson, have you been able to observe, as an overall picture, whether or not Communist influence, as it has been manifested through the operations of the ILWU and the United Public Workers, whether it is remaining approximately the same? I would like to point out that that is an important consideration for us. Much of your evidence has dealt with facts which have taken place over the last few years. I am wondering if you, sitting as Chairman of the Territorial Commission, are in a position to appraise the extent of Communist influence, with respect to its proportion?

MR. STEPHENSON. I should like the record to show that I must of necessity speak as an individual when I give an opinion. And our commission was set up and has always operated on the premise that it is a deliberative body that is meant to find facts, and if we commissioners go around the community giving our individual viewpoints, we might have seven different viewpoints on the same question.

By deliberate consultation and analysis of materials, we try to reach a common statement of facts. So with that understanding, I will state my personal impression.

I would like to put it this way. I see no significant diminution in the Communist power in Hawaii. I don't care what date you start at—1946, 1948, 1950—if two men will agree on the starting point, my opinion is that since that particular date, whatever you pick, up to now there has been no significant diminution.

There followed a lengthy informal discussion of possible remedial legislation, which Senator Watkins capped with a gracious word of thanks.

SENATOR WATKINS. I think that your suggestions that you have just made, all of them in fact, have merit. I personally will state to you now, and to the people here, that I intend to go into them very carefully, and if my preliminary impressions are finally confirmed by more mature consideration, I certainly intend personally to try to do something about it.

But no realist, reading the account of the Subcommittee's hearings in Hawaii, can suppose for a moment that the Communist dry rot in those lovely islands will long be checked by the cumbersome processes of legislation. Such a task would require an exertion of the popular and the legislative will that history, in Hawaii and elsewhere, teaches us is both unprecedented and unlikely.

The palms still nod in the warm breezes below Diamond Head. But the way those breezes are blowing was clearly indicated in the fall of 1964—eight years after the Subcommittee's hearings in Honolulu. As it happened, death came almost simultaneously that autumn to Bill Stephenson, forty-eight, and to Tadashi Ogawa, fifty-three, one of the ILWU officials who had pleaded the Fifth before both our Subcommittee and the House Committee. Among the friends at Stephenson's funeral was one major Hawaiian official: Attorney General Bert Kobayashi. Among those on hand at Ogawa's, to say their last alohas, were: John A. Burns, Governor of Hawaii; Neal S. Blaisdell, Mayor of Honolulu; U.S. Senator Hiram L. Fong; Congressman Spark M. Matsunaga; and numerous legislators and councilmen. It was really quite a tribute.

7

The Redefector

As already explained, it was understood by all hands that I would not be present in Honolulu for the actual Subcommittee hearings there. On my return to Washington, therefore, I resigned myself as philosophically as possible to the daily routine, and even played an active part in planning the surprisingly complex logistics of transporting five United States Senators to Hawaii. I also found time, on weekends, to attend a college football game or two, most notably the Princeton-Yale game on November 17. It was played in New Haven that year, and I accepted the last-minute invitation of *National Review's* editor-publisher, Bill Buckley, to be his weekend guest in nearby Stamford. Not even the score (a depressing 42-20 in favor of Yale) could spoil the occasion for me. Buckley, whom I had known only slightly theretofore (largely through his sister Patricia and her husband Brent Bozell, who lived in the Washington area), introduced me to his spectacularly beautiful and intelligent wife, Pat; and among their other guests that weekend was my fellow Princetonian Frank Meyer, whose *National Review* column "Principles and Heresies" had long been a favorite of mine.

In the world at large, there was plenty going on during that autumn of 1956. Eisenhower was re-elected President on November 6, with another Democratic Congress—which merely meant, as far as our Subcommittee was concerned, that Senator Eastland would continue as Chairman, instead of being replaced by Senator Jenner. Abroad, the calm of late October had been shattered by two historic events: the Anglo-French-

Israeli attack on Egypt, and the Hungarian Rebellion. The former quickly fizzled; the latter flared until, in early November, Khrushchev sent Soviet tanks rumbling into Budapest and brutally slaughtered the rebels. Across the border from Hungary into neutral Austria poured a horde of refugees, stirring the hearts of free men everywhere with their testimony to the hell Communism had made of their native land.

Among the refugees, one in particular attracted the notice of the U.S. investigators of domestic Communism. John Santo (or, to give the original form and spelling of his name, Szanto Janos) had emigrated to America as a youth and had been raised by relatives in Ohio. Joining the U.S. Communist Party, he quickly became a powerful and articulate labor leader. He was associated with Mike Quill in the foundation of New York City's Transport Workers' Union, and by the early 1940's was Secretary of the Greater New York Council of the CIO. Then John Santo's Communist affiliations caught up with him and, after a dogged years-long battle, he was deported to Hungary in 1949 as an undesirable alien. With him went his American-born wife.

The Hungarian Communists welcomed Santo as a martyr of capitalist persecution, and he was soon an official of the Agriculture Ministry of the Communist (Rakosi) government of Hungary. Nothing further was heard of him in the West until mid-November 1956, when Barrett McGurn, Vienna correspondent of the *New York Herald Tribune*, ran into the ex-CIO official in the Austrian capital. Santo, it seemed, had fled Budapest with his wife and two small children, in the refugee horde. He told McGurn that he had had his fill of Communism and was eager to come back to America. In return for that privilege, he vowed, he was ready to "tell all" about his days in the U.S. Communist Party. McGurn filed a dispatch on his interview with Santo, which the *Herald Tribune* carried on page one.

On Saturday, November 24, I was in our Subcommittee office at the usual hour, to see Senator Eastland and Bob Morris off for San Francisco and Hawaii. Then, feeling rather definitely like The Little Pig Who Stayed Home, I went out to dinner and a movie with a couple of friends. I had scarcely returned to my apartment, about 10:30 p.m., when the phone rang. One should beware of phone calls. They all sound alike in the beginning, but the similarities end there! This one, most likely, was from some friend, calling to ask what I was doing for supper Sunday. If anyone had told me, at that moment, that within 38 hours I would be in Frankfurt, Germany, en route to Vienna, I would have humored him until I could call a doctor.

The caller was Jay Sourwine, the Subcommittee's former chief counsel, who, having lost his bid for the Democratic nomination to succeed his old mentor, the late Senator Pat McCarran of Nevada, had returned to our legal staff late in October. Like me, he was not going to Hawaii; and as my senior in years and experience, he was in *de facto* charge of our office in Bob Morris' absence.

His first question was characteristically blunt:

"How would you like to go to Vienna?"

That was easy. I had already been to Europe once, a four-week visit in 1954, on vacation from my Manhattan law firm. But that trip had been confined to England, France, Switzerland and the Rhineland. Vienna lay far away to the east, on the very fringe of the Iron Curtain— redolent of Strauss waltzes, Wiener schnitzel and (especially just then) international intrigue.

But Sourwine was, as usual, in no mood for schmaltz. Quickly he reminded me of the McGurn story about John Santo and said that the Subcommittee had decided to see what Santo had to say. I was to recruit a staff investigator to accompany me, and leave for Vienna by the first available government transportation. Assignment: John Santo.

"And, Bill," Jay concluded, "while you're over there, try to find out if there are any Russian defectors among the Hungarian refugees. We might want to bring some of them over too."

As luck would have it, there was a power blackout in my section of Washington late that night, and I did my essential packing by flashlight. Mercifully, however, the telephone system was unaffected. Frank Schroeder was out of town but Ed Duffy was available. He quickly agreed to accompany me. Then it was necessary for me to reach the night duty officers at the State and Defense Departments and enlist their help in the crash program to transport two Senate staff members to Vienna. By 4 a.m., when I finally slumped into bed for a very few hours' sleep, the State Department had notified its consulates and embassies en route, and especially in Vienna, to expect our arrival and extend all appropriate courtesies. The Pentagon, on its part, had done as much for the various military installations, and in addition had arranged to fly us to Europe on a regularly scheduled flight of the Military Air Transport Service Sunday afternoon.

Sunday morning I was up at 8, and at 11 witnessed a minor miracle of bureaucratic fence-trampling when the State Department's Passport Office on H Street was specially opened just long enough to renew the expired passports that Ed Duffy and I presented. At 1:15 that afternoon an Army car drove us to National Airport. At the MATS Terminal there a twin-engine Aero Commander and a smiling Japanese-American Air Force officer, Captain Kishi, were waiting to fly us to Maguire Air Force Base near Trenton, whence our plane was scheduled to depart for Frankfurt. Unfortunately, Captain Kishi explained, icing conditions in the atmosphere over Maguire made the approach hazardous; it was by no means certain that our small plane would be able to land there.

Unwilling to risk an indefinite delay (or for that matter our necks), Duffy and I asked our Pentagon friends to reschedule us for a later MATS flight from Maguire to Frankfurt (the last was at 9 p.m.) and caught the 3 p.m. train from Washington to North Philadelphia. We also arranged to be met at North Philadelphia by an Air Force car from Maguire; but we missed it, or vice versa, so we commandeered a North Philadelphia taxi instead and zoomed off across the flatlands of the Delaware valley in the general direction of Trenton. At last we found Maguire, only to discover that the vast airfield was a complex of roads (and, for all we knew, runways) leading, apparently, nowhere in the misty night. There was a nightmarish quality about that last half hour or so, but finally we found the appropriate building, signed the last-minute forms, and scrambled aboard the 9 o'clock plane for Frankfurt. The door slammed shut behind us, the plane roared down the runway and into the air, and we were on our way.

It was less than 23 hours since my phone rang.

The jet age was still a couple of years away, and our DC-6B took nearly four hours to reach Harmon Field, the U.S. Air Force base at Stephenville, Newfoundland. After refueling there we were off again, bound nonstop for Frankfurt, Germany. The late-autumn sun rose after we left Stephenville and was setting seven hours later as we turned southeast across the dun-colored Southern Uplands of Scotland and the cloud-covered shires of England. The sky was dark again when we crossed the Belgian coast above Ostend and landed, at 6:30 p.m. local time, at the great Rhein-Main base of the U.S. Air Force near Frankfurt.

We were put up at a "hotel" for transients at the base and, after a steak dinner in the Air Force Officers' Mess, tumbled, exhausted, into bed. The next morning (Tuesday the 27th), we presented ourselves at the airfield at 8 o'clock for transportation to Vienna. Once again, the Pentagon's arrangements were flawless: a DC-3 was standing by. Unfortunately the weather was once more against us; crosswinds at the Vienna airport were so severe that the pilot assigned to us was reluctant (though not, if pressed, flatly unwilling) to risk landing there. So, quickly changing plans again, we left Frankfurt for Vienna at 11:07 that morning aboard the *Danube Courier* of the German Federal Railways, bound east through the industrial Main valley, then southeast through Wurzburg, Nuremburg and Regensburg amid the rolling hills of

southern Germany. Crossing into Austria at Passau, we reached Vienna
at 10 p.m.

The Vienna railroad station, like virtually all others in former Axis
territory, is a model of modernity: a monument to the accuracy of the
Allied bombers that destroyed its baroque predecessor. Unfortunately
there had been a failure of communications regarding the change in our
arrival plans, so Duffy and I searched out a taxi and, speaking slowly
and distinctly in English (our poor substitute for a knowledge of German), begged the elderly driver to take us to the American Embassy.
That did the trick, and a few minutes later we pulled up in front of an
imposing building on Boltzmanngasse, where a large circular medallion
with an eagle in its center reassuringly proclaimed the "Embassy of the
United States of America." In due course Ed and I were installed in the
ornate Hotel Bristol on the Ringstrasse.

My own room was probably nothing more than one of the Bristol's
better singles, but to me it might as well have been the set for a Strauss
operetta. There was a huge bed, a daunting *chaise longue,* an escritoire,
a whole wallfull of closets faced with dressing mirrors, and a white
telephone in a Continental style of which Western Electric would never
have approved. From the windows, I looked directly across Kaerntnerstrasse at the handsome baroque facade of the Vienna State Opera,
carefully reconstructed after the war. To the left, the life of Vienna
coursed along the famous Ringstrasse.

The second day we were there, I experienced a sharp reminder of the
world of power and intrigue into which we had been plunged. My fancy
white telephone rang, and a heavily accented voice inquired conspiratorially whether it was addressing "Mr Roother." I replied that I was
Mr. *Rusher.* The voice then asked, in evident puzzlement, whether it
was not speaking to Mr. *Victor Reuther.* I explained, as the light flooded
in upon me, that my name was William, not Victor, and Rusher, not
Reuther. End of conversation. Evidently the Viennese grapevine—a
concierge? an embassy secretary?—had swiftly (if not surely) reported
to someone that Victor Reuther, brother of the powerful U.S. labor
leader Walter Reuther, was staying at the Bristol. What a letdown the
truth must have been! (And to whom, by the way, would Victor Reuther's supposed presence in Vienna have been so important?)

Vienna, as Ed Duffy and I saw it on that first morning (Wednesday,
November 28), was a cold and cloudy metropolis, fairly bursting with
reminders of the great imperial capital it had once been. The central
city, on the west bank of the Danube, had once been ringed by a protective wall. Now the wall was gone, but a broad avenue, the famous

Ringstrasse, had replaced it. Within the circle described by the Ringstrasse, narrow cobblestone streets were the rule, and majestic old palaces and churches loomed on every side. Rounding a corner in this antique maze, it was easy to imagine that at any moment one might glimpse the carriage of the Emperor Franz Josef rattling ceremoniously across the ancient stones.

Austria had of course been occupied by the victorious Allied armies at the conclusion of World War II in 1945, and like Germany had been divided into four zones of occupation, with Vienna quartered into sectors on the (pre-Wall) model of Berlin. In 1955, however, the Soviet Union and the three Western powers had withdrawn their troops, and Austria had once more become a free and independent nation, pledged to neutrality in the Cold War. Now suddenly, just one year later, it found itself thrust into a prominence it can hardly have relished, as the only non-Communist neighbor of tormented Hungary and thus the logical refuge for the scores of thousands of brave Hungarians who had rebelled against their oppressors. Vienna, for this brief moment, was the beating heart of the free world.

Duffy and I spent that first day making our presence known to the relevant American authorities in the Austrian capital, and then on Thursday moved to make contact with John Santo. We had learned that he and his wife and two young children were staying (under an alias) at the Hotel Astoria, not far from the Bristol. From the lobby we phoned his room, and a few minutes later Santo joined us. He was a slightly built man, seemingly in his late forties or early fifties, with graying hair and haunted eyes. He was obviously edgy, and Duffy and I suggested that the three of us repair to one of Vienna's justly famed coffee houses for a long and leisurely chat.

We spent five solid hours talking to John Santo that first day, and additional long hours on subsequent days. It was a totally new experience, and a fascinating one. One of the rarest of all birds, in the field of Communist subversion, is the knowledgeable ex-Communist who is willing to talk. To be sure, there is no lack of peripheral defectors—political philanderers who kissed and are now willing to tell. But comparatively few really dedicated, hard-core Communists ever defect: the sense of alienation from their society, and of commitment to the Communist ideal, is too powerful to permit of reversal. When a break *is* made, moreover, it is often a terribly long and painful process: beginning with faint doubts, hardening slowly into resentment, but often retaining shreds of proletarian doctrine (the oppressing classes, the idealized workers, etc.) for years, or forever. Frank Meyer, now a senior editor of *National Review,* broke with the Communist Party in 1945 but continued for several years to regard himself as a doctrinaire socialist. In 1948 he decided to vote for the organization Democrat, Truman; by 1952 he was a Republican. In general it is the rule, rather than the exception, for a break with Communism to be a gradual and wrenching experience, rather than a cleanly surgical one.

Ed Duffy and I were well aware of this as we sat down across the table from John Santo, in a little coffee house just off the Ringstrasse. Here was a man who, three weeks before, had been an official of the Agriculture Ministry of the Communist dictatorship of Hungary. Behind him stretched a lifetime of service to the Communist cause. It was simply not reasonable to suppose that, in two or three weeks, he had been transformed into the sort of Eisenhower Republican who would feel at home in (say) Scarsdale, New York or Atherton, California.

For his part, and quite aside from his own stage of anti-Communist development, Santo obviously had certain preconceptions about us. We were the employees of a subcommittee of the U.S. Senate charged with investigating Communism. Years of caricature in the press—and not only in the Communist press, but in the press of America and the rest of the free world as well—had left an impression of hard-eyed bigots trying to brand as subversive every idea generated since the Dark Ages. One could be through with Communism and still view such witch-burners with distaste.

Fortunately Duffy and I were able to convince Santo rather quickly that we were neither bigots nor fools, and that we were capable of listening sympathetically to the story of a man who had trod the Communist path for many years and then turned decisively away from it. His account of his life, as he gave it to us that first day, contained few surprises but rang wholly true. Emigrating to America as a boy to settle with his relatives in Ohio, Santo had soon become a Communist. In all of his subsequent years in the labor movement, helping to organize the New York transport workers and serving as Secretary of the Greater New York Council of the CIO, he had been an obedient Communist, serving his Communist masters and, wherever necessary, subordinating the cause and principles of honorable unionism to the requirements of the Communist dialectic and the Party line.

Evidently Santo had taken it rather hard that his subversive record kept his service in the armed forces during World War II from paving the way toward U. S. citizenship. Since Soviet Russia was our ally in that struggle, many American-born Communists fought in our armed forces with a bravery which they later cynically cited as proof of their superpatriotism. (Robert Thompson, New York State Chairman of the Communist Party, even won a Distinguished Service Cross for heroism in the Southwest Pacific—and years later on his deathbed authorized his wife to use that fact to give his native country a final scandal-stirring kick in the teeth on his posthumous behalf, by requesting that he be buried in Arlington National Cemetery as a veteran!) But Santo was an alien well identified as a Communist, and thus he failed to acquire U.S. citizenship despite his military service.

Santo described to us the emotions with which he and his wife accepted deportation to Hungary in 1949. Very well, so be it. There was fruitful work to do in the People's Republic that was being constructed in his native land. John Santo would help to do it. But doubts set in swiftly. At the Hungarian border, as the Santos entered, a tremendous bureaucratic fuss was kicked up over some Kleenex they were bringing with them. Evidently it was a "luxury" by the standards of the People's Republic, subject to a stiff surcharge or even confiscation. John Santo—who was, of course, culturally a thoroughgoing American, despite his politics—was appalled but held his tongue.

Life in Budapest was one long lesson in disillusion. The petty tyrannies of a Communist bureaucracy, let alone the greater ones implicit in any Communist society, weighed heavily on a man whose entire adult life had been spent in a free Western community. Slowly he came to realize what a despotic fraud Communism is, what a cruel betrayal of the hopes of the "proletariat." When rebellion erupted in the streets of Budapest late in October 1956, it resounded in the mind of John Santo like a long-awaited bell. When Soviet tanks moved in to quell the uprising, he bundled his wife and two young children into a car and headed westward for Austria—and freedom.

His account of their progress on foot across the last few miles of borderland—terrified lest a wail from the baby should give them away to the Communist guards—seemed eerily real, there in the little Viennese coffee house. At last they reached Austrian territory and comparative safety. But Santo was under no illusions about his former masters; they would, he was sure, find him and his family and kill them all if they could. He forbade his wife and children to leave their cramped hotel room for any reason whatever. He himself left it only rarely, to buy food or other supplies—and occasionally to read American periodicals in Amerika Haus, the USIA library on the Kaerntnerstrasse. John Santo was a very homesick guy.

Duffy and I heard him out, in that first session. There was no doubt about the completeness of his break with Communism, and yet there was something pathetically paleo-Marxist about his notion of what he should do next. Santo was obsessed with the idea that he should be allowed to return to the United States to give a great "message" to the

American working class: namely, that Communism was a fraud and would betray the workers. He was in deadly earnest about his role as conveyor of this message; he was convinced that "the American workers" were bemused by Communism's siren song, and that they would be powerfully impressed by the news that they were being deluded.

In subsequent talks with Santo, Duffy and I asserted our own interests and opinions a bit more. We first pointed out that we were the agents of a Senate subcommittee, and that if we recommended his return to the United States it would be in order to take his testimony before that subcommittee. Santo (as already noted) was well aware of the Congressional committees investigating Communism, and he was frankly of the opinion that it would weaken the force of his message to America's workers if he was compelled to give it from such a supposedly discredited platform. However, if that was the only way he could arrange to deliver the message at all, he would agree.

We then reminded him that this particular subcommittee was headed by Senator James O. Eastland, a well-known and vociferous segregationist whose views on racial matters, while totally irrelevant to the work of the ISSC, were a favorite target of attack in our domestic press. Santo would have to be ready to face the false but deadly accusation that he was merely serving the cause of Southern racism. He indicated he realized this and was prepared for it; then, as his mind wandered back across the years and forward to his present terrible dilemma, he first stiffened with the old arrogance, then wilted in an astonishing (and unnecessary) submission: "I never liked that racism stuff," he began sharply. "But then . . . I've been so wrong about so much else, maybe I'm wrong about that too." Clearly, John Santo was through laying down the law—even to racists.

Next we began probing deeper into Santo's Communist past in the United States. It was here, if anywhere, that he might have information to offer that would justify his return to America, reversing the 1949 deportation order. Not surprisingly, we soon ran into a major level of resistance. Up to this point Santo had sincerely been under the impression that he was talking to us freely and frankly about his Communist past. But now, quite casually, Ed Duffy asked Santo whom he had paid his Communist Party dues to, while he was Secretary of the Greater New York Council of the CIO in the early 1940's. Santo replied that he didn't know—then, more precisely, that he did not remember. The truth was that he had simply not realized that a break with Communism, and an offer to "tell all," is fundamentally inconsistent with a determination to avoid naming names. He was in precisely the situation in which Whittaker Chambers had found himself: eager to tell the truth about

Communism, but humanly reluctant to implicate his fellow Communists by name.

This particular dilemma has a great appeal for liberals; and indeed every man feels a natural distaste for exposing others whose crimes, however great, seem after all no greater to him than the crimes of the one doing the exposing—and were done, moreover, in complicity with him, and in the bond of mutual trust and secrecy. The short answer is that, in this highly unsatisfactory world, we are not granted the luxury of placing our obligations to our friends on a level equal to, let alone higher than, our obligation to the society that shelters both them and us; and when we join with them in a conspiracy to destroy that society, and then break with them, our obligations to them and to it are fundamentally inconsistent—and the obligation to the society (which includes all posterity: theirs as well as ours) is paramount.

In due course Santo brought himself to this recognition, and thereafter spoke more freely about individuals, rambling easily over the labor and Communist scenes of the 1930's and 1940's. Only once did he seem to balk, and then it was only for an instant. We had been chatting about various aspects of the Communist conspiracy, and I mentioned the activity of Communist spies in government. Suddenly Santo bristled:

"I don't know that I believe all that espionage stuff. I never saw any of it."

To which I replied: "Of course not, John; you were assigned to labor work. But if a dedicated Communist is in the government and has access to information that would be useful to the Soviets, you know darned well he will give it to them if they ask for it."

Santo stared off into the mid-distance, obviously grappling with the hypothesis. Then, frankly conceding the point, he said slowly and softly: "I have no doubt of that."

At every meeting, Santo was visibly nervous. His fear, quite simply, was for his life—and for the lives of his wife and children. He was sure, as I have said, that the Communists would kill him if they could. Moreover, he was inclined to think they probably could. To Duffy and me, coming to Vienna from the free Western world of which it was now an outpost, this seemed a bit melodramatic. To Santo, a few score miles and less than three weeks from a murderous despotism, it seemed the most natural thing in the world.

On one occasion, as we were talking to him in a coffee house, he suddenly stared at a man across the room and literally turned pale. "That man over there!" he gasped.

"What's wrong?" I inquired. Santo's eyes never left the man.

"That man—he's an Austrian businessman. I've seen him often in Budapest. He does business with the Communists—he's a Communist himself. He'll recognize me, and they'll try to kill me."

Duffy and I tried to reassure him, and the "businessman"—who, to be perfectly fair, seemed to be acting quite normally and never appeared to glance in our direction—finally left. Only slowly, however, did Santo regain his composure.

As far as this aspect of our assignment was concerned, it was soon clear that we would be warranted in urging the Subcommittee to take steps to return John Santo to the United States, to testify publicly. One night, therefore, I reported as much by telephone to Jay Sourwine in Washington—and in return received from him a progress report on the Hawaiian hearings which were then taking place, under the aegis of the same Subcommittee, on the other side of the globe.

But our mission in Vienna was only half over. In those days all of eastern Austria was swarming with Hungarian refugees. The Austrians responded warmly to the plight of these former compatriots of theirs in the old Austro-Hungarian Empire. Perhaps only a nation which has itself experienced Soviet occupation can ever fully sympathize with its other victims. No doubt the ancient antipathy of Teuton and Slav was lurking below the surface as well. Whatever the reasons, Vienna in that cold, gray November of 1956 throbbed with sympathy for the thousands upon thousands of refugees who clogged its bureaucratic hallways, its charities and its makeshift soup kitchens—families and broken pieces of families, often with no clothes other than those on their backs, and hungry, always hungry. In a great convulsion of sentiment that rippled westward across free Europe, people everywhere sent money, food, and clothing to the refugee rebels of Hungary.

But of what, exactly, did this vast refugee horde consist? They streamed across the border every night and were collected in camps under Austrian governmental supervision: men, women and children, of high rank and no rank whatever, with memories of death and despotism behind them and not even a coherent dream of their possible future. Were there Russians among them—Red Army deserters, perhaps, or disillusioned political commissars? Or failing that, were there individual refugees with a worthwhile story to tell the American people? We turned our attention from John Santo to these questions.

First, what about Russian defectors? Discreet inquiries among American diplomatic and military officials in Vienna drew a blank. Nor were the overburdened charity organizations, public and private, any more helpful. Twice, however, we were asked: "Have you talked to Ross

Cogswell?" When we said we hadn't, and asked who he was, we were met with a blank, "Oh! Well, never mind. He was just somebody I thought you might have spoken to."

It didn't take a double-zero classification to deduce that Ross Cogswell (needless to say, I am not using his real name) was the head of America's secret intelligence operations in Vienna, and that he would in fact be an excellent person to talk to. Duffy and I decided that a frontal assault would be our likeliest bet and, walking up to the receptionist on the ground floor of a particularly promising office building, asked for Mr. Ross Cogswell. Incredibly, it worked. The receptionist smoothly asked who wished to see Mr. Cogswell, and was advised that we were staff employees of the U.S. Senate Internal Security Subcommittee. A few minutes later we were ushered into his office.

America's intelligence chief in Vienna that crucial autumn—and, for all I knew, with a jurisdiction extending across large areas of central Europe—was a handsome and prepossessing man in his late forties or early fifties, with steady gray eyes, black hair tinged with silver, and the relaxed manner of an athlete sure of his condition. He greeted us with no pompous pretense of secrecy, made us feel at home, and asked what we wanted of him. I explained that our Subcommittee was eager to interview any Russian defectors in the refugee horde, and ruefully added that I had been unable to find traces of even one. "Now," I concluded, "if I go home and report that there *are* none, and a few weeks from now some turn up, I'm going to be in mighty hot water."

Cogswell laughed.

"Well, Mr. Rusher, there'll be two of us in hot water, because I'm reporting exactly the same thing to my own superiors."

He went on to say that, in point of fact, two Soviet soldiers had crossed the border in recent weeks and were at the moment in custody. One was not really a defector at all; he was simply a Russian dogface who had accidentally wandered over the line and been picked up on the Austrian side. He wanted to go back, even though "his general attitude is," as Cogswell told us with a smile, " 'Boy, the sergeant is gonna be mad at me!' " The other was an authentic deserter, but distinctly poor witness material—an Azerbaijani Moslem, drafted into the Red Army, who got thoroughly fed up with his lot and fled to Austria in the general confusion. Unfortunately he was a high-grade moron who knew nothing of the slightest interest, and certainly did not qualify as an important ideological defector.

We thanked Mr. Cogswell and took our leave, convinced that we had now beaten the bushes as hard as they could be beaten and that there simply were no significant Russian defectors to be found. During the next day or two we concentrated on interviewing various Hungarian refugees suggested to us by our contacts in the charitable agencies, and eventually invited one of them to come to the United States to tell his story to the Subcommittee and the American people.

But the Case of the Missing Russians still troubled me. The Red Army is a huge organization, and large bodies of its troops had been stationed in Hungary on garrison duty for over a decade. Some of these men, at least a handful, were bound to have developed strong ties to the people whose land they were occupying, and when the Hungarians rebelled, it simply beggared belief that there were not at least a few Russians sympathetic to their cause and eager to flee with them to the West. Why were those Russians not in Austria now? It was to be several days before the answer dawned on us.

Meanwhile Sunday, December 2, was a day of rest, even for two weary Subcommittee staffers in Vienna, and Duffy and I made the most of it. During the morning we watched the famous Lippanzer stallions of the Spanish Riding School go through their grave and stately paces in the converted ballroom of the old Hofburg, Franz Josef's palace in Vienna. That afternoon we paid quick visits to Stephandom, Vienna's great baroque cathedral, where Prince Eugene—Marlborough's ally—is buried; to the incredible Kaisergruft, or Emperors' Crypt, beneath the Capuchin church, were 142 members of the ancient House of Hapsburg lie in great pewter sarcophagi; and lastly to Schloss Schonbrunn, the imperial summer palace a few miles outside the city, where the tastes and personality of Maria Theresa have survived the onslaughts of two centuries. Finally, that evening, we watched a performance of *Tosca* in the State Opera House, a building which had been superbly reconstructed, after the war, in faithful duplication of the curving staircases and red velvet trim that had made it for many decades one of the great sights of Europe. Unfortunately I was coming down with a truly majestic head cold, and Tosca's scornful words as she stood over Scarpio's corpse were punctuated by a series of vehement "hah-choos" directly traceable to the Senate Internal Security Subcommittee.

The next day we gratefully accepted an offer by the U.S. Embassy's military attaché to arrange an inspection trip for us southward toward the Hungarian border, with stops at various refugee camps. The first such stop was at Wiener Neustadt, approximately 35 miles south of Vienna, where some thousands of refugees were quartered in barracks-type one-story buildings amid a flat and dismal landscape. More interesting, however, in many ways, was our subsequent stop at Traiskirchen. Here, in a large building which had once been an Austrian military school, and which had later served as quarters for troops of the Red

Army (from 1945 to 1955 this area had been a part of the Soviet occupation zone), the Austrian government had set up a "collection center" for refugees. It was here that they were brought, direct from the border stations, to be sorted out and assigned in a day or two to more permanent locations like the one we had seen at Wiener Neustadt.

The building itself was in a sad state of disrepair. I particularly remember the water pipes sticking nakedly out of the walls and floors of certain rooms, and the disgust in the voices of our Austrian guides as they explained the phenomenon. The conquering heroes of the Red Army, it seemed, had never known such Western luxuries as radiators and flush toilets before; and when they left Traiskirchen to return to Mother Russia they simply took the precious fixtures with them, wrenching them bodily from the masonry.

We were ushered into a gigantic hall—the former dining room, no doubt, of the military school—which had been converted into a dormitory for the newly arrived refugees. A few bare light bulbs swung limply from the ceiling. From one end of the hall to the other, row upon row of triple-decker bunks had been installed, and here the refugees were preparing to settle down for the night: men, women and children all scrambled together, clutching what few pitiful belongings they had been able to bring with them from Hungary.

Our guides soon found an English-speaking Hungarian for us to talk to—a chemist, a highly educated man with dark Magyar eyes, accompanied, as I recall, by a daughter in her early teens. But the comment I remember best—which summed up, in fact, the whole experience—was made, not to us, but to the Austrian who had chauffeured us down from Vienna. While we talked to the chemist, he had fallen into conversation with an elderly Hungarian who spoke German. As he told it to us later, he had thought to offer his sympathy to the old fellow.

"Pretty rough here, isn't it?" he had asked, waving his hand around the hall. "I mean—the light, the noise, the crowding."

But the old gentleman was having none of that. "Listen," he snapped, "this is the first decent night's sleep anybody here has had in years."

Duffy and I left Vienna by train on Wednesday evening, December 5, and spent the next day in Salzburg, visiting among other things still another refugee camp at nearby Roder. It was in Salzburg that I learned, to my satisfaction at least, why there had been no Russians in the refugee horde.

"I can explain it," said a young American aid official. "No Russian soldier would have had a chance among these refugees, no matter how hard he protested he was on their side. Just his uniform—or even his accent—would have been enough to set them off. They would have killed him first and asked questions afterward. To these people, the only good Russian is a dead Russian.

"And if you don't believe it," he went on, "let me tell you something that happened right here a few days ago. As you might expect, the Communists have planted a few of their own people—Hungarians, I mean—in the flood of refugees, just to keep an eye on things and report when they cool down. Well, several days ago some of the refugees here spotted two Hungarians in the camp whom they had known back home as hardened Communists. They reported the fact to us, but just the other night, while we were still mulling over what to do about it, the decision was taken out of our hands." He paused, to see if I grasped his implication.

"You mean . . ." I began.

He nodded, sucking on his pipe. "Sometimes," he said, with the faintest suggestion of a smile, "you just can't stop 'em."

After various delays in Frankfurt, owing to the postponement of successive MATS flights, Duffy and I returned to Washington in the early hours of Tuesday, December 11. On Wednesday the 19th, a young Hungarian resistance fighter whom we had interviewed in Vienna and invited to America appeared in public session before Senator Johnston.* Bob Morris courteously accorded me the privilege of questioning him, the first time I had interrogated one of our witnesses in public. He was a brave young man, and he had suffered much.

MR. MORRIS. Will you give your name to the reporter.
MR. RUFF. Lajos Ruff.
MR. MORRIS. And that is your true identity; is it not?
MR. RUFF. That is my true identity.
MR. MORRIS. Senator, before getting into the concrete details of the particular subject for which the witness was called, the witness has a very interesting background, which I think would be of great interest to the subcommittee in connection with this general subject of the tactics of world Communism.

Mr. William Rusher, of our staff here, went to Vienna, and while there encountered Mr. Ruff, and has spent many hours with him, and I think Mr. Rusher is qualified to bring out the underlying background facts which I think are rather essential at this time, Senator. So if Mr. Rusher may take over—
SENATOR JOHNSTON. Mr. Rusher will take over.
MR. RUSHER. Mr. Ruff, what is your age?

* His testimony is set forth in full in Part 47 of the ISSC's inquiry into "Scope of Soviet Activity in the United States."

MR. RUFF. Twenty-five and a half.

MR. RUSHER. You were engaged at one time in resistance activities against the Communist government of Hungary, were you not?

MR. RUFF. Yes.

MR. RUSHER. Will you tell us, in a general way, the kind of activities that you engaged in, and what years they were, what time?

MR. RUFF. I took part from 1951 on. This took the form of preparing the leaflets, in the 1953 election, against Rakosi at that time. In 1952 and 1953, for the May 1 demonstrations, we also prepared leaflets, and I also gave certain information to a Western correspondent friend of mine.

MR. RUSHER. In the course of these activities, ultimately you and the people you were working with were apprehended by Hungarian Communist authorities; is that correct?

MR. RUFF. Yes.

MR. RUSHER. Can you tell us in a general way how you came to be apprehended by them?

MR. RUFF. After I had become suspicious, a secret policeman had gotten me acquainted with a secret police captain, the AVH, and then he arrested me.

MR. RUSHER. You say when you became suspicious; you mean, after they had become suspicious of you?

MR. RUFF. Yes; after they had become suspicious of me.

MR. RUSHER. And how did the Hungarian Communist police find out about your activities?

MR. RUFF. Without suspecting it, I became a personal friend of Mr. Bela Roezaboeldyi. I didn't suspect that he was a member of the AVH, and I probably mentioned things to him which caused my arrest.

MR. RUSHER. In other words, this AVH agent won your friendship and eventually betrayed you; is that what you mean?

MR. RUFF. Yes.

MR. RUSHER. When were you arrested?

MR. RUFF. On August 10, 1953.

MR. RUSHER. Will you tell us where you were taken and what happened to you, in the first period after your arrest?

MR. RUFF. They took me to the secret police headquarters in the Fo Utca, and that is known as the Special Matters Investigation Department of the Ministry of the Interior.

MR. RUSHER. Is that the AVH police?

MR. RUFF. That was the AVH police, known under the pseudonym of Special Investigations Department of the Department of the Interior.

MR. RUSHER. And what happened there?

MR. RUFF. There, for approximately 6 to 8 weeks, closer to 8, they tried to get information out of me with common methods of torture, and were particularly interested in whom I had given information to.

MR. RUSHER. What sort of torture, that you call common?

MR. RUFF. They burnt my hand—

MR. RUSHER. Is that the scar you showed us on your hand yesterday?

MR. RUFF. That is the scar.

MR. RUSHER. Would you hold it up, please; just hold up your hand?

MR. MORRIS. Let Senator Johnston see it.

MR. RUFF. They knocked my teeth out.

MR. MORRIS. How many teeth did you lose?

MR. RUFF. Two on the left side.

They also burnt my feet. For 5 days I stood in a cell 60 centimeters by 60 centimeters, without food or water, or being let out.

For 2½ days I was in a room up to my waist in water, cold water.

SENATOR JOHNSTON. Sixty centimeters would be something in the neighborhood of 2 feet, wouldn't it?

THE INTERPRETER. Two feet by two feet.

MR. MORRIS. And how many days were you in the room of those dimensions?

MR. RUFF. Five and a half days.

MR. MORRIS. Go ahead.

MR. RUSHER. These are the methods that you call common; is that right?

MR. RUFF. This is what I call common methods of getting information.

MR. RUSHER. So, is this what happened to you during this first period of 6 to 8 weeks after your arrest?

MR. RUFF. This happened for the period of 6 to 8 weeks, and in the meantime, of course, they always took me out of the cell to ask me questions and grill me. One of the hearings lasted 36 hours without stop.

MR. RUSHER. How did they come to knock out your teeth?

MR. RUFF. After I had refused to answer 1 question, 1 of my inquisitors threw an iron ashtray at me, which I couldn't duck.

MR. RUSHER. I think you were about to tell us what happened in the second period, after the stage of 6 to 8 weeks of customary methods of obtaining information. What happened next?

MR. RUFF. Then I was taken into special investigation, psychological investigation room, which we nicknamed the "bewitched room," in which they applied special psychological methods to us.

MR. RUSHER. How long did that last?

MR. RUFF. Also 6 weeks.

MR. RUSHER. Will you tell us something about this room?

MR. RUFF. One lived in this room day and night without getting out, and there was complete darkness outside the 1 ventilation—no light came in through the 1 ventilation hole in the wall. For this purpose there were special films designed which were shown to us inside that room. There were lamps whose shades had holes in them and were continuously revolving on the ceiling.

They gave us constantly shots of scopolamine and mescaline.

MR. RUSHER. I think, Senator, scopolamine is known in this country as a drug that weakens the will and weakens a person's power to resist.

Will you tell us, Mr. Ruff, how long this lasted? You said 6 weeks?

MR. RUFF. Six weeks.

MR. RUSHER. And this was in the "bewitched room" in which you lived during that entire period; is that right?

MR. RUFF. I was in this room day and night, and a doctor of Russian descent, called Laszlo Nemeth—he was a Hungarian who was a Russian citizen—took care of me, and as far as I know, this is the only—he is the only expert of this method in Hungary.

MR. RUSHER. He is an expert in these methods of psychologically inducing a person to reveal information; is that correct?

MR. RUFF. In these psychological methods.

He came in every day and spoke to me for hours on end in a very friendly way.

MR. RUSHER. Was he a Hungarian?

MR. RUFF. He was probably of Hungarian descent, because he spoke very good Hungarian. He told me that they brought people into this room only in various special cases, because this method could only be used on a very intellectual sort of people.

He also told me that Cardinal Mindszenty had been in this room.

MR. RUSHER. The "bewitched room?"

MR. RUFF. The "bewitched room."

They told me that by perfectly ordinary methods they could also find out what I had done, but they were not interested in what I had done but also in how I was thinking.

MR. RUSHER. Where did you go at the end of that 6 weeks in the "bewitched room?"

MR. RUFF. At the end of these 6 weeks I pretended to be insane, I broke things and made noise, and then they thought—thinking that I was insane, they transferred me to the insane asylum of the AVH, the secret police.

MR. MORRIS. Before you go on, was that Laszlo Nemeth?

MR. RUFF. Yes.

MR. MORRIS. And I understood you to say he was a medical doctor?

MR. RUFF. He is probably a psychiatrist.

MR. RUSHER. So you then feigned insanity, and were sent ultimately to the mental hospital of the AVH; is that correct?

MR. RUFF. It was their insane asylum.

MR. RUSHER. And how long were you there?

MR. RUFF. Approximately 7 weeks.

MR. RUSHER. Seven weeks. Before the trial?

MR. RUFF. Before the trial.

I met 5 people there who had all been in the "bewitched room," and all of them were schizophrenic.

MR. RUSHER. As a result of their experiences?

MR. RUFF. As a result of that.

MR. MORRIS. They were not pretending?

MR. RUFF. They were not pretending. They had been there for a number of years.

MR. RUSHER. And there were others like yourself who, however, had pretended?

MR. RUFF. As far as I know; no.

MR. RUSHER. Now, then, were you left relatively alone in the mental hospital, or were further tortures inflicted?

MR. RUFF. There were times when I was just plain locked up together with normal criminal-type people, who were mentally ill, and sometimes they had special little tortures. They gave us electric current shocks, shock treatment. They wrapped us in wet blankets, and when the wet blankets had dried, the skin was usually so dried out that it split and cracked.

The head of this insane asylum was a Mr. Istvan Nemeth.

MR. RUSHER. But not the same man?

MR. RUFF. Not the same man.

MR. RUSHER. Now, from this mental hospital or prison, you were taken, as I understand it, to trial; is that correct?

MR. RUFF. They took us back to the special section of the Internal Ministry of the Interior at Fo Utca.

MR. RUSHER. Will you tell us the circumstances of your trial, how long it lasted, and what you had in the way of defense counsel?

MR. RUFF. In 1954, January 18, is when it approximately started.

MR. RUSHER. How long did the trial last?

MR. RUFF. Three-quarters of an hour, approximately.

MR. RUSHER. Did you have defense counsel?

MR. RUFF. I had defense counsel in the form of a man appointed by the Defense Ministry, and I had no chance to talk to him or even meet him beforehand.

MR RUSHER. Do you know whether or not he was himself a Communist?

MR. RUFF. He had a large party insignia on his lapel.

MR. RUSHER. Did he make any serious effort to defend you?

MR. RUFF. He did absolutely nothing, and spoke only 3 or 4 minutes in all.

Two members of the judges' bench were in secret police uniform.

MR. RUSHER. They were members of the secret police?

MR. RUFF. They were members of the secret police.

MR. RUSHER. And I take it then, that under those circumstances, you were found guilty; is that correct?

MR. RUFF. Yes.

MR. RUSHER. What were the charges of which you were found guilty?

MR. RUFF. I was condemned for 15 years for having organized against— having plotted against the People's Republic, for the downfall of the People's Republic, and for having disseminated leaflets.

MR. MORRIS. In connection with an election campaign, or generally?

MR. RUFF. Elections, and with May Day demonstrations.

MR. RUSHER. Now, after your sentence to a term of 15 years were you then taken to prison, to begin serving it?

MR. RUFF. They took me the very next day to the collecting prison, so-called, in Kobanya.

MR. RUSHER. And how long were you there?

MR. RUFF. I was there until November 1, 1956, when in connection with the revolt, I was freed.

MR. RUSHER. Now, was Cardinal Mindszenty in that same prison while you were there?

MR. RUFF. He was in the same prison until 1955 when, in connection with the Geneva conferences, he was taken away.

MR. RUSHER. Did you have occasion to see him and, if so, would you tell us about those occasions, or occasion?

MR. RUFF. Since they still considered me slightly insane, and thought that I wouldn't have the memory to say anything, they chose me for domestic work in the prison. As such, I was transferred to the hospital of this collecting prison, where, in a special wing, they were guarding Cardinal Mindszenty. And in this connection, I was detailed to clean out his cell every single day.

MR. RUSHER. And how long did this go on?

MR. RUFF. Approximately 3 months I was doing this.

MR. RUSHER. And what caused you to stop?

MR. RUFF. On each of these occasions, Cardinal Mindszenty was standing in a dark suit, in the corner, and in one instance he dropped his handkerchief. I picked it up and handed it to him, and he fairly softly said, "Thank you, my boy." From that point on, they immediately took me away, they didn't let me finish my work.

MR. RUSHER. Did they see this particular incident?

MR. RUFF. There was always a guard in the cell, as well.

MR. RUSHER. So what did they do; they immediately stopped having you clean the cardinal's cell?

MR. RUFF. They immediately stopped having me clean the cardinal's cell, took me out, stripped me and searched me, and I was never allowed to return.

MR. RUSHER And never saw the cardinal again?

MR. RUFF. I never saw him after that.

MR. RUSHER. Now, then, you served, you say, in that prison until you had served 3½ years of your 15-year sentence, and you were released by the revolutionaries on November 1, 1956? Is that correct?

MR. RUFF. On November 1; that is correct.

MR. RUSHER. And they released all the prisoners; is that correct?

MR. RUFF. Only the political prisoners. That was done by forming five committees, on one of which I took part, and we investigated the prisoners to see whether they really were political prisoners or just common criminals, and the common criminals were not released.

Ruff then described how, as a released prisoner, he had helped inspect the villa of the deposed Communist dictator, Matyas Rakosi; and he reported a chilling discovery there:

MR. RUFF. Rakosi's villa was furnished in the greatest luxury. He had a private theater, not movie but players.

MR. RUSHER. Was there a barracks nearby?

MR. RUFF. On the large grounds of the villa there were three buildings occupied by the AVH. Farther down the hill, about three or four hundred yards away—meters away—there was another large building which was in constant ultrashortwave contact with the villa itself.

MR. RUSHER. Where exactly was the villa? Can you give us an address or description?

MR. RUFF. It was a former cloister for nuns.

MR. RUSHER. Where; in Budapest?

MR. RUFF. It was in the suburbs of Budapest, on Szechenyi Mountain.

MR. RUSHER. I think you told us yesterday, when we first spoke to you [in executive session], about a bodyguard barracks—will you tell us about that?

MR. RUFF. Excuse me. About bodyguards?

MR. RUSHER. About a barracks for bodyguards.

MR. RUFF. In the 3 smaller houses on the same property there were approximately 130 bodyguards of the secret service. All of them lived there all the time. And there were approximately 150 more in the other barracks, which were 300 yards away, with radio contact.

MR. RUSHER. Was there anything in these barracks except the living quarters of the bodyguards?

MR. RUFF. In the larger of these buildings, which was off the grounds, there were a number of cells, and a small-sized crematorium.

MR. RUSHER. A small-sized crematorium?

MR. RUFF. A small-sized crematorium, one person at a time.

MR. MORRIS. You saw all these things with your own eyes, did you not?

MR. RUFF. Yes; I did.

MR. RUSHER. Can you describe the crematorium to us, the small crematorium?

MR. RUFF. The crematorium was in the basement of the cloister, which adjoined the Rakosi villa, and was probably the former central heating apparatus of the building.

MR. RUSHER. Do you happen to know who this crematorium was for?

MR. RUFF. In the second little slot next to the furnace itself we found 12 bodies. These had shown signs of beating, but were obviously waiting to be burned.

MR. RUSHER. Do you know who these people were or what the particular reason or purpose for this crematorium was?

MR. RUFF. I don't know who these people were. As far as I know regarding the crematorium, it was to completely erase traces of those special prisoners who had been taken for interrogation in this place.

MR. MORRIS. In other words, they were prisoners?

MR. RUFF. They were prisoners.

Ruff was only one of perhaps a dozen Hungarian witnesses who were heard by the Subcommittee in public session during the four months following the revolt. As more and more refugees reached the United States, it became possible to put in the record almost any desired amount of eye-witness information concerning Communist perfidy and brutality toward the indomitable people of Hungary. But the relevance of much of this data to our specific preoccupation—namely, internal security—was debatable, once the pattern of Communist behavior and techniques (which might be applied wherever they had the chance) was established. Slowly, reluctantly, our attention turned away from the Hungarian agony.

But meanwhile what of John Santo? Duffy and I had left him in Vienna, promising to recommend strongly that he be returned to the United States for at least the limited purpose of testifying before the Subcommittee. Once here, it might be possible to take further steps to regularize his status and give him permanent residence, if not the citizenship he coveted.

To be entirely frank, the matter seemed to us to involve much larger issues than merely Santo and his marginally useful recollections of Communism in the U.S. labor movement fifteen to twenty years previously. Here was a major figure in the world Communist movement, who was at long last ready—nay, eager—to denounce it as a fraud and a delusion. He was in technical terms a "redefector," and it seemed crucial to us—and I may add, to Bob Morris when he heard the story—that the door should not be slammed shut against such a man. Not only for his sake, but as an example to all the others like him who might even now be watching his case and assessing developments in it as a guide to their own conduct, it was essential that the possibility of political redemption and social acceptance in the West should be held open.

I am sorry to say that it was not, for several years. The Subcommittee duly requested Santo's return, but it soon became plain that somewhere in the bureaucratic hierarchy that makes the final decision in such matters there were powerful forces working against us. Slowly we came to suspect that Immigration Commissioner Joseph Swing, knowing how long the struggle had been to deport John Santo, was simply unable to adjust to the notion of having him back in our midst again.

So Santo gradually drifted into a sort of Viennese limbo—a refugee from Communist Hungary, debarred from returning to America, hungrily reading American newspapers and magazines in the free library of Amerika Haus on the Kaerntnerstrasse. His wife and two children, all American citizens, returned to this country and to her family. Santo scraped along on translating jobs tossed to him by sympathetic USIA officials, and kept a wary eye out for his former Communist colleagues. Early in 1957, Ben Mandel was dispatched to Vienna to interview him further, to lay if possible a firmer foundation for his return. But once again the effort was fruitless.*

In 1958, Santo's luck at last began to turn. In that year Roland Elliott, director of refugee activities for Church World Service, who had interested himself in Santo's case, took him to Geneva for a conference with Representative Francis E. Walter (D., Pa.), the powerful chairman of the House Committee on Un-American Activities and also of the

---

* Mandel's trip did have one serio-comic by-product, which served to remind me just how slight is the regard in which our powerful Executive branch holds the Congress. By the time Mandel arrived in Austria, the hectic atmosphere of November and December had been replaced by more normal moods. The U.S. diplomats in Vienna, perhaps beginning to fear that the ISSC would develop a permanent taste for those little Viennese coffee houses, declared that the Austrian authorities were annoyed at having an agent of a Senate subcommittee, unaccredited in any official way to Austria, questioning a refugee who was under the protection of the Austrian government. Accordingly, Ambassador Llewellyn Thompson formally "ordered" Mandel to stop talking to Santo, and Ben cabled for further instructions. The matter was soon ironed out amicably enough, by talks between the Subcommittee and the State Department; but I remember with special vividness a call paid on us, at the height of the crisis, by a young attorney representing the Legal Division of the State Department. Turning the problem over in my mind, I remarked genially to him that we seemed to have here a rare and interesting conflict of interests, in a foreign capital, between two constitutionally equal branches of the federal government, the Executive and the Congress. The young man, who was really quite friendly, put me in my place with a smirk and a single supercilious sentence: "Congress . . . Congress . . . I've heard that word somewhere . . ."

Immigration Subcommittee of the House Judiciary Committee. Representative Walter, who had previously been cool to pleas for Santo, talked with him at length, but did not immediately change his mind. But in April 1962, four years later, on the occasion of another visit to Geneva, Walter had a second long conversation with Santo, who by this time was established in business in Vienna with an Austrian partner, engaged in importing goods from the United States. This time Walter promised Santo that he would intercede for him with the Attorney General when he was satisfied that the statutory requirements for immigrant ex-Communists (five years of demonstrated active opposition to Communism) had been complied with. In January 1963, John Santo returned at last to America.

One of Santo's first steps after his return was to hold a lengthy "consultation" with HCUA, which was published as a part of the Committee's public record. Curiously, while dealing at great length with his experiences in Communist Hungary from 1949 to 1956, Santo was almost entirely silent about his previous Communist activities in this country. And the unwritten rule which prevents one Congressional committee from poaching on the territory of another prevented the ISSC from asking Santo—who had, after all, become HCUA's witness—about these extremely interesting matters.

John Santo now lives in America again, trying to build a new life in the country it had once been his supreme ambition to destroy. I disagree profoundly with those who are coldly indifferent to the fate of ex-Communists like Santo. No doubt it can be argued that whatever it may be, they deserve it. But I cannot accept such a view, either from the practical standpoint already discussed or from the purely human one. Santo's manifest talents, his wide experience, his transparent idealism (so long misplaced, but at last so totally refounded)—these are assets the West can use in the struggle against Communism; and it needs every asset it has. And at the end, in such cases, there may also be saved another human soul.

8

The Norman Case:
Prelude

By March 1957 I had been with the Subcommittee a year, and while a certain amount of controversy had swirled around our activities, no major attack had yet been mounted against us. I realized that this was very largely due to the care with which Bob Morris chose his subjects and prepared his groundwork; but I confess that I was also beginning to wonder whether I hadn't overestimated the hostility of our non-Communist critics. Perhaps they weren't such bad fellows after all. Be fair, play a clean ball game, and they would leave you alone—or even commend you, as certain discriminating liberals were in fact already beginning to commend Bob Morris.

Unfortunately, as I was soon to learn, many other liberals were simply waiting patiently for us to make a mistake. In April 1957 they decided we had made one—and swiftly moved to pillory Morris and to destroy the Internal Security Subcommittee altogether. It was a very near thing, and we were ultimately saved only because Morris, as usual, hadn't made a mistake after all.

What the world was to come to know as "the Norman Case" began for us, early in 1957, as the Emmerson Case. John K. Emmerson was a career officer in the U.S. Foreign Service who, by the time he was asked to testify in executive session before the Subcommittee on March 12, 1957, had achieved the highly responsible position of Deputy Chief of Mission and Counselor of the United States Embassy in Beirut, Lebanon. At that particular moment, however, he was and had been for some months on special assignment as a member of the U.S. delegation to the General Assembly of the United Nations, charged with maintaining liaison with the delegations of the Middle Eastern nations.

Emmerson's career had naturally extended over a period of many years and involved service in a number of different countries. In 1951 his name had been among those mentioned in testimony before the Subcommittee as close to the notorious Institute of Pacific Relations (IPR), the fountainhead of pro-Chinese Communist propaganda in America. What particularly interested the Subcommittee in 1957, however, was a certain dispatch Emmerson had sent to his State Department superiors from Yenan, in the Communist-held fastness of western China, late in 1944. A copy of this dispatch had been found by a Subcommittee investigator in 1955 in a filing cabinet at the Treasury. The cabinet in question contained various official papers of our old friend, the late Harry Dexter White, whose death in 1948 had by no means ended Congressional interest in his career.

At the executive session on March 12 (the transcript of which was later made public), Morris' introductory question to Emmerson concerned the circumstances of his assignment to Yenan:

> MR. MORRIS. Mr. Emmerson, the reason the subcommittee has asked you to be here today is that there has accumulated in the public record of the Internal Security Subcommittee since 1951 statements, testimony about you and certain documents of yours, so we felt in order to have a full story, that it would be well if you would appear and give testimony on these various items.
>
> This testimony and these items relate to a period of time when you were—and shortly thereafter—in Yenan, which was the Chinese Communist headquarters in China during the recent war. I wonder if you could begin your testimony today by telling us about your general assignment to Yenan and the nature of your duties there.

Emmerson's reply seemed straightforward enough:*

> MR. EMMERSON. I was assigned toward the end of 1943 as a political adviser to General Stilwell. I was concurrently second secretary of Embassy in Chungking and political adviser to General Stilwell.
>
> As a Japanese language officer and Foreign Service officer who had had experience in Japan, my duties in the theater were concerned en-

---

* Here, as throughout this book, I have risked exhausting the reader's patience by setting forth large segments of the transcript verbatim, rather than paraphrase the the testimony of a witness who may subsequently object that his statements were misinterpreted or deliberately misrepresented.

tirely with Japanese matters, interrogation of prisoners of war, psychological warfare particularly.

In the fall of 1944 our Government, or the Army, the United States Army, established in Yenan, the Communist headquarters, a United States Observers' Mission. This was done with the consent of General Chiang Kai-shek, and consisted of an Army unit in Yenan.

My assignment to the observers' section was concerned exclusively with psychological warfare matters. It was known that there was a group of Japanese prisoners of war who had been taken by the Chinese Communists and who were operating in Yenan. The head of this group was a well-known Japanese Communist by the name of Okano. That was the name he used at this period. He later used the name of Nozaka. It is one and the same person. So that, when I arrived in Yenan, the purpose of my assignment was to find out the kind of activities which were being conducted by this group of Japanese prisoners of war. At that time in 1944 we were, of course, concerned with the prosecution of the war against Japan.

The presence, I think, of an American observers' mission in Yenan indicated that there was cooperation between the Chinese Communists and ourselves as far as the war against Japan was concerned, so that we were eager to find out the kinds of activities which the Japanese prisoners of war there were conducting, the psychological warfare that they were engaged in, and whatever information or intelligence they might have with respect to Japan.

Senator Jenner was presiding, but Senator Watkins, who was also present (quite obviously at the request of the Eisenhower State Department, which was eager to protect Emmerson from our Subcommittee's fell designs, whatever they might be), now intervened to explore the function of these prisoners of war, who had been formed into an organization called the Japanese Peoples Emancipation League:

SENATOR WATKINS. Were the Chinese Communists working with them at the time?

MR. EMMERSON. Yes; they were under complete control of the Chinese Communists, but the Chinese entrusted the actual operation to the direction of this Japanese Communist, Okano, who was then present in Yenan and who directed the whole operation. He was a Japanese himself, but again he was subject to the orders.

SENATOR WATKINS. What was the operation they were doing?

MR. EMMERSON. It consisted largely of two things. One was the psychological warfare.

SENATOR WATKINS. Against whom?

MR. EMMERSON. Against the Japanese.

SENATOR WATKINS. In the homeland?

MR. EMMERSON. In the homeland and in China; that is, the Japanese Army operating in China and the Japanese homeland.

SENATOR WATKINS. These Japanese prisoners of war were conducting a psychological campaign, according to what you have just said, against the Japanese at home?

MR. EMMERSON. That is right.

SENATOR WATKINS. And those on the mainland?

MR. EMMERSON. They had been indoctrinated to the extent that they accepted the idea of the end of the war, opposition to militarism, and readiness to work for what they called a democratic future in Japan.

SENATOR WATKINS. In other words, they were seeking to undermine the armed might of Japan at that time.

MR. EMMERSON. That is right.

SENATOR WATKINS. And stop the war?

MR. EMMERSON. That is right; exactly.

Watkins' point here was, of course, that these Japanese and their Chinese Communist captors were both working against Japan, and hence were in a broad sense "on our side" at the time Emmerson became acquainted with them.

But Morris now moved to the heart of the matter: a memorandum written by Emmerson from Yenan under date of November 7, 1944, and forwarded to the U.S. commanding general of the China Theater and to the United States Embassy in Chungking—from which, in due course, it was transmitted to the State Department in Washington and circulated there to various officials, including Harry Dexter White. In this memorandum, Emmerson did not once mention the outright Communist nature of the Japanese Peoples Emancipation League, and actually recommended the employment of its members to assist the American military government in controlling Japan when that country was finally occupied. Following is the full text of Emmerson's memorandum:

Proposed Projects Against Japan

My short study of the activities of Susumu Okano and the Japanese Peoples Emancipation League in Communist China convinces me that we can utilize the experience and achievements of this group to advantage in the prosecution of the war against Japan.

Without going into the details of methods and materials, all of which are being carefully investigated here, we can suggest the following proposals:

(1) Effect the organization of an international "Free Japan" movement. The Japanese Peoples Emancipation League (Nihon Jinmin Kaiho Renmei) has an estimated membership of 450 Japanese prisoners

in north and central China. Its declared principles are democratic. It is not identified with the Communist Party.

Upon completion of a course of indoctrination, the more able members voluntarily prepare propaganda leaflets and engage in propaganda activities on the frontlines. There is no doubt that most of them are sincere converts to the anti-war principles of the league.

Intelligence shows that the league is well known to the Japanese Army and its influence is respected and feared.

Organization of chapters of this association, or a similar one, among Japanese prisoners, internees, and others, in the United States, India, Australia, and other countries, should be carried out.

The result would be widespread dissemination of democratic ideas, the creation of a powerful Japanese propaganda organ. (It is indisputable that propaganda from a Japanese source and written by Japanese is more effective than that from enemy sources.)

(2) Encourage the organization of cells within Japan to spread defeatism and thereby reduce resistance at the time of the invasion.

Preparations are now being made to send agents directly to Japan from this (Yenan) area.

Simultaneous organization needs to be undertaken of underground cells within Japan on the same principles as the free-Japan group on the outside. Such activities would necessarily be on a small scale, but ample evidence exists that there are such elements which can be useful to us. Careful preparation is obviously essential.

(3) Set up a radio transmitter in a Communist base area such as Shantung Province for broadcasts to Japan, Korea, and Manchuria.

A transmitter on the Shantung promontory would be 400 miles nearer Japan proper than Saipan and 600 miles nearer than the northern tip of Luzon.

The Japanese Peoples Emancipation League has a strong unit in Shantung Province and is now establishing a school there. Consequently trustworthy Japanese personnel is already on the spot to operate such a station. Additional trained personnel could be recruited from the school in Yenan and sent to any designated spot.

Identification of the station with a free-Japan group would insure broadcasts of immeasurably greater effect than those of stated American (enemy) origin.

(4) Train units of Japanese for activity with American pacification operations and with military government officials during occupation.

Eighth Route Army experience has clearly proved not only that Japanese prisoners can be converted but that they can be satisfactorily and extremely effectively used in propaganda operations on the front lines. Approximately 350 are now training and engaging in such activities on the north and central China fronts.

Such Japanese personnel, with invaluable knowledge of particular areas and of the language, could be extremely useful in assisting American Army officers in reestablishing order among the Japanese population.

Recruitment of these persons can be made from the personnel of Japanese Emancipation League chapters in China, already trained, and from prison camps under American, Australian or British jurisdiction.

A course of training would be necessary. Issei and Nisei in the United States could serve as instructors. Materials and the experience of the 8th Route Army would be of inestimable assistance in setting up such a project.

Now, with all due allowances for the proverbial acuity of hindsight, this was a truly astonishing document. Here was an American Foreign Service officer recommending, in November 1944, as the war thundered toward its close, that our military governors in Japan make use of a group of dedicated Japanese Communists in "reestablishing order" in Japan. Given the known methods of the Communists, such a course of action could only have had one outcome: a Communist Japan. But Emmerson, writing from Yenan, did not even inform his superiors of the trifling detail that he was talking about a Communist organization. On the contrary, he flatly asserted that "Its declared principles are democratic. It is not identified with the Communist Party."

I was interested, to put it mildly, to see how Emmerson would explain this extraordinary memorandum. As he read it aloud to the senators, Morris intervened to stress the point that particularly interested us:

> MR. MORRIS. May I break in? You knew it was a Communist organization?
> MR. EMMERSON. I knew it was a Communist organization. I felt that the fact that they had been successful in indoctrinating prisoners of war to the point where they were willing to participate in activities directed against the Japanese military and against the Japanese regime meant that the use of such people was a possibility, and, therefore, might contribute to our effort against Japan.
> [Continuing to read the text aloud:]
>
> Without going into the details of methods and materials, all of which are being carefully investigated here, we can suggest the following proposals:
> (1) Effect the organization of an international "Free Japan" movement. The Japanese Peoples Emancipation League (Nihon Jinmin Kaiho Renmei) has an estimated membership of 450 Japanese prisoners in north and central China. Its declared principles are democratic. It is not identified with the Communist Party.
>
> I would like to point out here I wrote a number of other reports

which gave in detail the program and the principles of this propaganda organization. They were, to a large extent—if I can recall them after this period of time—antagonism toward the militarists, the ending of the war, peace, freedom, democracy, that kind of thing.

Now, I say these were the declared principles of this organization. It was obviously a Communist organization, and that was completely known to me at the time.

An interesting concession, but it only added to the confusion.

MR. MORRIS. But there is nowhere that you say that in that document?
MR. EMMERSON. I say, "Its declared principles are democratic." The next sentence I say, "It is not identified with the Communist Party."

I might say here that the Communists deliberately did not identify it as being a Communist organization, because they expected that, by so doing, the effect would be greater among the Japanese, because, as I say, the leaflets, the material which they scattered and used in China contained the kind of platitudes which I have mentioned, "down with the militarists, surrender of Japan, democratic principles, peace," that sort of thing which, after all, in a general sense, were the same kind of things that we were talking about with respect to Japan.

Apparently, then, Emmerson was not going to try to deny that he had been perfectly familiar with the Communist nature of the Japanese Peoples Emancipation League. On the other hand he was staring straight at words of his own which any rational reader would interpret as denying flatly that the organization was Communist. In this rather ludicrous state of affairs he resumed reading, and in due course Morris pounced on another striking sentence:

[Emmerson reading:]

The result would be widespread dissemination of democratic ideas, the creation of a powerful Japanese propaganda organ. (It is indisputable that propaganda from a Japanese source and written by Japanese is more effective than that from enemy sources.)

MR. MORRIS. May I break in there? Do you think that the Japanese Communists would dispense and propagate democratic ideas?
MR. EMMERSON. Certainly, not basically. As I said, the leaflets which they were disseminating, if you read the text, it is simply a matter of "down with the militarists" and "end the war" and so on.

But, of course, knowing Communists, their objectives would be quite different. So I would like to say right here that this suggestion was made when I was only in Yenan a short time, and was made on the experience of what they were doing, was made in the atmosphere of our great concentration upon the war effort against Japan, and our general desire to get collaboration and cooperation wherever it might be found, and I am quite aware that this does not indicate the ultimate objectives of the Communist move or of Communists anywhere.

And I may say that, when I worked on this project a little later, and a few months afterward came to Washington and presented the project to the War Department and to the State-War-Navy Coordinating Committee, there was no suggestion of any participation by Communists or any use of Communists or Communist material whatsoever; so I am quite aware the ultimate objectives of the Communists are far from democratic.

I was not aware and did not express here the risks which would be involved in collaboration, close collaboration, with the Communists either in the war period or afterward.

There were many people at that time who spoke in favor of the coalition governments in which Communists might participate. I think that there was a general feeling among many quarters, and some perhaps high statesmen, that collaboration with the Communists was possible. We later found out, certainly, that that was not possible, and that any collaboration with a coalition government in which Communists had a part was a danger and meant the eventual efforts of the Communists to dominate.

So that was it! Emmerson's basic plea was naivete, i.e., that in November 1944, when he had only been in Yenan "a short time," he "was not aware and did not express here the risks which would be involved in collaboration, close collaboration, with the Communists." Well, that was possible, though naivete could hardly explain, and Emmerson never did get around to explaining, why he not only "did not express here the risks," but actually misled his superiors by concealing what even in 1944, and aside from the question of risk, was certainly not a negligible datum: the Communist nature of the Japanese Peoples Emancipation League. But there was more to come.

Emmerson had served as a Foreign Service officer in Japan before the war. He spoke Japanese, and was by way of being rather a specialist in Japanese affairs. Early in 1945, as he had already testified, he was sent back to Washington at his own suggestion "to discuss these specific ideas, the indoctrination program and the psychological warfare organization." With him, he brought an interesting document:

> MR. MORRIS. At that time, I think I asked you a while ago, did you bring any letter from Okano back?

Okano, it will be recalled, was the Japanese Communist who headed the puppet League.

MR. EMMERSON. I brought, as examples of activities of this organization, I brought back a number of materials including charts, pamphlets, leaflets, as objects of the work they were doing. I also brought back 2 or 3 letters, as I recall, which were simply statements of the principles and ideas of these psychological warfare organizations.

MR. MORRIS. Okano gave you this before you left?

MR. EMMERSON. Yes.

MR. MORRIS. Did he tell you to deliver it to anyone?

MR. EMMERSON. As I recall it, there was one which had the name of a Japanese in the United States.

MR. MORRIS. Was that Fujii Shuji?

MR. EMMERSON. Fujii Shuji.

Morris thereupon put into the record the fact that, according to evidence in the possession of the Subcommittee, Fujii Shuji had been at that time (1945) an employee of the U.S. Office of Strategic Services, and that in 1956 he had pleaded the Fifth when asked whether he had also, simultaneously, been a member of the Communist Party. It was to this man (of all people) that Emmerson, in 1945, had delivered a letter from the Japanese Communist, Okano.

Next Morris turned to a period in late 1945, just after the surrender of Japan, when Emmerson had been assigned by the State Department to Tokyo as a civilian political adviser to General Douglas MacArthur. Another Foreign Service officer in Tokyo, Eugene Dooman, who subsequently retired, had given the Subcommittee during the IPR hearings in 1951 a vivid description of Emmerson's seeming eagerness, while in Tokyo, to release certain prominent Japanese Communists from internment, presumably so that they, like the Japanese Peoples Emancipation League, could be "useful" to our military government there. Morris now virtually invited Emmerson to give his version of this episode:

> MR. MORRIS. Did you visit in Japan subsequently when you were General MacArthur's aide, the Japanese prisons there? Did you visit the Japanese Communists in their cells?

Emmerson, of course, had known all about Dooman's testimony for more than five years, and had his own version ready:

> MR. EMMERSON. Shortly after I arrived in Japan—this was immediately after the surrender in 1945—we heard that there were some Japanese Communists in a prison camp just outside Tokyo and at that time Mr. Herbert Norman, a Canadian diplomat, was working in the Counter Intelligence Corps. He is a well-known Japanese scholar and speaks

Japanese, was born in Japan. He, as I say, was working for Counter Intelligence, and so, under orders of the Counter Intelligence Corps, he and I together, in an Army vehicle, went to the prison camp to find out whether in fact these prisoners were there.

We discovered that they were, that there were two very important Japanese Communists, Mr. Shiga and Tokuda. After talking briefly to these prisoners, we returned to headquarters and reported this to the Counter Intelligence Corps.

It was felt that perhaps these prisoners might have some intelligence value that might be worth while interrogating them, so it was arranged that military cars from the Counter Intelligence Corps should go out to the prison, and again Mr. Norman and I went out, since we spoke Japanese.

Prisoners were placed in the cars and were brought back to headquarters itself by officers of the Counter Intelligence Corps.

At the end of the interrogation, they were taken back to the prison. That is the complete extent of my association with the interrogation of those prisoners of war or any visits to Japanese prison camps.

Morris now summarized the key points of Dooman's quite different account:

MR. MORRIS. Are you acquainted with Mr. Dooman's testimony to the fact that these Communists were driven around in Tokyo in Army staff cars, which was the equivalent of 100,000 votes to the Japanese Communists in their election?

MR. EMMERSON. I have read that testimony, and all I can say is that the only time the prisoners were ever driven in Army cars was when this group was driven from the prison to the headquarters and back again.

MR. MORRIS. Were they observed, do you think?

MR. EMMERSON. There was no reason for them to be observed. They were in khaki-colored Army sedans and they went through the streets of Tokyo, but there was no reason for them to be remarked any more than any other Army cars would have been.

Furthermore, Mr. Dooman, I believe, states that on October 10, I went out in an Army car and liberated these prisoners and drove them to their homes. That is completely false. I was not in the vicinity of the prison on October 10, and at no time ever drove these people to their homes. They were freed under the order of General MacArthur which liberated all political prisoners under the date, I believe, of October 4, 1945, and what happened at the prison at the time of their liberation I am not aware.

And that was how the name of Herbert Norman came to be introduced into the 1957 interrogation of John K. Emmerson. (Like Emmerson's, however, as we shall see, it had earlier appeared briefly in the 1951 hearings on the IPR and its friends.) In the ensuing colloquy, it developed that Emmerson had known Norman for quite a while:

MR. MORRIS. When did you first meet Mr. Norman, Mr. Emmerson?

MR. EMMERSON. I think about 1940. It was prewar Japan. He was, at that time, at the Canadian Legation in Tokyo when I was at the American Embassy in Tokyo. He was already a well-known writer on Japan, has written a number of books on the Government of Japan. He was born in Japan and speaks Japanese, of course, fluently, and has always been widely known.

MR. MORRIS. Had he attended Columbia University?

MR. EMMERSON. I assume so. That I don't know. He was already in the Canadian Foreign Service in 1940, that is the prewar period. He is a very well-known scholar, but I just say I have no reason to think he was a Communist in my association with him.

SENATOR WATKINS. Did he ever give any indication in conversations with you that he was pro-Communist?

MR. EMMERSON. No, not to my recollection. I don't remember any conversation which would indicate that he was a Communist.

Before turning aside from the interrogation of Emmerson to trace the career of Herbert Norman, let us review and summarize what the Subcommittee had established, thus far, concerning this American Foreign Service officer:

1. As early as 1940 Emmerson had known Canadian diplomat Herbert Norman in Tokyo. The significance of their friendship remains to be assessed below, in the light of Norman's own record.

2. In November 1944, Emmerson had recommended to the State Department the utilization, in postwar Japan, of the Japanese Peoples Emancipation League, an organization which, by his own much later admission, he knew to be Communist, yet which he had, at the time, described as follows: "Its declared principles are democratic. It is not identified with the Communist Party."

3. In early 1945, on returning to the United States, Emmerson had delivered a letter from Susumu Okano, the (Communist) head of the (Communist) Japanese Peoples Emancipation League, to Fujii Shuji, an OSS employee who subsequently pleaded the Fifth when asked whether he himself had been a Communist at the time.

4. In late 1945, in Tokyo, Emmerson and Norman had plucked two leading Japanese Communists from an internment camp for interrogation, assertedly on the theory that they "might have some intelligence

value." The precise details of the episode, and the prestige value it might have had for the Communists in question, were disputed however.

It would take, surely, a pretty intransigent foe of Congressional investigations to argue that there was no security question here worth investigating. Moreover, it was soon to appear that Emmerson and Norman had met yet again, years later, in another highly suggestive area of the globe: in October 1956, in the explosive Middle East, scant hours before the ill-fated Anglo-French-Israeli attack on the Suez Canal. What happened or may be conjectured to have happened at their meeting on that occasion, we must refrain from speculating on for the moment. The time has come to look at the brilliant and ultimately tragic career of Herbert Norman, whose name was so soon to eclipse Emmerson's in the annals of this particular investigation.

Norman was a Canadian, born in 1909 in Japan, the son of missionary parents. Whatever his political opinions and activities, they would not in the normal course have attracted the attention of a subcommittee of the United States Senate charged with an overview of *internal* security problems. But Norman's contacts included, as we have seen, an American Foreign Service officer, John K. Emmerson, whose own conduct had quite understandably aroused the curiosity of the ISSC. Moreover, Norman himself had spent years in the United States. It was, in fact, his activities while living and working in New York in 1938-39 that had first brought his name to the attention of the Subcommittee back in 1951.

On Tuesday, August 7, 1951, the ISSC was taking the testimony of Professor Karl August Wittfogel of the University of Washington, in connection with its aforementioned investigation of the Institute of Pacific Relations and the IPR's pro-Communist influence on American policy regarding China. Wittfogel, a German by birth, was and remains today one of the world's great experts on Chinese history. He had been a member of the Communist Party in Germany from 1920 to 1932, and remained close to the Communist movement, though no longer a Party member, after his emigration to the United States in 1934. By 1951, however, he had broken utterly with his Communist past, and was happy to be able to furnish the Subcommittee with valuable insights into the pro-Communist activities of the IPR and some of its allies in the years preceding World War II. He described, for example, a Communist study group he had belonged to in 1938:

MR. MORRIS. Now, Dr. Wittfogel, where did you stay later on in the summer of 1938? That was early in 1938?

DR. WITTFOGEL. That is right. Then I went to Provincetown.

MR. MORRIS. Where did you stay there?

DR. WITTFOGEL. I stayed in the house together with a gentleman who was a graduate student at Columbia. His name was Moses Finkelstein.

MR. MORRIS. Did Moses Finkelstein in the summer of 1938 run a summer camp or a summer study session?

DR. WITTFOGEL. Not that summer. He later became a very active organizer of some academic front organizations, of which you know, and which had many prominent persons of the campus and I think of some other campuses in them. He was a very skillful man that way. He had sometimes, it seems, study groups assembled in his house.

MR. MORRIS. Was he a Communist?

DR. WITTFOGEL. Yes.

MR. MORRIS. Did he tell you he was a Communist?

DR. WITTFOGEL. Sure.

MR. MORRIS. Was this study group that he ran a Communist study group?

DR. WITTFOGEL. Well, it was a discussion among a group of friends, of people who belonged to his political creed. There was no problem about that.

MR. MORRIS. Now would you tell us who some of the members were of that particular study group which you have just characterized?

DR. WITTFOGEL. It was a very small group. There were just a very few people that I met there. . . .

After a luncheon recess, Dr. Wittfogel resumed testifying. Morris began by recapitulating the morning testimony:

MR. MORRIS. Mr. Chairman, at the termination of the last session, chronologically, we had gotten as far as Dr. Wittfogel relating his experiences at a certain Communist study group in the summer of 1938. We had mentioned that the school was run by Moses Finkelstein. . . .

Who were some of the other students at this study group?

DR. WITTFOGEL. There was a talented and pleasant young man who was studying in the Japanese Department at Columbia. His name is Herbert Norman.

MR. MORRIS. Was he a member of this study group?

DR. WITTFOGEL. Yes.

MR. MORRIS. To your knowledge, did he know it was a Communist study group?

DR. WITTFOGEL. Yes, it was obvious.

MR. MORRIS. To you?

DR. WITTFOGEL. I think it was obvious, in general.

MR. MORRIS. Was it obvious therefore that he was a Communist?

DR. WITTFOGEL. Yes.

Morris thereupon introduced into the record IPR documents (correspondence and the like) indicating that a Canadian specialist in Japanese history named Herbert Norman had been a close friend and ideological ally of the dominant IPR personalities in and prior to 1940.

It is a singular fact, however, that neither Morris nor Wittfogel nor the members of the Subcommittee even dreamed what a devastating impact this testimony, which they must have regarded as useful largely for the historical record, would have in Canada. By nightfall the wire services had reported Wittfogel's testimony to our northern neighbors, and the next morning Canadians awoke to the sickening realization that this same Herbert Norman—whom Wittfogel described as being in 1938 "a talented and pleasant young man who was studying in the Japanese Department at Columbia," and as being simultaneously a Communist, and a member of a Communist study group—was now (i.e., 1951) Chief of the American and Far Eastern Division of the Department of External Affairs of Canada, and acting head of the Canadian delegation to the United Nations!

Great was the consternation in Canada, and especially in Canadian government circles—greater, even, than the Subcommittee and the astonished Canadian public realized. For though the world at large did not know it, security officers of the Royal Canadian Mounted Police had had their eye on Norman for a number of years, and in 1950 had lost a major behind-the-scenes battle concerning him.

According to information developed by the Mounties over a period of years, Norman had probably been a member of the Canadian Communist Party as early as 1935. In that year he had married Laura Irene Clark, and one of the official witnesses at their marriage had been Charles P. H. Holmes, a well-identified Canadian Communist.

In 1936 Norman was publicly listed as Secretary of an organization known as Canadian Friends of the Chinese People, the Canadian affiliate of a notorious U.S. Communist front called, correspondingly, American Friends of the Chinese People.

The next item, chronologically, in Norman's record was his membership in Moses Finkelstein's Communist study group in New York in 1938-9, when Dr. Wittfogel had noted him as "talented and pleasant"— and a Communist. But information concerning this aspect of Norman's record had not yet reached the Mounties when they were assembling their dossier on him in 1950.

In February 1940, however, an underground source of the RCMP had identified Norman (by now a Canadian Foreign Service officer and about to leave for service in Japan) as a member of the Canadian Communist Party.

Then in 1942 there had been a strange episode at Harvard involving Norman, who had just been repatriated from Japan. Shigeto Tsuru, a Japanese economist who had his own long history of involvement with Communists in both Japan and the United States, had been at Harvard that year, but—being technically an enemy alien—was scheduled for repatriation to Japan on the Swedish liner *Gripsholm*. Apparently he had to leave some of his papers behind, for very shortly, as the RCMP later learned,

> . . . the FBI was approached by Norman who represented himself as an official on highly confidential business of the Canadian Government in an effort to take custody of Tsuru's belongings.
>
> One main item of these belongings was a complete record of the Nye munitions investigations, largely prepared by Alger Hiss.
>
> Norman later admitted to the FBI agents in charge that his was only a personal interest, and that he was not representing the Canadian Government as stated.
>
> Another item among these belongings, as reported by the FBI, was a letter dated May 9, 1937, which related to a series of studies being promoted at Harvard by Tsuru which provided for the study of American capitalists from a Marxist viewpoint. The studies were conducted by a group of young instructors and graduate students which had met five times. They discussed certain papers which included *American Imperialism*, by E. H. Norman.

In short, Norman had lied in representing himself to the FBI in Massachusetts in 1942 as an authorized representative of the Canadian government, and on this basis had made a desperate but unsuccessful effort to bluff his way into possession of the compromising documents of a Japanese Marxist.

Next in chronological order was the suggestive behavior of Norman—accompanied this time by his American friend Emmerson—in postwar Japan: most notably their visit to the Japanese Communist leaders, Shiga and Tokuda, in their internment camp in October 1945, and the subsequent interrogation of these men, with all the disputed political implications of that action. This episode, however, like Dr. Wittfogel's information, was still unknown to the RCMP in 1950.

Finally, Norman had been briefly recalled from Japan by the Canadian government in 1947, to explain his close friendship with Israel Halperin, a Canadian citizen implicated by a Royal Commission with the Soviet military intelligence operation uncovered following the defection of Soviet code clerk Igor Gouzenko in Ottawa in 1945.*

This highly suggestive material on Norman (excluding the Columbia

---

* Halperin was later acquitted of statutory violations in this connection.

and Shiga-Tokuda episodes, of which they were then still unaware) had been set forth in a memorandum by the RCMP in October 1950 for the information of the Canadian government. But Norman—still, despite all setbacks, rising rapidly in the Canadian Foreign Service—had powerful friends. Specifically he was the protégé of Lester Pearson, then Minister of External Affairs in the St. Laurent government of Canada. A blow at Norman was, willy-nilly, a blow at Pearson; and Pearson moved vigorously to fend off the blow. Assailing the unknown 1940 RCMP informer as unworthy of credence, and the rest of the data as insubstantial or conjectural, Pearson actually succeeded in forcing the RCMP to issue a second report in December 1950, modifying and softening its October memorandum; and Norman sailed serenely on. Of this struggle behind the scenes, of course, the Canadian public was told nothing.

It is now possible, however, to appreciate why Professor Wittfogel's testimony in August 1951 (and Eugene Dooman's testimony, which followed it in September) fell like thunderbolts in Canada and hardest of all behind the scenes in the St. Laurent government. Here was fresh confirmation of the "discredited" October 1950 memorandum! This time not even the puissant Mr. Pearson could save his protégé. Despite official assurances that Norman had been subjected to "the normal security investigation" and "given a clean bill of health," and despite Pearson's personal avowal of "complete confidence" in him, Norman was recalled from New York to Ottawa and then, after a graceful pause, assigned in 1953 to innocuous desuetude as Canada's High Commissioner to New Zealand. There he languished until, in 1956, deeming it safe at last, External Affairs Minister Pearson assigned him to the key post of Canadian Ambassador to Cairo, with concurrent accreditation as Minister to Lebanon. In Beirut on October 27, presenting his credentials in the latter capacity, Norman (as already noted) had a reunion with his old friend Emmerson.

Thus did the tangled skein of time and circumstance bring these two men—Norman, the Canadian Communist, and Emmerson, the American Foreign Service officer—together at three widely separated times and places: in prewar Tokyo; in Tokyo again during the postwar American occupation; and in volatile Beirut in October 1956. It can hardly be much occasion for surprise, in view of Emmerson's own ambiguous behavior, that the ISSC wanted to know all about his decades-long friendship with Norman, its origins, its depth, and its significance.

To lay a foundation for this line of questioning, Morris, interrogating Emmerson in March 1957, accordingly put into the record what the Subcommittee had learned over the years concerning Herbert Norman. Since taking Professor Wittfogel's testimony in August 1951, the Sub-

committee had come into possession of the substance of the RCMP
memorandum of October 1950, which had been suppressed at the insistence of Lester Pearson. There is reason to believe that Pearson (who
today, of course, is Canada's Premier) still wonders how this particular
leak occurred, and I will certainly not enlighten him here. What matters
is that the ISSC knew what the RCMP had reported, and that Morris
(without identifying the RCMP as the author of the memorandum)
summarized it for the record in the 1957 investigation of Norman's
American crony, Emmerson. Combined with the other aspects of Emmerson's record already discussed, it certainly raised questions of the
gravest kind.

Senator Jenner for example probed, without much success, the question of what (if anything) had passed between Norman and Emmerson
in Beirut in October 1956:

> SENATOR JENNER. In October when you saw him in Beirut when he
> came to present his credentials, did you have dinner with him or did you
> visit with him at any length?
> MR. EMMERSON. Very briefly, because I was leaving the same day for the
> United States.
> SENATOR JENNER. Did he pass any opinion upon the problems confront-
> ing the world in the Middle East at that time? This was in October
> 1956?
> MR. EMMERSON. He was extremely concerned about the developments in
> the Middle East, about the danger of an explosion taking place.
>   As a matter of fact, I believe that this outbreak occurred while he was
> in Beirut and he was delayed in getting back to Cairo.
> SENATOR JENNER. Which outbreak now do you refer to?
> MR. EMMERSON. I am referring to the Israeli invasion at the end of
> October, and the British and French action.
> SENATOR WATKINS. Did he go back there before the trouble?
> MR. EMMERSON. He could not leave because no one could go to Cairo.
> After the invasion had taken place there was no plane service between
> Beirut and Cairo. I am not sure how long he had to stay there, but no
> one could go from Beirut to Cairo.
> SENATOR WATKINS. What were your duties in Beirut?
> MR. EMMERSON. I am deputy chief of mission there, counselor of em-
> bassy.
> SENATOR WATKINS. Is that in effect a deputy Ambassador?
> MR. EMMERSON. That is right. That is the No. 2 position in the Em-
> bassy.
> SENATOR WATKINS. Yes.
> SENATOR JENNER. Did he criticize our country for the attitude we took
> on the English and French invasion?

MR. EMMERSON. No; because that had not taken place.

SENATOR JENNER. That was not discussed?

MR. EMMERSON. The British and French invasion had not taken place when I saw him. As I recall it, we discussed the general situation in the Middle East.

SENATOR JENNER. I thought you were referring to the outbreak when Israel broke into the Sinai Desert and so forth and at the same time, as I recall it, and I may be wrong, the French and British moved into Suez.

MR. EMMERSON. As I recall the chronology, that did not happen until about the 30th or 31st October. I was in London, in fact I was in the House of Commons on the 30th, which was the day Prime Minister Eden presented his ultimatum, so that he did not know, at least in Beirut, about the Israeli—in fact, I think that mobilization in Israel had taken place, but we had not got the news yet when I left Beirut.

SENATOR JENNER. So that matter was not discussed?

MR. EMMERSON. That matter was not discussed.

SENATOR JENNER. Do you recall what you did talk about?

MR. EMMERSON. The general situation, and I am sure that we did discuss the general situation in the Middle East, and our concern about developments and about the dangers to western interests in the Middle East.

I am sorry I cannot recall any specific statements that he may have made, but there was certainly nothing which would excite my curiosity or which would strike me as being strange or being pro-Communist.

I am sure that I would have remembered any statement of that sort.

Not all of those present shared Mr. Emmerson's confidence on this latter point, but we had to let it go at that for the time being. After a few more desultory questions, the hearing was adjourned.

Two days later (on March 14), the Subcommittee voted to make the transcript a part of its public record. The new material concerning Emmerson (and especially his 1944 memorandum) was indisputably thought-provoking. However, this was the first time the full story on Herbert Norman had ever been made public, and its impact, especially on Canadians, was bound to be powerful, even though Morris had carefully *not* identified the RCMP as the source of most of it. The Norman aspects of the matter were further tenderized by the fact that an election was scheduled in Canada for the late spring, with Lester Pearson as the Liberal Party's candidate for Premier to succeed the venerable Louis St. Laurent. In such a state of affairs, fresh security information involving a well-known Pearson protégé was bound to loom large on the Canadian scene.

On the other hand, it should be emphasized, the Senate Internal

Security Subcommittee would certainly not have been warranted in discontinuing or hushing up a thoroughly justified investigation of an American Foreign Service officer merely because his story involved close contacts with a Communist who happened to boast Canadian citizenship and powerful friends currently running for high office.

The first impulse of America's liberal press—hostile, as always, to investigations of Communism—was, predictably, to minimize the whole affair. On March 15 the *Washington Post* carried a short medley of wire service reports on page 5 under the ho-hum headline, "Old Charges Against Envoy Aired":

> A Senate subcommittee yesterday made public the transcript of a hearing in which it was alleged the Canadian Ambassador to Egypt is a Communist.
>
> John K. Emmerson, United States deputy chief of mission in Lebanon, testified in the same hearing that he understood the Canadian government had announced in 1951 that the envoy, E. Herbert Norman, had been cleared of such charges. Emmerson also said he has known the Canadian since 1940 and had never heard anything indicating Norman is or was a Communist.
>
> The statements involving the Canadian were contained in the transcript of a hearing held Wednesday by the Senate Internal Security Subcommittee.
>
> [In Ottawa, Foreign Secretary Lester Pearson said the testimony appears to repeat slanders the Canadian government has rejected, the Associated Press reported. He declined further comment.]
>
> Emmerson also was questioned about his World War II service when he was assigned to the Chinese Communists.

Among other things, the *Post*'s story did not do justice to the sweep and power of Lester Pearson's denunciation of our hearing. Quoth he:

> This record contains a great many innuendoes and insinuations that Mr. Norman was a Communist. We knew all about these charges years ago, as a result of which Mr. Norman was subjected—in his own and the public interest—to a special and exhaustive security check.
>
> As a result of that check our confidence in Norman's loyalty was not weakened in any respect. Nothing he has done since has affected—unless to increase—the confidence we have in him as a devoted efficient and loyal official of the Government, who is doing extremely important work at a very difficult post in a way which commands my wholehearted admiration and deserves my full support.
>
> These slanders and unsupported insinuations against him contained in this United States Senatorial Subcommittee report we can treat with the contempt they deserve.

The next day (March 16), the vigilant *Post* followed up its news story with an editorial entitled "Smear, Inc.," firing a shot across the Subcommittee's bow:

> The Senate Internal Security Subcommittee is at it again. Apparently not having enough to do in internal security, it has gone into the business of vilifying friendly foreign diplomats. On Thursday it released a transcript of what Senator Jenner had said was an executive hearing about the activities of the Canadian Ambassador to Egypt, Herbert Norman. Subcommittee Counsel Robert Morris said that "We have quite a few security reports which have a great deal of information to the effect that he is a Communist . . ."
>
> These are stale and repudiated charges. As the Canadian government has made clear, they were thoroughly investigated in 1951 and Mr. Norman was found to be completely loyal. Apparently his offense in the eyes of the Subcommittee is that he is an expert on the Far East and once was a member of the Institute of Pacific Relations. The action of the Subcommittee embarrasses Canada and indeed the Western position at a time of extremely sensitive relations with Cairo.
>
> Entirely rightly, Canadian Foreign Secretary Pearson has retorted that the "slanders" and "unsupported insinuations" of the Subcommittee will be treated with contempt. The strong protest to the United States which he promises is thoroughly justified. If the Subcommittee had had new security information, its proper course was to transmit the data to the State Department for relay to Canada instead of to broadcast it publicly. No one has given the Subcommittee a mandate to meddle in diplomacy. When is the Senate going to put a bridle on this sort of rampaging irresponsibility?

Not a word, of course, about the true subject of our inquiry: Emmerson, and his memorandum from Yenan.

It was in this supercharged atmosphere that the Subcommittee held a second executive hearing with Emmerson on March 21. He wanted to make certain corrective changes in his previous testimony, and once again Senator Watkins hovered solicitously in the background, asking helpful questions. The changes themselves were largely trivial: Emmerson now recalled that he had left Beirut on October 28 rather than October 27; he had forgotten an exchange of letters with Norman about their prospective meeting in Beirut; Norman had mentioned, at the meeting itself, that he had been "cleared" of security charges growing out of the ISSC's 1951 hearings; and so on. Perhaps the most interesting moment occurred during a discussion of Dr. Wittfogel's 1951 testimony. Morris casually remarked to Senator Watkins:

MR. MORRIS. Senator, I also think it is appropriate at this time to mention that I have since spoken to Professor Wittfogel, since last week, and he said that to this day no official of the Canadian Government has ever called him up or asked him whether or not any of his testimony was, in fact, accurate.

One could be pardoned for wondering just what sort of "special and exhaustive security check" the Canadian government had performed on Norman in 1951, following Wittfogel's devastating testimony about him, that did not even involve a talk with Wittfogel! Senator Watkins' response was appropriately cautious:

SENATOR WATKINS. I see. Well, that is very interesting. It may have some significance.

The session ended without further incident, and a week later (on March 28) the Subcommittee voted to include the transcript of this hearing too, in its public record. Both Emmerson hearings are set forth in Part 56 of the Subcommittee's investigation into "Scope of Soviet Activity in the United States."

At this delicate stage in the investigation, a new line of inquiry suddenly suggested itself. As it happened, Shigeto Tsuru, whose papers had been of such consuming interest to Herbert Norman when Tsuru was repatriated to Japan in 1942, was back in the United States in that spring of 1957, as a visiting lecturer in economics at Harvard, on leave of absence from his professorship of economics at Hitotsubashi University in Tokyo. Quite independently of the 1942 episode, the files of the Subcommittee's 1951 IPR hearings bulged with evidence that Tsuru, both as a graduate student of economics at Harvard from 1935 until his repatriation to Tokyo in 1942, and in postwar Japan, had been (like Norman himself) a pillar of the pro-Communist Institute of Pacific Relations and a close associate of various American Communists. Moreover, accounts of his activities in the postwar period (when he was first a research economist for the occupation regime and had later risen to be Vice Minister of Economic Stabilization) suggested that he had then followed a vigorously anti-American line, quite consistent, of course, with the policies and program of the Japanese Communist Party.

Tsuru had not been in the United States during the IPR hearings of 1951, and had thus escaped interrogation by the ISSC at that time. But now the Subcommittee, pursuing its inquiry into the strange behavior of Herbert Norman at Harvard in 1942, had obtained copies of certain of the documents Tsuru had left behind when he was hastily repatriated.

They not only explained why Norman had tried so desperately to pre-empt them; they inspired in the Subcommittee a renewed and powerful desire to talk with Professor Tsuru. A subpoena went forth, and Tsuru appeared before the Subcommittee, first in executive session and then in public, on Tuesday, March 26.

I daresay the subpoena came as a rude surprise to him. Certainly it landed on the Japanese press corps in Washington with devastating effect, for when we entered the hearing room for the public session we noted a number of clearly flabbergasted Orientals at the press table. The McCarthy Era had ended, officially, with the Senate's condemnation resolution of December 1954, and no doubt Japan's journalists in Washington, like so many of their American colleagues, had learned to sneer contemptuously at all congressional investigations of Communism. That these continued despite the sneers was bad enough; that one such investigatory body should actually have the audacity to subpoena a noted Japanese citizen while he was on a visiting lectureship at Harvard was, evidently, just too much to be borne—even though he had once spent many years in this country. But our Japanese friends, and the world at large, had not read Professor Tsuru's correspondence during those years. We had.

Morris took Tsuru briskly through his career to date, then turned to the matter of the documents he had left behind in Cambridge in 1942. It had become obvious in the executive session that Tsuru had, quite humanly, forgotten just how damaging they were, and he and his attorney were still visibly nonplused as they struggled to adjust to their astonishment. The Subcommittee, on the other hand, (represented on this occasion by Senators Johnston and Jenner) knew the indisputable significance of the documents, and there was a no-nonsense air about them as Morris took up the prickly subject:

> MR. MORRIS. Now, Mr. Chairman and Senator Jenner, the purpose of this hearing here today is to ask Mr. Tsuru to identify for the public record, which he has already done in executive session, portions of his papers and books which he left behind at the time of his repatriation in 1942, about which he has just told us.

Morris thereupon asked Ben Mandel to read portions of a letter Tsuru had written from Madison, Wisconsin on August 31, 1936, to Professor W. T. Parry, who was at that time on the philosophy faculty at Harvard. (Parry had later been identified under oath as a Communist, and had pleaded the Fifth before HCUA when asked about it.) The letter was a long discussion of the general utility of a new Marxist publication called *Science and Society*, with which both Parry and Tsuru were connected, and was studded with references which were only intelligible on the assumption that the author regarded himself as for all practical purposes a Communist:

> We already have various forms of organization for the educational purposes, for example the Worker's School [a Communist school] . . .
>
> The existing forms are adapted mainly for the members of the working class and the lower middle class or for the members of the party and YCL [meaning the Communist Party and its youth arm, the Young Communist League] . . .
>
> [Then, after recommending the formation of *Science and Society* "study groups":] No less important than the foregoing point, however, is the necessity of leading ordinary members of these study groups into a more mature form of organization or of activities. To be a member of a study group may be a step toward enrolling [in] the worker's school; it may be a step toward joining the American League Against War and Fascism; it may be a step toward becoming a member of YCL or of the party. It is absolutely necessary to keep a study group from becoming a self-perpetuating, stagnant cloister for the few.

In the teeth of these damning sentences, Tsuru protested feebly that he personally had never been a Communist. But Morris was not through. After a lengthy digression into Tsuru's postwar actions and views, which Tsuru admitted had caused him to be "known as anti-American in Japan," Morris read a portion of a letter from Parry, dated September 6, 1936, replying to Tsuru's of August 31:

> [Morris reading:]
>
> It is the duty of the more advanced members of the groups to draw the others closer to the revolutionary movement by involving them in activities, as you suggest. If anyone raises any objection to these study groups, see to it that his position is corrected, if necessary appealing to the district leadership.
>
> Now isn't that advice to you to take the problem up with the district leadership of the Communist Party if you have any dissension whatever in following out your plan?
>
> MR. TSURU. Well here again, the only way I can answer, I think, is I committed excesses, and I have committed mistakes in widening too much my association with various people, and probably I was too eager to make *Science and Society* a success at the time. But truthfully, I never was a member of the Communist Party; I never identified anyone as a member. . .

Senator Jenner now broke in to stress the giveaway phrase, "district leadership":

> SENATOR JENNER. Did *Science and Society* have a district leadership?
> MR. TSURU. No, it did not, sir. Well, we had a number of people who were interested in developing this magazine, *Science and Society*, in different districts.

It was really pretty lame. Tsuru's ordeal was over for that afternoon, however; the Subcommittee adjourned, and he was instructed to return the next day. By the next morning Professor Tsuru had had time to do some further thinking, and was ready with a written statement which he asked and was given permission to read. Its key portion was the following:

> As I have testified, I am not and never have been a member of the Communist Party. Attention has been called to a handful of letters written by, and to, me in 1936-37, some 20 years ago when I was a student at Harvard. These letters were apparently among the possessions which I left behind in my apartment in Cambridge when I was repatriated on the *Gripsholm*. During that period of time, as these letters indicate, I was acquainted with some individuals who were Communists or Communist-sympathizers, and, for a brief while I showed interest in the publication, *Science and Society* (some of whose editors were Communists), and in groups in Cambridge which discussed, among other things, Marxist doctrine.
> Looking back over 20 years, I can only explain such interests during my student days in terms of youthful indiscretion of which I am ashamed.
> I soon lost interest in *Science and Society* and saw less and less of those individuals in Cambridge and elsewhere who had been active in it. As I matured, my attitudes changed.

Morris was unwilling to let such a self-serving declaration go into the record unrebutted:

> MR. MORRIS. These papers don't reveal youthful indiscretion or any such thing. The witness, in his own [1936] statement [read] yesterday, was talking of the necessity of leading ordinary members of study groups into a more mature form of organization or activities. He went on to say that to be a member of a study group may be a step toward enrolling in the workers' schools; may be a step toward joining the American League Against War and Fascism. It may also be a step, he said, toward becoming a member of the Young Communist League or of the party. "It is

absolutely necessary," said Mr. Tsuru, "to keep a study group from becoming a self-perpetuating stagnant cloister for the few."

Morris thereupon introduced into the record still other documents in the cache Tsuru had left at Harvard, and which Norman tried so hard to obtain. Chief among them was a lengthy memorandum to the editors of *Science and Society*, which Tsuru had handed personally to Parry on January 30, 1937. It was signed by Tsuru and two other members of the Marxist clique: Karl Heinrich Niebyl, then a professor of economics at Carleton College, Northfield, Minnesota, and Constance Kyle, a lecturer in psychiatry at the University of Illinois. In it, Tsuru and his co-authors proudly reported on their success in forming *Science and Society* study groups at various Midwestern universities. One brief paragraph will suffice to convey the general flavor:

> In Minneapolis we got a foothold at the University of Minnesota where a group of a few economic historians, political scientists, and a philosopher was meeting with N. [Niebyl] fairly regularly. The discussion revolved mainly around an interpretation of history coupled, of course, with an understanding of present events. Fairly good headway has been made. There is a possibility that the group will have to be reorganized because two of the members will go to Washington, D.C., after Christmas.

One cannot help wondering which two members of the Minnesota study group went "to Washington, D.C." at the end of 1936, and how loyally they served their country there!

Lest anyone be left in doubt for whom the memorandum was really intended, Morris inserted in the record a long letter from Tsuru to Niebyl dated February 22, 1937, which read in part:

> Not only your letter made it clear that the memorandum is addressed to the fraction, but I also repeated it verbally to Parry. Parry explained to me, however, practically all of the members of the editorial board either are or once were members of the Party, and that the fraction and the editorial board are almost identical.

Not, apparently, identical enough, however, for we find Tsuru writing from Harvard to Professor Kyle (copy to Niebyl) on April 9, 1937:

> Have you received an answer from N.Y. to our memorandum? I have repeatedly inquired Parry about it, but no avail. Finally I suggested that

> I shall go down to N.Y. in the weekend of April 10 to discuss the matter. . . . I have persistently repeated to Parry that the matter of the memorandum is of immediate and primary importance and that according to my impression their slow response is partly due to their slipshodness with which they distinguish the party fraction from the editorial board. The memorandum is addressed to the fraction; and it seems to me that it is a breach of discipline for them to have laid it aside for more than two months. I have no authority to say anything further on this matter. So, I hope that you and Karl-Heinrich will press this matter and work toward dispelling any misunderstandings.

The interesting point of course is that, although the memorandum was addressed formally to the "Editors of S. and S.," Tsuru insists that it was really "addressed to the fraction," i.e., to the Communists who actually controlled the publication, and even blames the failure of communication on the "slipshodness with which they distinguish the party fraction from the editorial board." He goes so far as to charge the party fraction with "a breach of discipline" for not responding more promptly, but notes that he has "no authority" to say more.

There was, by this time, little reason to wonder why Herbert Norman, at Harvard in 1942, tried so desperately to prevent these and related documents from falling into the hands of the FBI when Tsuru was repatriated to Japan. There remained, however, the task of exploring Tsuru's relations with Norman over the years; and to this task Morris now turned.

Tsuru testified that he had met Norman at Harvard, through a mutual friend, in the spring of 1936. Within a year they were both members of a study group—yet another of those famous study groups!—at Harvard, founded (according to a letter from Tsuru to Niebyl dated May 9, 1937) "for the study of American capitalism from the Marxist point of view." (This was the letter that had been singled out for special attention in the RCMP's October 1950 memorandum, since the subject of one meeting of the group, it asserted, had been a paper composed by Norman entitled "American Imperialism.")

Subsequently, as we have seen, Norman had joined the Canadian Foreign Service and been posted to Tokyo, where in 1940 he first met the chief object of our inquiry, John K. Emmerson. Interned by the Japanese upon the outbreak of war in the Pacific, Norman was soon repatriated to Canada in an exchange of diplomats. Meanwhile, Tsuru had applied for his own repatriation to Japan, as an enemy alien. In the rush to leave Harvard, he had to leave much behind, including the correspondence we have been quoting, which was by then at least five years old and probably had slipped his mind altogether. One tries to catch a glimpse of those musty letters, as Tsuru's account proceeds:

> MR. TSURU. . . . suddenly, I believe it was June the second, 1942, we received a telegram from the State Department saying that we are to be repatriated by the first boat and we are to report to Ellis Island by June the 7th, I believe, the exact date I am not quite certain now. Which meant that I had only a few days between the receipt of the telegram and the date of my departure . . . I instructed the janitor of the apartment that he can have my furniture, kitchen utensils, radio, and other things he wanted. Books and documents I was certain that he would have no use, so I suggested to him he can dispose of them in second-hand bookstores or just dispose of them as he liked.
>
> One other item which I took care of was the making out of a box full of Japanese books which I intended to give to Mr. Norman because he had indicated while he was in this country a few years back of that period, that he wanted to obtain those books very much, but they were very difficult to get.
>
> The major item in this box of books was volumes on source materials on the economic history of early Meiji period, that is to say, the third quarter of the 19th century.
>
> I believe I included some other source books and economic history books and I left this box in care of International Student Association, it might have been called institute, I am not certain, which was located on Phillips Place, Cambridge. Director at the time was Mr. Lawrence Mead. And I asked him if he would be willing to keep it until Mr. Norman calls for it.
>
> Immediately, that is at the same time, I wrote a letter to Mr. Tarshis, whose name I mentioned earlier, who I knew to be a friend of Mr. Norman, asking him to get in touch with Mr. Norman when the latter returns.
>
> I knew Mr. Norman to be in Japan at the time and gave him my instructions to proceed to International Student Institute to take that box. That is the way I more or less disposed or left behind my belongings.

But nothing in this bland testimony explains the fervor of Norman's subsequent effort to keep Tsuru's papers out of the hands of the FBI. Norman had, it will be recalled, falsely "represented himself [to the FBI] as an official on highly confidential business of the Canadian Government in an effort to take custody of Tsuru's belongings." Surely his zeal for source materials on the economic history of the early Meiji period could not have accounted for such conduct. But the highly compromising correspondence we have reviewed could easily have done so, and obviously did.

After the war, Tsuru testified, he had met Norman again, this time in Tokyo in late 1945, when Emmerson was also there and when all three were serving in various capacities in SCAP (Supreme Command, Allied Powers—the occupying authority). Over the next four and a half years, during which Norman returned to Canada and was then reassigned to Tokyo as head of the Canadian Legation there, Tsuru estimated that he met Norman about 20 times. Norman, he said, had confirmed receiving the box of books discussed (concerning the Meiji period) and added that he had voluntarily tried to question Tsuru's Cambridge janitor about his other papers. Here at last we seemed to be getting, second-hand, Norman's own version of the 1942 episode reported by the FBI:

> MR. TSURU. But after dealing with the janitor for a while, he did not get a very cooperative attitude he told me. The janitor looked somewhat queer and not very—he appeared to be equivocal about the whole matter. Although Mr. Norman pressed it, he couldn't get anywhere with it.
>
> MR. MORRIS. You say he pressed it with the janitor to have a look at all your papers and books?
>
> MR. TSURU. Well, I gathered that Mr. Norman pressed, "Did Mr. Tsuru leave other belongings here?" and if so he would like to find out if he could get hold of some more Japanese books.
>
> I do not remember the exact words which Mr. Norman said to the janitor.
>
> MR. MORRIS. Did he tell you he had represented himself as an official of the Canadian Government?
>
> MR. TSURU. Not that I recall.
>
> MR. MORRIS. He didn't indicate that at all?
>
> MR. TSURU. Not that I recall. But I believe he told me he visited the place twice or he first visited it once and then made an approach the second time, in what means I do not know, but I remember he said he made attempts twice.
>
> MR. MORRIS. And you did say he pressed on the point?
>
> MR. TSURU. Yes, he pressed on the point that he wanted to see it, but could not get anywhere so he went back. So he told me now he doesn't know what happened to my belongings which I left at the apartment.
>
> MR. MORRIS. And some of which have come into the record of the Internal Subcommittee and have given us valuable information.
>
> MR. TSURU. Yes, much to my own shame of the period which is covered.

Finallly, Morris took Tsuru through a long list of people whom Tsuru knew or might have known in IPR circles before and after the war, probing the depth of his contacts with each. For our present purposes, the most important name was that of Israel Halperin, because Tsuru testified he had been introduced to Halperin by Norman, and because of a further interesting fact having to do with Halperin's address book:

MR. MORRIS. Do you know a man named Israel Halperin?

MR. TSURU. Yes.

MR. MORRIS. Who was Israel Halperin?

MR. TSURU. I knew him as an instructor of mathematics at Harvard University. He might have been a research associate, the official title I do not know. He was introduced to me, I believe, by Mr. Norman. The year I cannot remember quite exactly, but possibly around 1937.

MR. MORRIS. Now this is the same man who was arrested in the Canadian espionage case in [1945].

MR. TSURU. That I did not know, but I knew it later because I was questioned about him by United States Government representatives in Japan.

MR. MORRIS. Did you know your name appeared in his address book at the time of his arrest?

MR. TSURU. I did not know my name appeared there.*

The first result of the Tsuru hearings was an explosive reaction in Japan, fully reported and ably exploited by American critics of Congressional investigations of Communism. The fact that this man had spent long years in the United States, conniving with American and Canadian Communists in half a dozen cities, was brushed aside as irrelevant. Here was a stick—Japanese national pride—with which to beat the dog of Congressional investigations, and the liberals of the world made the most of it. A United Press dispatch from Tokyo, dated March 30, summed it up:

TOKYO—March 30 (UP). A political storm brewed today as angry Diet (parliament) members pressed the government to explain why a visiting Harvard University professor, Shigeto Tsuru, was called to testify before U.S. Senator investigators on alleged Communist ties.

Government spokesmen, at loss for answers, promised to seek an explanation from the Japanese Ambassador in Washington . . .

Diet members in the Education Committee protested yesterday that Tsuru enjoyed the status of a government official while lecturing at Harvard. Other members said that the Japanese government should be entitled to question U.S. soldiers involved in incidents on U.S.

---

* For the full transcript of the Tsuru hearings, see Part 57 of "Scope of Soviet Activity in the United States," published by the ISSC in 1957.

military bases here if the Senate could subpoena a Japanese government official . . .

Socialist Diet leaders were expected to take up the issue today in a meeting of the Diet policy committee.

On April 4, under the headline "Japan Hits U.S. on Red Probe," the *Washington Star* carried an Associated Press story from Tokyo:

> TOKYO, April 4 (AP). Seiichi Inouye, parliamentary vice foreign minister, today accused the United States Congress of being rude to Japan and damaging United States-Japanese relations.
>
> Mr. Inouye assailed Congress for calling before one of its committees a Japanese professor now at Harvard University as a visiting lecturer. He is Shigeto Tsuru, a government official and professor at the National Hitotsubashi University . . .
>
> Mr. Inouye told the Japanese Diet (Parliament) the Japanese Embassy in Washington had been instructed to make a strong protest to the United States Government demanding that "such summons will not take place again without obtaining consent from us."

By April 5th, Reuters was able to report from Tokyo that the Eisenhower administration had crumpled:

> TOKYO, April 5—Chief Cabinet Secretary Hirohide Ishida said here today the United States "expressed regret" that the Japanese Professor Shigeto Tsuru had been called before the Senate Investigation Committee.
>
> Ishida said a formal United States reply to a Japanese Government protest had been received by the Foreign Office through the Japanese ambassador in Washington, Masayuki Tani.

As late as May, however, assorted liberals were still gnashing their teeth over the pity of it all. On May 20, four Harvard professors—John K. Fairbank (famed apologist for the Chinese Communists), John K. Galbraith (later Kennedy's Ambassador to India), Seymour E. Harris (Harvard Keynesian economist), and Edwin O. Reischauer (an IPR fixture who was later the U.S. Ambassador to Japan from 1961 to 1966)—complained bitterly to the *New York Times* that the Subcommittee's conduct in respect of Tsuru raised "new doubt about Congressional investigative procedures." By then, however, thanks to intervening developments, Tsuru's name had faded from public attention almost as completely as Emmerson's.

Nonetheless the immediate outlook was gloomy from the standpoint of the Subcommittee, as matters stood following the adjournment of the second Tsuru hearing on March 27. There was little reason to expect that the information we had so painstakingly developed concerning Emmerson would have any effect whatever. Although there were individuals in our State Department with other opinions, the Eisenhower administration as a whole obviously preferred the risks of leaving Emmerson in his job, whatever they might be, to the williwaw that would predictably follow any effort to remove him. In Canada, Lester Pearson's bland and total rejection of the massive evidence against Norman was quite enough to satisfy even those individuals and newspapers that were preparing to oppose Pearson in the election. Canada, firmly in the grip of political forces we may call liberal in the broader sense, was virtually unanimous in wanting no so-called "McCarthyism" in its public life. The information concerning Norman, accumulated by the RCMP in the years preceding 1950 and placed on the public record for the first time by the ISSC on March 14, 1957, was not really evaluated and rejected by Canadian opinion; it was simply ignored, on Pearson's repeated assurance that it was wholly false.

But we had instituted this particular investigation, and we were determined to follow wherever it might lead us. Once more a possible avenue of further inquiry appeared. Karl Heinrich Niebyl, Tsuru's co-author of the 1936 memorandum to the editors of *Science and Society,* was now living in New York City, employed as an economic consultant and also serving as a lecturer at the New School for Social Research. He was subpoenaed to appear before the Subcommittee on Thursday, April 4.

That morning, as I switched on my radio to hear the 8 o'clock news and began brushing my teeth, I anticipated nothing out of the ordinary as a result of the day's developments. Niebyl would dodge and minimize, or invoke the Fifth, and a complacent nation would go on ignoring what had happened—and might still be happening—to it. The radio's first news item caught my ear:

CAIRO: E. Herbert Norman, Canadian Ambassador to Egypt, leaped to his death today from the top of an eight-story Cairo business building . . .

At such moments, thoughts crowd in upon one another in a sort of psychic traffic jam.

There was, first of all, Herbert Norman, who had solved in this ghastly way the problems acquired during a lifetime of service to the cause of Communism. By any objective standard, and despite any degree of personal idealism one chose to credit him with, Norman had been my enemy, and the enemy of all who love freedom. In the name of a perverted world-view, he had placed his great gifts—his natural charm, his native intelligence, his profound learning—at the disposal of a murderous dictatorship that had been dominated, until just four years before, by Joseph Stalin. And yet, humanly regarded, it was impossible to consider his suicide, whatever had motivated it, as anything but a personal tragedy.

Whatever had motivated it . . . It was easy to assume—would inevitably be assumed—that his death was the direct consequence of our investigation. *Post hoc ergo propter hoc,* the oldest logical fallacy of them all. And yet, as a Communist, Norman might (for all we knew at that moment) have had a dozen reasons to commit suicide—blackmail, for instance, or imminent danger of exposure as a spy—that had nothing whatever to do with the actions of our Subcommittee.

Our Subcommittee . . . This would be the test. Would our friends rally to it now, or desert us? Would our foes play fair, or strike for the jugular?

I dressed hurriedly, and taxied to the Senate Office Building, visualizing, as the car sped along, that grim scene in a Cairo street. Now, and no fooling, the fat was in the fire.

9

The Norman Case:
Finale

At the office, that morning of April 4, I quickly huddled with Bob Morris. It was obvious that the press would soon be upon us in droves, and it was up to us to recommend to the members of the Subcommittee what statement, if any, should be made in the aftermath of Norman's suicide. On the one hand, the normal human impulse was to express regret. But we realized that any statement containing an expression of that perfectly natural sentiment would quickly be twisted, by our critics, into a seeming admission that the Subcommittee had erred, whereas it had done no such thing. Accordingly we drafted, and cleared with Eastland and Jenner, a brief statement which calmly restated the propriety of our investigation of Emmerson and Emmerson's connections—including Norman. It read:

> The Senate Internal Security Subcommittee, during recent months, has been hearing testimony about Communist activity in the United States which may have an important bearing on our internal security. In the course of this testimony, evidence has been received indicating that certain foreign nationals have engaged in such Communist activity in the United States.
>
> We would not be living up to our obligation of presenting a record to the United States Senate if we deleted references to foreign nationals in connection with these investigations of Communism in the United States.
>
> If foreign nationals enter the United States and join Communist units

here and participate with American Communists in the subversion of
our institutions, these facts should be known to the Senate. Furthermore, if they do not have diplomatic immunity they are subject to our
process like any other person in the United States. That is the practice of
the subcommittee and we shall continue this practice because it is our
duty to do so.

Armed with this statement, and determined not to go beyond it, Bob
Morris stepped out onto the mezzanine of the Senate Office Building's
rotunda to face the most hostile mob of reporters I can ever recall
seeing. There must have been twenty there, and virtually all of them
were obviously ready to draw and quarter the Subcommittee. Bob read
our statement, and distributed copies, and then began replying to a
barrage of questions with just two inflexible words: "No comment." I
particularly remember the correspondent of the *Toronto Star*, Harold
Greer, who later wrote a savage piece on the Norman affair for the far-
left *Nation*. His eyes were literally red-rimmed, quite obviously from
weeping, but his voice was merciless as he snarled, "Who's your next
victim?" Bob clung grimly to his formula: "No comment."

At last it was over. When there had been time for the wire service
correspondents to file their stories, I walked over to the Senate's Writing
Room, which (as already mentioned) was equipped with AP and UP
tickers, to see what they had reported. Fortunately we had given them
little to hang their hats on; the stories, while essentially hostile, were
factually skimpy. The effort, of course, was to make it appear that the
Subcommittee was callously indifferent to the tragic human implications
of Norman's suicide. But Morris' statement, which carefully spelled out
the circumstances under which the activities of foreign nationals might
properly attract the attention of the Internal Security Subcommittee, had
served its purpose well.

Sometime during those frantic hours, when it seemed that just about
every man's hand was against us, we received in our little office an
unexpected and most welcome visitor: Monsignor Bela Varga, a Hungarian Catholic priest who had served as a Small Holders' Party deputy
in the first Hungarian Parliament after World War II and had been
elected Speaker of that Parliament. Now, in exile from his Communist-
ruled homeland, he was a major figure in Hungarian circles in America,
serving as Chairman of the Hungarian National Council and as a member of the Hungarian delegation in the Assembly of Captive European
Nations. The previous autumn, following the Hungarian revolt, we had
encountered him often during our interrogation of Hungarian refugees.
Tall, commanding, with an absolutely bald head, a ringing baritone

voice, and magnificent eyes, he appeared, in his black clerical garb, almost like some messenger from On High. His mission—and it could not have been more welcome or better-timed—was simply to speak a word of encouragement when, as he sensed, we needed it most.

"You will be savagely attacked," he thundered, like an Old Testament prophet, "but you are *right*, and you must never forget it! This man killed himself because he was *guilty*—because he had blackened his soul in the service of Communism!"

Somehow we got through the morning. It was almost a relief, in an anticlimactic way, when the public interrogation of Karl Heinrich Niebyl got under way at 12:30 p.m. before Senator Hruska. It was soon clear that Niebyl would invoke the Fifth Amendment in response to just about every significant question, including all questions having to do with Shigeto Tsuru and the memorandum they had co-authored, concerning *Science and Society*, back in 1936-37:

MR. MORRIS. Now, Professor Niebyl, what is your present business or profession?

MR. NIEBYL. I feel that under the circumstances I must invoke the protection of the Fifth Amendment.

MR. MORRIS. You mean you cannot tell us what your present business or profession is, lest you would be surrendering your rights under the Fifth Amendment?

MR. NIEBYL. That is correct.

MR. MORRIS. And you will not tell us now what you are doing?

MR. NIEBYL. That is correct.

MR. MORRIS. Well, are you now a Communist, Professor Niebyl?

MR. NIEBYL. The answer to that is, under the protection of the Fifth Amendment.

MR. MORRIS. I see. Now, I have offered to you through your attorney a memorandum that purports to be written—have you still got it, Mr. Rein?

MR. REIN. I have it.

MR. MORRIS. Will you look at that, please. Now that is signed by—will you read the names of the three persons signing that. Just read the names. It appears on page 12. Just read the names.

MR. NIEBYL. Karl H. Niebyl.

MR. MORRIS. Karl H. Niebyl . . . Now, did you sign that memorandum?

MR. NIEBYL. I invoke the Fifth Amendment.

MR. MORRIS. You will not tell us, but instead you are invoking the privilege under the Fifth Amendment?

MR. NIEBYL. Yes . . .

MR. MORRIS. Well, Senator, I do not want to labor this too much. The whole thing is in our record. It has been described as a document that is obviously the work of a student of an, an advanced student of Communist propaganda, advanced student of Communist dialectics and, as has been described to the subcommittee, is obviously a person with very important experience in the Agitprop portion of the party. Were you a Communist at the date this memorandum was written, roughly 1937?

MR. NIEBYL. I refuse to answer.

MR. MORRIS. Had you any Communist training at the time this memorandum was prepared?

MR. NIEBYL. I refuse to answer.

MR. MORRIS. Had you attended the Chicago Workers School?

MR. NIEBYL. I refuse to answer.

SENATOR HRUSKA. On what grounds?

MR. NIEBYL. Based on the Fifth Amendment.

SENATOR HRUSKA. Does that apply to all of these refusals?

MR. NIEBYL. Yes, sir.

It also applied to Niebyl's entire career:

MR. MORRIS. Now, were you a Communist when you went to the University of Wisconsin in 1936?

MR. NIEBYL. I refuse to answer.

MR. MORRIS. Were you a Communist when you were research assistant at the University of Wisconsin in 1935 to 1936?

MR. NIEBYL. I refuse to answer.

MR. MORRIS. Were you a Communist when you were instructor and professor of economics at Carleton College, Minnesota?

MR. NIEBYL. I refuse to answer.

MR. MORRIS. Were you a Communist when you were advisor on monetary and fiscal policies, Consumer Division of OPA [in] 1940-41?

MR. NIEBYL. I refuse to answer.

SENATOR HRUSKA. The record will show that in each instance where the witness refuses to answer, it is made on the ground of the Fifth Amendment.

MR. MORRIS. Now were you a Communist when you were on the Advisory Commission to the Council on National Defense?

MR. NIEBYL. I refuse to answer under the Fifth Amendment.

MR. MORRIS. Were you a Communist when you were the associate professor of economics and chairman of the graduate department, Tulane University, in the years 1941-43?

MR. NIEBYL. I refuse to answer under the Fifth Amendment.

MR. MORRIS. Were you a Communist when you were a professor at the University of Texas in 1946?

MR. NIEBYL. I refuse to answer on the grounds of the Fifth Amendment.

MR. MORRIS. Were you a Communist when you were in Black Mountain College in North Carolina, 1946 to 1947?

MR. NIEBYL. I refuse to answer.

MR. MORRIS. Were you a Communist when you were professor and chairman of a department at Champlain College, State University, New York?

MR. NIEBYL. I refuse to answer under the Fifth Amendment.

MR. MORRIS. Were you at any time asked by State authorities if you have been a member of the Communist Party while working at the State University in New York?

MR. NIEBYL. No.

MR. MORRIS. Were you a Communist when you were chairman of the department of economics and business administration at Muskingum College in Ohio, 1953-1954?

MR. NIEBYL. I refuse to answer.

MR. MORRIS. Were you a Communist carrying on your work since 1954 for the Economic Historical Association in New York City?

MR. NIEBYL. I refuse to answer.

MR. MORRIS. Were you a lecturer in the New School of Social Research beginning in 1956?

MR. NIEBYL. I refuse to answer.

To all other substantive questions, Niebyl offered the same reply. It was plain that, whatever Tsuru thought of their common activities in 1936-37, Niebyl believed that an honest description of them might serve as a link in a chain of evidence helping to convict him of a crime.

The weekend came, and with it a comparative respite. But it was obvious, by now, that Norman's suicide was going to be used as a club to beat the life out of the Internal Security Subcommittee once and for all. In the United States, in Canada and abroad, the war drums were throbbing. *The Internal Security Subcommittee had hounded an innocent man to death*: that was the gravamen of the charge that rang out from scores and hundreds of liberal megaphones across the United States and Canada, and for that matter around the world. It was bad enough that this reckless Subcommittee had rudely manhandled an eminent Japanese economist lecturing at Harvard; now its charges, branded as false by the Minister of External Affairs of Canada himself, had driven to suicide a brilliant career officer of the Canadian Foreign Service. *O tempora! O mores!*

It soon became apparent, however, that our critics were relying heavily on Lester Pearson's assurances, less than a month earlier, that the charges against Norman were mere "slanders and unsupported insinuations," all of which had been negatived by a "special and exhaustive security check" on Norman *after* the Wittfogel and Dooman testimony before the ISSC in 1951. From our vantage point in the Subcommittee, of course, we knew how empty Pearson's assurances actually were. The truth was that there had been no security check worthy of the name, and that the full force of the case against Norman had never reached unbiased eyes and unfettered tongues until March 14, 1957, when our Subcommittee published the transcript of its first Emmerson hearing. Even then, a complaisant press had in effect conspired with Pearson to minimize the clear implications of the evidence. Now, however, Norman's suicide had focused upon the case a far brighter light than Pearson's breezy denials were able, or indeed had ever been intended, to bear. It was with an almost hypnotic fascination that we watched our critics inch out onto the limb Pearson had inadvertently provided for them.

A United Press dispatch from Cairo on the very day of the suicide (April 4) laid down the basic line. Its first paragraph, in full, read as follows:

> Canadian Ambassador Egerton H. Norman committed suicide early today because of charges in a U.S. Senate subcommittee that he was a Communist. The Canadian government denies the charges.

A Canadian Press story from Cairo, on the same date, put it this way:

> Canada's Ambassador to Egypt, distressed by accusations of Communist tendencies leveled at him by a United States subcommittee, plunged to his death . . .

Lester Pearson, naturally, was called upon for comment. It was too late, now, to retract all those earlier dogmatic assurances about Norman, but Pearson's statement on the suicide must have sounded strangely low-keyed to his fellow Canadians. Expressing his personal sorrow, and his sympathy for the dead man's family, he spoke at length of the heavy strain of Norman's work in Egypt. Not until paragraph four did he make the inevitable reference to the Subcommittee's hearings, and even then he did not give it the sort of emphasis many must surely have expected:

> [Norman] also had been deeply and understandably depressed by the resurrection by one or two persons in Washington of certain old charges affecting his loyalty, which were disposed of years ago after careful investigation.
>
> The reasons for these renewed attacks may be obscure, but the tactics used degrade only those who adopted them.

The leader of the opposition in the Canadian Parliament, John Diefenbaker, was at this time ignorant of the truth and therefore a good deal more vehement—ironically, in view of the role he was later to play:

> [Norman's] tragic death seems to be attributable to the witch-hunting proclivities of certain Congressional inquisitors in Washington, who, lacking local targets, felt impelled to malign and condemn Canadian public servants.

And Alistair Stewart, a Socialist (CCF) M.P. for Winnipeg, was quoted by the *New York Herald Tribune* as saying that Norman "was 'murdered by slander' as surely as though someone had put a knife in his back."

The United Church of Canada (a merger of 21 Methodist, Presbyterian, and Congregational denominations) promptly called upon the President and Congress of the United States to stop "politicians and partisans from assassinating the characters of innocent men." In New York that Sunday, preaching at the (Episcopal) Cathedral of St. John the Divine, Dean James A. Pike accused the Subcommittee of "assassination by insinuation."

In Toronto, meanwhile, according to the *Montreal Star* of April 6:

> The well-dressed dummy of Robert Morris paid the price of "cancelling Canada's freedom" early this morning—a flaming death on the University of Toronto campus....
>
> Morris' immaculate papier-mache-and-bedsprings effigy was created in a university residence. Launched toward a vigilante trial by a student party, the dummy-Morris was ridden on rails to the main campus, not far from where Herbert Norman studied 20 years ago.
>
> An indictment scathing Morris and Senate investigators was read to 50 students in Ku Klux Klan-style bedsheets. The kangaroo court's double-barrelled verdict—"hang him; burn him!"
>
> In dark glasses, with well-polished shoes, coat, tie and jacket, Morris-in-effigy was hanged until dead, then burned till his bedsprings showed.

All over the United States and Canada, the next day, wire service photos of the effigy in flames enlivened the newspapers.*

---

* Ironically, I later became a fast friend of the young Canadian who organized that effigy-burning: Donald G. M. Coxe, of the University of Toronto. Years afterward, when I was publisher of *National Review* and wrote a friendly appreciation of Morris for the magazine (see p. 27, *supra*), Coxe sent us a letter identifying himself as a loyal reader and a staunch conservative but condemning Morris for his supposedly unjust treatment of Norman. I replied, and out of our correspondence grew not only a valued personal friendship but Coxe's employment, in 1962-63, as an associate editor of *National Review*.

As the hysteria mounted, Pearson—who knew only too well where it might lead—tried desperately to slow the stampede. According to the *Washington Star* of April 5, Pearson now "issued a call to Canadians for forbearance. 'Let's not make an international incident of this,' Mr. Pearson cautioned. 'The people who persecuted him were only one or two. Most people in Washington knew his worth.' " Alas for Lester Pearson, it was too late. The Subcommittee's critics had scented its blood, and they were determined to demand the forfeit of its life. The news stories had done their work; now it was the turn of the editorial writers.

The *Washington Post*'s editorial page on Friday, April 5, contained a Herblock cartoon of a grinning figure with a death's-head (representing the Subcommittee) pulling a file entitled "Herbert Norman" from a cabinet labeled "Hearsay Reports," and also a lead editorial which said in part:

> The death, by suicide, of Herbert Norman, Canadian Ambassador to Egypt, is a multiple tragedy. There is tragedy in the anguish of mind and spirit which led this gifted foreign service officer to take his own life, apparently in despair over a persecution which he had no means of arresting. There is tragedy in the loss to Canada of a public servant characterized by Foreign Minister Pearson as a "highly respected and trusted senior official." And there is tragedy in terms of Canadian-American relations because the Internal Security Subcommittee of the United States Senate is directly responsible for the persecution which may have led to Ambassador Norman's death. . . . In an extraordinarily vigorous protest to the State Department, the Canadian government declared that Mr. Norman had been cleared of all Communist suspicion by a double security check of the utmost severity. . . . The cruel and tragic event to which these [Subcommittee] tactics seem to have led ought at last to lead the Senate of the United States to put an effective check upon the irresponsibility of its Internal Security Subcommittee.

The *Toronto Globe and Mail* on the same day:

> Canada's Ambassador to Egypt took his own life in Cairo yesterday because liars and calumniators persisted in branding him as a Communist. No proofs were offered, no evidence was brought forward. Nothing but the unsupported statements of a United States attorney, quoting what he alleged, without proof, to be reports from various agencies whose identities he did not reveal.
>
> In Canada's House of Commons, Mr. Lester Pearson declared that the tactics of United States Senatorial investigators "degrade only those who adopt them." Perhaps it is more reasonable to assume that the degradation preceded use of the tactics followed by committee counsel

Robert Morris in repeating charges which had been twice investigated by Canadian authorities, twice rejected as false, and at least once made the subject of strongly worded protests to the United States Government.

Beside the editorial, a staff artist had drawn a picture of the Statue of Liberty, her torch quenched and hanging downward, her face buried in shame in her other arm.

The *Montreal Star*'s lead editorial that day was entitled "This Tragic Age":

Once fear enters the heart of man, all balance, and much decency flies out of it. It was fear—the curse of our age—which destroyed Herbert Norman, our ambassador to Cairo. Not, we think, fear of discovery that he was in fact a Communist. The strict scrutiny of every investigating organ our Government possesses had given him a clean bill, and, in these uncertain times, this can be our only solid point of departure. It was fear of other things and expressed by other men which at last entered his own spirit and corroded it until it broke.

These relentless inquisitors in the U.S. Senate have much to answer for. . . .

The *New York Times* waited until Saturday to speak out editorially; but its line was predictable. Under the title "Reckless and Unfair," it wrote:

The suicide of E. Herbert Norman, Canadian Ambassador to Egypt, has brought shame to the Government and people of the United States. Whether Mr. Norman was literally driven to his death by the actions of Senator Eastland's Internal Security subcommittee and its chief counsel, Robert Morris, may not be susceptible of proof. Certainly many Canadians—with understandable vehemence—hold the committee guilty of "assassination by insinuation." But Americans who believe in fair play must agree that Senator Eastland and his associates had no moral right to bring Mr. Norman under suspicion by the release of testimony at a Congressional hearing—testimony given under circumstances which did not allow Mr. Norman either to confront his accusers or defend himself against their accusations.

That this should have been done after the Canadian Government had cleared Mr. Norman of even the suspicion of subversion and that the State Department thought it necessary to say that the United States "has every confidence in the Canadian Government's judgment in the selection of its official representatives" show also how reckless has been the Eastland subcommittee's disregard of the first principles of civilized diplomacy. . . .

The Government and people of the United States own a deep apology to the Government and people of Canada—most especially to Mr. Norman's family—for the un-American misconduct of Senator Eastland, his colleagues and their chief counsel, Robert Morris.

The *Milwaukee Journal,* too, ran true to form:

The Canadian charge that the Senate Internal Security Committee is responsible for the suicide of the Canadian ambassador to Egypt can never be proved, of course. No one can know what drives a human being to take his life. Herbert Norman, always nervous, had been suffering from overwork and overstrain in his important Cairo post.

To say, however, that the subcommittee bears some responsibility for the Norman suicide seems logical.

And to say that its methods in the Norman case, as in so many cases in the past, were unjust, cruel, outrageous and a disgrace to the United States is a certainty.

Norman is another victim of this subcommittee's long and irresponsible record of endless harassment and persecution of individuals.

Behind the giants, as ever, trooped the dwarfs. The *Youngstown (Ohio) Vindicator,* always a hot pitcher in the liberals' Little League, was one of the first:

Americans have reason to feel ashamed about the death of Herbert Norman, Canada's ambassador to Egypt. While his suicide was the act of a depressed mind, the Senate internal security subcommittee apparently was a prime mover in the tragedy . . .

It is useless to expect Senators Eastland and Jenner and Committee Counsel Morris to change their ways; all three are willing to go to any lengths in a search for headlines.

Surely, however, the Senate itself has the power to curb the subcommittee's abuses. This country has enough to do to mind its own affairs without meddling in the business of friendly, respected allies.

And so it went. Abroad, the formidable *Times* of London added its denunciation in an editorial headed "Reckless Persecution:"

The persecution came from the Senate Internal Security Subcommittee in Washington—a body whose methods are as strongly resented by decent Americans as by anyone else. There will be as much sorrow in America as in Canada at this terrible consequence of the committee's recklessness.

Mr. Norman's death emphasizes again the nastiest aspect of the committee's investigating technique. It is bounded neither by the forms of law nor by the abstract principles of justice.

Not surprisingly, the prize for the harshest headline went to an apprentice liberal journalist on the *Harvard Crimson*. "Suicide by Slander" was the title; and the editorial (dated April 9) kept the pace:

> The punishment by publicity technique has paid another dividend. This time it is awarded to the Senate Internal Security Subcommittee, which, in reviving discredited accusations against Canada's Ambassador to Egypt, E. Herbert Norman, not only recklessly abused his reputation, but virtually drove him to suicide . . .
> It would seem, moreover, that the gentlemen of the subcommittee are proud of it. They see their "duty," they say, and they are bound to do it. They ignore the fact that their techniques are completely antagonistic to any high moral purpose, and they refuse to acknowledge the gravity of their mistake. Their recent activities have caused a substantial rise of anti-Americanism in Canada, our closest ally, and in the rest of the world. We have grudgingly tolerated investigative irresponsibility on a national level, but we cannot allow it to affect foreign relations.

Well, retribution would be swift and sure: there was at least, many liberals reflected, that consolation. On Wednesday, April 10, President Eisenhower was to hold his regular press conference. It was certain that a question concerning the Subcommittee's treatment of Norman would be raised, and it seemed equally certain that Mr. Eisenhower would denounce the Subcommittee as the malignant thing it had proved itself to be. On that basis, an attack could then be mounted against the very life of the Subcommittee, and against the whole rotten process it represented.

Imagine, then, the chagrin and frustration of the international liberal community when the question was duly raised at Mr. Eisenhower's press conference and he replied as follows:

> . . . I think they [the Canadians] do not hold such things too much against the government when they occur and, indeed, I have no way of knowing that anybody in Congress deliberately did anything that he thought would damage our relations abroad. Now, in this particular case, it, I think it is a great sorrow to all of us that misunderstandings should occur . . . I am sure that part of this came, this difficulty came, from inadvertence. As usual, I shall not criticize anybody. Indeed, it is my hope that the thing can now be dropped, if possible, even though I know that in Canada it has become a matter of far graver popular and public importance than it probably has in this country. But I think all of

us should do our very best to restore as rapidly as we could the fine, firm character of our relationships with Canada just as rapidly as we can.

The liberal press erupted in new fury, and this time a fury directed, not at the Subcommittee, but at President Eisenhower. On April 11, the *Toronto Globe and Mail* (which styles itself "Canada's National Newspaper") declared:

> Canadians will read President Eisenhower's statement on the death of Mr. E. Herbert Norman with a mixture of incredulity and disgust. No one expected the President to say anything memorable on the tragedy, but it might have been thought he would at least express some regret that a distinguished servant of Canada had been hounded to destruction by the irresponsible and slanderous attacks of a branch of the United States government. Instead of this, his statement—apart from a stock profession of "great sorrow"—was essentially a defense of Senators Eastland and Jenner, Mr. Robert Morris, and the rest of the Senate's Internal Security troupe . . . the President had the effrontery to hope that the emotions aroused by this revolting business would die down . . .

To be perfectly frank, we were almost as incredulous as the *Globe and Mail*, though by no means so disgusted with Mr. Eisenhower. We presumed, of course, that he possessed the relevant facts concerning Norman as developed in our hearings. What we did *not* know, and were not to learn until some months later, was that Eisenhower also had the benefit of a dispatch radioed from Cairo by American intelligence sources less than 48 hours after Norman's suicide—in other words, on or before Saturday, April 6. According to this dispatch, Norman had dined with a friend, a doctor, the night before his death and had told this friend that, as a result of the impact of our hearings on the forthcoming Canadian elections, he feared that a Royal Commission would be appointed to investigate the entire matter; that, if called before such a Royal Commission, he would be forced to implicate "sixty or seventy" Canadians and Americans; and that, rather than do this, he would kill himself. Small wonder that Eisenhower, possessed of this information, refused to follow the world's liberals out onto the limb they were so eagerly trooping to occupy!

Still, the limb would be firm enough to hold them all *if only the fiction of Herbert Norman's total innocence could be preserved.* This, in turn, depended upon everybody—or at least everybody important—ignoring the devastating material read into the record by Robert Morris on March 12 and made public by the Subcommittee on March 14. For the rest of that week, the world's press did its best to cooperate. Seven days, now, had passed since Herbert Norman's suicide, and scarcely a word concerning his published record of Communist activity had reached a public shocked by his death. Even among leading conservative publicists, among the very members of the Subcommittee, there was an ominous silence. Were we to be sacrificed to a howling mob, like Bob Morris' effigy at the University of Toronto?

I hardly need say that those were feverish days in our little office off the rotunda. Eastland had ordered a complete suspension of hearings—on any subject—for the duration of the crisis, but there was certainly no lack of things to do. The phone ran incessantly, like some crazy klaxon. Friends passed and repassed, with words of encouragement and advice, most of the latter contradictory. More than once we were assured that Senator So-and-so was about to take the floor in our defense; more than once we drafted ourselves, at their request, speeches for members of the Subcommittee to make. This or that columnist was rumored to be writing an exposé. But somehow the speeches were not made, the exposés never written; and it seemed possible that they never would be, that Morris (and I with him, if anybody cared) would simply be cast aside, as a burnt offering to the Subcommittee's furious foes.

And then a quite miraculous thing happened. Perhaps, on second thought, it was inevitable; but I must say that to us it seemed, at the time, as gratuitous and as welcome as manna from Heaven. On Friday, April 12, the Canadian Parliament was to be prorogued for the election (which was scheduled for June 10). On that day John Diefenbaker, leader of the Conservative opposition and *ipso facto* its candidate for Premier of Canada, rose to address a simple question to his prospective rival, Mr. Pearson, the Minister for External Affairs in the retiring Government: "Will the Minister say that the allegations before the Subcommittee of the United States Senate on March 12 and 21 specifically were untrue, unjustified and had no basis in fact?"

It was a shot straight to the mark. I do not know what information Mr. Diefenbaker (who on April 4 had been one of our severest critics) had in his possession when he asked his question. Certainly the specific allegations of our Subcommittee—and possibly the original October 1950 memorandum of the RCMP—were by now available to him. In any event, he had somehow hit upon the one demand Pearson dreaded most: namely, that he reiterate in April, in the uncompromising glare of world attention, the sweeping denials he had made in the comfortable shadows of March.

Pearson could not do it. More precisely, he did not dare to do it. Instead, he struggled desperately to evade the central issue by making marginal concessions—always a risky procedure. Norman, he told the

Commons in his carefully prepared reply (for Diefenbaker had filed his question in advance), "as a university student was known to have associated with Communists or persons thought to have been Communists, and he made no secret of it. These associations were of course known to us. We examined Mr. Norman's record on the basis of confidential information. I examined this information more than once myself." Pearson added that as a result of a security check the government was left with no doubt that Norman was a loyal Canadian, suitable for important posts.

But Diefenbaker was not to be so easily put off. Pearson's bland references to Communist associations during Norman's university days did not even attempt to deal with the wealth of other statements concerning Norman in the transcript of the Subcommittee's hearings. Diefenbaker sternly repeated his question: would the Minister say that those statements were "untrue, unjustified and had no basis in fact?"

Pearson, "whose face," as one reporter put it, "grew pink as crowds in the public galleries stared down at him," would not. "I've made my statement," he replied. "I will stand on that. I am not going to say at this moment whether any single statement made in a United States subcommittee is accurate or not. I have not got the statements before me."

"The answer is an equivocal one," Diefenbaker shot back. "He equivocates. He has the statements released by the subcommittee in connection with its hearings of March 13 [actually March 12] and March 21. He knows what charges and allegations were made. He has come into this house with a prepared statement, but *he has not denied those charges.*"

That afternoon Parliament was prorogued for the election campaign, and the Norman case was sure to be an issue.

The disintegration of the imposing facade of silence and denials concerning Norman, begun by Diefenbaker's shrewd question and Pearson's lame reply, now swiftly gathered momentum. As matters stood when Parliament was dissolved, Pearson had conceded that Norman, in his university days, had associated with Communists—not a terribly damaging admission in itself, but a devastating footnote to all those earlier assurances, which the world's liberals had so serenely relied on, that the Subcommittee's statements were *totally* false. Small wonder that Saturday's *Montreal Gazette*—the leading English-language Montreal daily, which was supporting Diefenbaker—carried the news of Parliament's reaction in a banner headline on page one: "COMMONS STUNNED AS PEARSON TELLS OF NORMAN'S RED TIES."

By Monday the 15th, Pearson's astonishing remarks on Friday had been tardily reported in Washington and their implications digested, and the sun rose on a week when the Subcommittee's friends regained their voices. David Lawrence, doyen of conservative columnists, broke the silence that Monday with a column which began: "Many Canadians are having second thoughts about the case of E. Herbert Norman . . ." Those were very nearly the first kind words we had seen in print in twelve days.

Now the counterattack began in earnest. Where, the week before, even our closest friends in the press had been either preternaturally cautious or totally silent, now they all but fell over one another in their eagerness to recount the great story of how the Subcommittee had been maligned and then vindicated. To be perfectly fair, I suppose I should acknowledge that their caution had been justified; after all, if we *had* made a mistake, there would have been no point in going over the side with us. But it had been a lonely week.

On Wednesday the 17th, in a telegram to the *Montreal Gazette*, Pearson strove to repair the irreparable, and only succeeded in making matters—from his rather special standpoint—infinitely worse. He now revealed at last that the Subcommittee's statements concerning Norman were based on (indeed were largely quoted from) an October 1950 report of the RCMP, which the Canadian public, of course, had never heard of prior to that moment. He then went on to insist that this report had been based on a 1940 tip from an RCMP informer in the Communist Party, placing Norman *in the Party*. This tip, one gathered, had rattled around the police bureaucracy in isolated splendor until it was finally enshrined in the memorandum in October 1950 and circulated to high officials in Ottawa—and also, Pearson surmised, to certain of their American colleagues, whence it found its way to the malignant Subcommittee. What made everything all right, he concluded triumphantly, was that the RCMP itself (as already recounted, see page 198) had modified its view of the informer's accuracy in a *second* memorandum, dated *December* 1950, of which our Subcommittee was (he assumed) unaware and from which he proceeded to quote:

> [The RCMP] have made extensive inquiries concerning the information originally supplied by our secret agent and have arrived at the decision that the information given is one of either mistaken identity or unfounded rumor by an unidentified subsource.
>
> Of the numerous points supplied at the time, the majority have been absolutely determined to be in error, the remaining few have not been confirmed, nor does there appear to be any answer to them. The source does not recall the matter. We have therefore deleted the reference in so far as Norman is concerned.

There were, however, several troubles with Pearson's painstaking exegesis. The first and worst, of course, was that Pearson had by now taken so many successive and inconsistent positions on the Norman affair that his reputation for veracity was, to put it mildly, suffering. Then too, the Canadian public now suddenly had to adjust to the fact that the charges against Norman, true or false, had originated, not with our much-excoriated Subcommittee, but with Canada's own beloved Mounties.

Less obvious, though perhaps in the long run more dangerous, was the fact that Pearson was once more up to his old trick of replying to only a portion of the question. The 1940 tip was one of the major items in the October 1950 memorandum, but it was by no means the only one. The Mounties had likewise cited, in their October memorandum, Norman's Communist associations as far back as 1935, as well as information (e.g., concerning the 1942 episode in Cambridge) supplied to them by American security agencies, or obtained by them independently, through the entire decade of the 1940's. Pearson could not hope to demolish the whole October memorandum by an attack, however successful, on one isolated part of it. Moreover, neither the October nor the December memorandum of the RCMP could, in the nature of things, take into account the subsequent and highly damaging testimony of Wittfogel and Dooman before the ISSC in 1951—testimony which tended to support the conclusions of the October memorandum, and which Pearson simply ignored.

But not even Pearson's attack on the 1940 informer was indisputably successful. There promptly stepped forward one Pat Walsh, a former Communist courier who had simultaneously served the RCMP as an undercover agent. He identified himself to newsmen as the source of the 1940 report, insisted that it was accurate, and placed the blame for its downgrading in December 1950 squarely on the drooping shoulders of Lester Pearson.

"I met Norman personally in Toronto in the thirties," Walsh declared, "when I was with the Canadian League Against War and Fascism and he was secretary of the Canadian Friends of the Chinese People, a Commie front. He was introduced to me as 'Comrade Norman.' A chap by the name of A. A. McLeod, who later became a Communist member of the Ontario Legislature and editor of the Communist *Canadian Tribune,* told he me he had sponsored Norman as secretary."

But Lester Pearson's cup of woe was not yet full. The very next day (April 18) the *New York Daily News* released the full texts of two suicide notes allegedly left by Norman. Reynolds Packard, a *News* correspondent in Cairo, had obtained the texts from the Cairo police. Neither note forthrightly explained Norman's motive for killing himself, but they were certainly not inconsistent with the massive evidence of his Communist Party affiliations. To his wife he had written in part: "I wanted so much to tell you all about my troubles during these last few days of my life . . . I have no more hope in life, no more future." And to his close friend, Brynolf Eng, Swedish Minister to Egypt: "I wanted to . . . tell you about what has been worrying me, but I am afraid that even in this letter I cannot bring myself to tell you the true reasons that impel me to commit suicide." Hardly the words of a man tormented by slanders!

The original notes themselves had, in due course, been turned over by the Egyptian authorities to the Canadian government, and on the 19th Pearson caused a statement to be issued by A. D. P. Heeney, Canadian Ambassador to Washington, branding the *News* texts as "complete fabrications." But the Canadian government refused—and has refused to this day—to release the verbatim texts of the notes, and we are left with the plausible assumption that the *News* versions (which had apparently been translated by the Cairo police and then retranslated into English) are at variance with the originals in minor, but only minor, particulars. In any case the aforementioned American intelligence report, based on Norman's talk with a close friend the evening before his death, leaves little doubt as to the real motive for his suicide.

The far-reaching repercussions of the Norman case rolled on through the balance of the spring and even into the summer. The first victim of the fallout was Scott McLeod, administrator of the State Department's Bureau of Security and Consular Affairs, whom President Eisenhower had just nominated to be America's Ambassador to Ireland. McLeod, who was a protégé of veteran New Hampshire Senator Styles Bridges, was no favorite of the liberals anyway; he was a hard-core anti-Communist and for years had made life uncomfortable for State Department officials who weren't. Now, however, in the aftermath of Norman's suicide, and just as the Senate Foreign Relations Committee was preparing to conduct hearings on his appointment, a new stick for beating him came to hand: it was one of McLeod's subordinates, the liberals charged, who had consented on behalf of the State Department to publication of the transcripts of the Subcommittee's executive sessions with its Foreign Service officer, John K. Emmerson, including the damaging material on Norman. Senator Hubert Humphrey, girding his loins on April 10 for the hearings on McLeod, was especially determined to probe his relation to the Norman affair: "There are many questions," he growled, "that need to be asked about the matter." But while the vote in the Foreign Relations Committee on May 2 was unusually close—nine to six—McLeod was duly approved, and subsequently the full Senate followed suit.

Less fortunate, and deservedly so, was the cool, moon-faced opportunist who had quarterbacked Herbert Norman through the Canadian Foreign Service, bullied into silence the Canadian security officials who knew the truth concerning him, and all but succeeded in concealing from the world forever the facts about his protégé's long Communist record. On June 10, 1957, the people of Canada trooped to the polls and installed the Conservative Party of John Diefenbaker in power. For six years Lester Pearson was compelled to occupy the Opposition bench until, in April 1963, the Liberals squeaked back into office with 130 seats to 135 for the combined (but divided) opposition, and Pearson achieved at last his fierce ambition to be Prime Minister of Canada. By then, however, he was 66 years old, and the sun that had shone so brightly on him over the years was clearly setting. His administration has been rocked by scandals and party dissension; even John Diefenbaker, who never had but one shining hour, fought him almost to a standstill in the election Pearson called in 1965 in an effort to strengthen his feeble grip on Parliament. As for the other, higher possibilities that once seemed almost within his grasp—prestigious office in some great confederation of the Atlantic powers, perhaps even of the world—these have gone glimmering . . . with the years . . . and with Herbert Norman.

As in the case of Japan after Tsuru's interrogation, so in that of Canada our State Department abased itself and the United States with unjustified apologies and uncalled-for assurances. The Canadian government had protested on April 10 what it took to be the improper conduct of some arm of our Executive branch, which had apparently handed over to the Subcommittee classified security information (i.e., the RCMP memorandum of October 1950 on Norman) provided by a friendly power. On April 18, when the truth about Norman was painfully obvious to all, and again on August 13, when it was practically ancient history, the State Department beat its breast guiltily and promised Canada: never again! In the words of its August 13 note:

> . . . the United States Government gives its assurance that none of its agencies or departments will pass such information concerning Canadian citizens, received from Canadian sources, to any committee, body or organization in the United States over which the Executive Branch of the United States has no control, without the express consent of the Canadian government in each case.

Actually the assurance was rather hollow, for the truth is that neither the Canadian government nor the Executive branch of the U.S. government had (or has yet) the foggiest notion how the Internal Security Subcommittee came into possession of the RCMP memorandum, and consequently both have precious little actual control over whether the same thing happens again. But should the U.S. Executive make such promises?

And what about the larger question raised by the outcries of the Subcommittee's critics? If a Canadian citizen is welcomed to this country, and so abuses its hospitality as to aid the Communist cause while here, should the Canadian government, as a matter of comity, be accorded some sort of veto over whether the unpalatable truth about him is revealed?

That these questions are not purely academic is sufficiently indicated by a little-noticed dispatch of David Sentner, a top Washington correspondent for the Hearst newspapers, which was published on April 1, 1957. Norman's suicide, occurring just three days later, drew attention away from the Sentner story, and may also have misled the inattentive into supposing that Sentner was talking about Norman. His dispatch, however, was as follows:

> The State Department is trying to get top Senate leaders to keep the lid on the secret committee testimony of Elizabeth Bentley charging a high Canadian official leaked American wartime data to a Soviet agent.
>
> During the past decade, Miss Bentley, former Communist spy queen, spilled the works before various Congressional committees, in public and private sessions.
>
> It was Elizabeth Bentley who exposed the Moscow-directed espionage ring in which she served as courier as well as the Red underground cells operating in the U.S. Government.
>
> Her committee testimony, further developed by Whittaker Chambers, also a former Red espionage courier, led to the infamous Alger Hiss case.
>
> However, there is one piece of testimony by Elizabeth Bentley which has been sat on for six years.
>
> It has been kept from the American public on the grounds it would rock the boat of international relations.
>
> Now, a new element has entered the case which may either bury the testimony deeper or blow it out.
>
> Miss Bentley testified that a certain uppercase Canadian official fed a known Soviet spy (linked with the Canadian Soviet atomic espionage ring) details of what occurred in wartime huddles among the Allied powers in Washington.

Did diplomat———know that H———was a Soviet agent?" Miss Bentley was asked by one Senator.

"Yes," she replied, "He did."

The State Department sent one of its foreign service officers to Ottawa to warn the Canadian Prime Minister of this testimony.

The foreign service officer went straight to the Canadian official whose name had been mentioned by Miss Bentley and bypassed the Canadian Prime Minister. The official was informed of the testimony.

The current pressure to stand—not sit—on the Bentley executive committee testimony stems from upstairs-in-the-State Department presumably just learning that the Canadian Prime Minister was never informed of how one of his top aides was trucking with a Soviet agent.

That same aide is now in a post of great diplomatic importance and has his hands deep in the Middle East situation.

But let us end this sad and intricate story as we began it: with John K. Emmerson, Herbert Norman's American friend, who in November 1944 had assured his State Department superiors that the "declared principles" of the Japanese Peoples Emancipation League were "democratic," and that this organization, which he knew to be Communist-controlled, should be given a large role in the postwar life of the Japanese nation. Where is Emmerson today?

Why, he is where an expert on Japanese affairs ought to be: in Tokyo, as Counselor Minister (or #2 man) in the American Embassy there. I do not suggest that Emmerson is or ever was a Communist, or that in his work in Tokyo these days he necessarily favors policies helpful to the Japanese Communist Party, or to the Red Chinese, or to the world Communist enterprise. But I do submit that a man with his proven inability to tell a hawk from a handsaw has no business guiding the policies, or guarding the interests, of the United States in respect of Japan. And I am unreservedly glad that there was a subcommittee of the United States Senate ready to publish the truth about him.

10

The Last Days
of Joe McCarthy

Not long ago, a reviewer of a new novel by Irwin Stark reported a striking resemblance between the book's principal character and the late Senator Joseph McCarthy. Comparing Mr. Stark's novel with another, the writer observed:

> Mr. Stark's horizons are wider, his figures larger, especially the central one: a red-neck, power-driven Senator, a pitiless demagogue, callous, cynical, full of animal appetites, incapable of love or decency, who buys loyalty to himself by fear, money or blackmail. Armed with the subpoena power of an investigative committee of Congress, pledged to root out Communism at home and in any of our agencies abroad, he has a high old time as he crushes those he can bring into the committee room and slanders those he cannot.
>
> Born in a dairy state west of the Mississippi, a World War II veteran, a none-too-squeamish district attorney and judge, he bears a strong resemblance to an active Senator of a decade or so ago—a resemblance the author does not bother to deny.

This passage interested me because it sums up, as succinctly and earthily as anything is ever likely to sum up, what many of McCarthy's critics sincerely thought of him, and because the picture is so wildly at variance with the man as I knew him when I was working in Washington during the last fourteen months of his life.

Whatever one may choose to think of McCarthy, there is no gainsaying the fact that he came to be identified, in the climactic years of his political career, with a tremendous crisis in American history. Whether the eventual outcome of that crisis was for better or worse, his countrymen at the time could not bring themselves to agree. Indeed, nothing in my recollection—not even the great isolationist-interventionist debate of 1940-41—and perhaps nothing in our national history since the Civil War has divided them so deeply or so bitterly. Less than fifteen years have gone by since the quarrel was at its height, and I am under no illusion that sufficient time has passed to permit a truly calm and unemotional discussion of this man and his actions. Impassioned partisans on both sides, who have forgiven and forgotten nothing, will crowd forward to weigh every word, hail (and distort) every shred of fresh "evidence," and praise or damn, as the case may be, any conclusion indicated, and any writer reckless enough to indicate one.

Yet time is rolling on. Even today, few Americans under thirty can have any balanced recollection of that furious controversy, let alone of the man at its epicenter. To them, McCarthy must seem an almost mythological figure—perhaps the Giant, perhaps Jack, but certainly not just an ordinary human being who was active in our national political life slightly over ten years ago. But that is what he was; and it is for the sake of this new generation, primarily, that I would like to set down here my comparatively few personal recollections of him, and to offer a tentative appraisal of the roots of the great crisis with which his name will forever be identified.

I trust that the reader who has come this far with me will not need to be reminded that McCarthy was never a member of the Senate Internal Security Subcommittee, or even of its parent Judiciary Committee, and that accordingly he played no part whatever in our investigations. Rather, he was a member—and ultimately the ranking Republican member—of the Senate's Government Operations Committee and its investigative arm, the Permanent Investigations Subcommittee. As such, when the Republican Party took control of both Houses of Congress in the Eisenhower sweep of 1952 McCarthy automatically became chairman of the Government Operations Committee and its subcommittee. In that capacity he enjoyed the usual latitude that the Senate accords the chairmen of its committees: he hired the members of the staff, directed their work, and in general decided what subjects would be investigated.

Since McCarthy's national involvement with the issue of domestic Communism is usually (and rightly) dated from his speech in Wheeling, West Virginia on February 9, 1950, it may be a little startling at first to realize that he never conducted any Congressional investigations of Communism whatever until the Republican majority organized the Senate three years later, in January 1953. Moreover, since the Republicans promptly lost the Senate again in the mid-term elections of November 1954, McCarthy lost control of his committee to the Democrats (and specifically to Senator John McClellan, its ranking Democrat) at that time. In short, McCarthy's whole career *as a Congressional investigator* of Communism (in the sense of conducting official inquiries, armed with the subpoena power and the research facilities of a committee staff, and having access to a committee budget) was wedged into the two years 1953 and 1954.

For the rest, strange as it may seem, McCarthy waged his battle over the issue of domestic Communism simply as an individual senator, and a member of the minority party at that. Most of the really violent controversy had been kicked up in the years 1950, 1951, and 1952, *before* his brief term as a committee chairman. By the time he stepped down, the Senate had passed its famous resolution of condemnation against him, and thereafter, from 1955 to his death in May 1957, McCarthy was notably less active in this area, though no less interested in it.

I emphasize the point because the savage caricatures of McCarthy (like the one I quoted at the outset of this chapter) tend to dwell on his supposed villainies *as a Congressional investigator*; and thence to spread outward into a generalized condemnation of *all* Congressional committees that investigate domestic Communism. Actually, McCarthy was hotly engaged in his famous struggle before he ever picked up a chairman's gavel, and the story of his career would probably not have been different in any major particular if he had never held one in his hand.

For this reason it also follows that McCarthy was never, in a strict sense, the leading Congressional investigator of domestic Communism (once again limiting that term to the chairmen or other members of investigating committees). Over in the House Committee on Un-American Activities, a whole series of chairmen, both Republicans and Democrats, wielded their gavels as long or longer, and presided ably over many more hours of explosive investigations. Even in the Senate, few would doubt that the ablest investigator by far was silver-maned old Pat McCarran, the Nevada Democrat (and former Chief Justice of the Supreme Court of his state), who chaired the Internal Security Subcommittee from its establishment in 1950 until the Republican takeover in January 1953. Joe McCarthy, to be sure, was to become far better known than any of these men, but not by virtue of his activities as chairman of an investigating committee.

By the time I came to work for the ISSC in March 1956, McCarthy was, of course, already a legendary figure to me, as he was to every American, friend and foe alike. I had watched his career closely ever since he first captured national attention with his Wheeling speech early in 1950, and it would be idle to pretend that I was neutral on the subject. I had not been primarily influenced by McCarthy's specific charges concerning domestic Communism; the seriousness of the problem had already been established, as far as I was concerned, long before McCarthy spoke at Wheeling. Rather, it was the character of the counterattack unleashed on McCarthy that had shocked and sickened me. Recuperating from a bout with pneumonia at a resort in the Poconos in April 1954, I had watched the televised hearings investigating alleged preferential treatment of a member of his staff who had been drafted into the Army, and read with care the newspaper accounts of them. Many others, I know, watching the same hearings and reading the same newspapers, were sure they were watching someone very like Satan himself; but all I could see was a collection of trivial charges ballooned out of all proportion to distract national attention from far more serious matters.

My immediate boss at the Subcommittee, Bob Morris, had first come to Washington in 1950 as minority (i.e., Republican) counsel to the Tydings Committee, which had been set up by the Senate in February of that year to investigate McCarthy's charges concerning security risks in the State Department. The Republican members of the Tydings Committee (including some, like Henry Cabot Lodge, who were later destined to win acclaim as "moderates") were determined not to permit the whitewash of the State Department on which Chairman Tydings seemed bent; and Morris was their chosen instrument. It was on this assignment that he caught the eye of Senator McCarran who, though a Democrat, promptly invited him to become counsel to the newly constituted Internal Security Subcommittee.

Morris, then, had known McCarthy since 1950. In addition, soon after coming to Washington I had become acquainted with L. Brent Bozell, who at this time was on McCarthy's staff as a speech-writer with the nominal title of "legislative assistant." Bozell, a tall, carrot-topped former Nebraskan who lived in Chevy Chase with a growing family, all of whose members were as red-headed as he, is the brother-in-law of Wm. F. Buckley Jr. With Buckley, Bozell in 1954 had co-authored *McCarthy and His Enemies,* a painstaking analysis of the numerous charges that had been made against McCarthy up to 1953. Late in 1955 Buckley, with Bozell and others at his side, had launched *National Review,* an intelligent and serious journal of frankly conservative opinion, of which I became a charter subscriber. I had met Buckley casually once or twice before going down to Washington in March 1956, but Bozell was only a name to me until I encountered him on Capitol Hill that spring. Thereafter we became fast friends, and I was often a guest in his home.

Through Morris and Bozell, it was inevitable that I would soon meet the fabled Senator McCarthy. The moment came one evening in May, not long before McCarthy was to appear before our Subcommittee as a witness in connection with certain proposed amendments to the Internal Security Act. Morris suggested that we drop over (it was after dinner) to see "Joe and Jeanie" in their pleasant but far from ostentatious house on Capitol Hill. The whole area to the east of the Capitol had declined rather sadly during the preceding half-century, but by 1956 a modest real estate boom was under way. Once-impressive homes that had deteriorated into little more than slums were being purchased, rehabilitated and tenanted by some of Washington's best-known names. (The same process had made real estate history when it occurred a decade or two earlier in Georgetown, on the western edge of the District of Columbia.)

McCarthy himself came to the door and shook my hand warmly when Bob introduced me. He was in his shirtsleeves, and I was soon to learn that this sort of informality was one of his characteristics. Of medium height, with rather hairy hands and a tendency to five-o'clock shadow, he was a thoroughly masculine example of the type called "black Irish." His manner was pleasant, soft-spoken, almost shy. His baritone voice mumbled along in a series of blurts, punctuated by deprecatory little chuckles. We briefly discussed his forthcoming testimony, and then the talk grew general. I was anxious to see whether he would express bitterness toward any of the individuals, senators and others, who had been instrumental in bringing about his condemnation by the Senate in December 1954; but bitterness simply wasn't in character for him. He would discuss this or that well-known liberal with what might be called a standard conservative awareness of the man's point of view and probable conduct, but never once did a really stinging phrase escape his lips. Perhaps, in view of all that has been said about him, I should add what ought to be unnecessary: at no point did McCarthy recklessly or casually impute Communism to non-Communists who disagreed with him, or whom he personally happened to dislike.

Of course this was 1956, and it is probably fair to assume that he had by that time acquired—as one inevitably does, in the investigative process—a pretty broad education in the relevant distinctions between liberals, socialists and Communists, and indeed between the various subspecies of each. But my impression of McCarthy's attitude was more positive than such experience alone could explain. He seemed quite devoid of any *urge* to mislabel political opponents as Communists. Rather, his general attitude was one of bewilderment, both amused and slightly sad, at the ferocity of his liberal foes, and at the security policies they endorsed.

If I had to single out one characteristic of McCarthy as the key to his role in our history, and to the tragedy of his death at forty-eight, I would say it was an ingenuous stubbornness. Most politicians, after all, are pretty adept at sensing when to stop riding an issue—quite regardless, mind you, of the real importance of the issue. When it stops paying dividends, when on straight pleasure-pain principles it ceases to yield a sufficient return in praise, all but the most exceptional politicians will quietly drop it. McCarthy wouldn't; and, studying him that evening, I slowly came to understand the origin of his intransigence. It was not sheer patriotism that forbade him to stop; he was certainly patriotic, but he did not burn with any particularly hard, gem-like flame on the subject. Rather, it was a strange and ultimately fatal innocence.

To McCarthy, senator from a prosperous Midwestern state with no Communist problem beyond the ordinary ones, the American Communist Party was, quite simply, a Very Bad Thing. He had discovered, moreover, as all Americans had discovered during the late 1940's, that dedicated Communists had, in the preceding two decades, effectively penetrated important areas of our national life—not only government but labor, communications, the entertainment industry, etc. McCarthy could see no earthly reason for ignoring this fact or its contemporary consequences; so he spoke out, and when, for reasons I shall analyze a little later, his charges evoked a furious counterattack, he simply hunched down and stuck to his guns. I am reasonably sure that, to the end of his life, he never developed a really satisfactory theory as to why the liberals (in contradistinction to the Communists, whose hostility was of course understandable) were so hard on him.

Blinded as he was by this perilous ingenuousness, it does not seem to have occurred to him to drop the subject of domestic Communism merely because it was violently controversial. In addition, of course, he did not lack for enthusiastic friends who encouraged him to press on. So Joe McCarthy and the American left continued on the collision course that was to destroy the former and severely inconvenience the latter.

Re-reading the above paragraphs, I am assailed by a feeling of hopelessness. It seems impossible, or at any rate highly unlikely, that any such mild description of Joe McCarthy can make headway against the savage caricatures of the man drawn by his enemies. One remembers Herblock's famous cartoon of McCarthy, a maniacal grin on his face, stealing up out of a sewer manhole clutching a brush and a paintpot of smears. One thinks of Richard Rovere's book on McCarthy, whose cover photo of the subject (far subtler than Herblock's cartoon) had been retouched in such a way as to blot out the pupils of the eyes; the effect was precisely that which Bela Lugosi achieved, in his horror films during the early 1930's, by the artful use of egg white on his eyeballs.

On the purely literary front, the anti-McCarthy canon has likewise reflected these two somewhat inconsistent concepts of the man. Read again the passage quoted at the outset of this chapter. There we are offered simply a picture of a publicity-hungry, power-mad politician: a conventional demagogue raised to the *n*th power. Now, McCarthy was indeed a politician, and no doubt shared the typical politician's taste for favorable publicity and the perquisites of senatorial power. To the end of his days, he was grateful for his huge public following. But it would have taken a man far crazier than his worst enemies ever alleged McCarthy to be, to have supposed that his public image was on balance being improved, or his personal power effectively augmented, by the furious struggle in which he found himself engaged from 1950 onward. Certainly in the months during which I knew him (long after the Senate's resolution condemning him), he remained entirely loyal to his view of the domestic Communist problem; but he never revealed in my presence any expectation that doing so would, at that point in his career, bring him either publicity or power—or the slightest interest in whether it did or not.

The other hostile picture of McCarthy depicts him rather differently: as a being so devoid of scruples, or even human feelings, as almost to forfeit the name of man, a conscienceless obscenity grinding up human beings as mechanically as a robot. Once again, any healthy person who was ever exposed to the flesh-and-blood McCarthy can only snort, "Nonsense!" McCarthy was typically Irish in his gregariousness and his sense of fun, and a typical politician in his readiness to check his razor (figuratively speaking) at the door before entering any party. He also shared with Bob Morris what I have concluded may be a characteristically Irish feeling that to decline to drink with him was truly and greatly unkind. Almost anyone, friend or foe, would be invited to join him in a drink, and the libation symbolically affirmed a friendship that, on McCarthy's side, easily rose above political differences. As for grudge-holding, as already noted it simply wasn't in his line; he did not possess, in this painful department, the pertinacity with which he clung to the dread issue of domestic Communism.

Nor am I impressed with that subdivision of McCarthyphobia which concedes that my description of his qualities is accurate as far as it goes, but insists that it merely throws into higher relief the essentially monstrous nature of the man who exhibited these qualities—much as Adolf Eichmann's sheer banality is said to have accentuated the ghastliness of his crimes. On the contrary: McCarthy's ingenuousness was not only real but entirely of a piece with his public actions as I saw them and understood them.

Very well then (I can hear the reader saying), but if you are right, has everybody else, during all these years, been wrong? Is it likely, is it even conceivable, that the whole concept of "McCarthyism" is based on a case of mistaken identity?

Well, in the first place not "everybody else," by a long shot, has shared these Grand Guignol notions of what Joseph McCarthy was like. His vast public following might perhaps been deceived about him, but those who knew him personally most certainly could not have been, and I have never met one of them who would seriously attempt, for a moment, to defend either of the hostile concepts of McCarthy that I have described. These fantastic caricatures are the products of the fevered imaginations of men who either had good reason to hate McCarthy (e.g., the Communists), or who sincerely believed they had, and accordingly saw him only through the haze of their own animosities and fears.

A more comprehensive and logically satisfying way of answering the question, of course, would be to make a careful study of what McCarthy actually did and did not do—in other words, a close analysis of his supposedly horrendous actions. But that would be another book, and a sequel or supplement, at that, to one which has already been written, and well written: *McCarthy and His Enemies,* by Wm. F. Buckley Jr. and L. Brent Bozell.* I have already indicated that, in my own view, McCarthy's substantive contributions to the documentation of the important story of domestic Communist subversion, while valuable, were not in most cases achievements of the first rank—not comparable, for example, to HCUA's brilliant probe of the Hiss-Chambers case, or the ISSC's investigation of the Institute of Pacific Relations. But there remains one more thing to be said—one that, to my mind, correctly describes the historical significance of McCarthy, and (almost incidentally) explains how this mild, rather soft-spoken man came to represent, to a large number of his fellow Americans and virtually all foreigners, evil incarnate.

To understand McCarthy's impact on his times, we must first understand those times. The leading personalities of the late 1940's and early 1950's were, by and large, liberals who had drunk deep of the heady wine of the 1930's and its predecessor decades. Almost since the turn of the century, the tide of intellectual opinion had flowed swiftly in the direction of Marxism and various related scientistic determinisms. As

* Chicago: Henry Regnery Co., 1954.

early as 1915, it was deliciously daring, rather than merely odd, to be a socialist; by 1925 it was highly fashionable. The Bolshevik revolution of 1917 in Russia, and the exile of Trotsky from the Soviet Union in 1929, created deep rifts in the socialist intellectual community, but they did not weaken it; on the contrary, the various currents of Marxist and quasi-Marxist thought flowed on, strengthened by the passions with which their enthusiasts asserted their differences. Among them, and *primus inter pares* by reason of their discipline and their ruthlessness, were the Communists.

The Roosevelt administration, reaching out among the intelligentsia for representatives of just about every point of view that could conceivably pass muster as "liberal," brought to Washington and installed in positions of power there exponents of the entire spectrum of Marxist and quasi-Marxist thought, including a substantial number of discreet but committed Communists. (See Chapter 8, p. 207, for a description of how one Communist study group, at the University of Minnesota, was weakened when two of its members "went to Washington" in December 1936.)

It is easy, in retrospect, to be contemptuous of the New Jerusalem these Marxists—Communists and non-Communists alike—believed they were building in Washington in the 1930's; but we should try to view the situation from their perspective. Marxism had profoundly impressed all but the most specialized intellectual circles with its brilliant if simplistic and fundamentally wrongheaded interpretation of human history. The Great Depression had thereupon struck America and the whole world, in and after 1929, in what must have seemed like an explicit confirmation of the Marxist critique. And if the Marxist critique had been confirmed empirically, who could doubt that the Marxist remedy was the right one? The infamous Moscow purge trials—the assassination of Trotsky—the Hitler-Stalin pact—the Cold War—the downgrading of Stalin: all these were still years, in some cases decades, away. The whole leftist movement in the United States was sure that there was much to do, and much, also, that must be undone. With intramural differences over details, and with differing degrees of sophistication, but with a magnificent will, they set about the job.

In later years it became fashionable to regard the New Deal in retrospect, not as the would-be destroyer, but rather as the savior of the free enterprise system in America: a reformist impulse which rescued and preserved an economic system that was otherwise doomed by the Depression. Well, perhaps; but it is only fair to note that the Marxist zealots who thronged Washington in the 1930's had no such narrow concept of their function. No doubt each had his own private vision of what ought to be accomplished, and perhaps a more modest notion of what was actually possible; but of the general direction of events there could be no doubt: America was to become at least a quasi-socialist society, in which all sorts of old icons would be pulled from the walls.

In this process, as viewed by their fellow Marxists, the Communists too had a role to play. They might be too rigid, too authoritarian, too doctrinaire, but they had at least the correlative virtues, fixity of purpose and the obvious advantages of carefully coordinated efforts. It is preposterous to pretend that their presence was unsuspected by knowledgeable people in Washington during the Roosevelt presidency. Rather, it was generally believed, even as today's sincere pacifists and civil-rights demonstrators too often believe, that the Communists could be worked with and yet kept within bounds. The world-wide Communist tactic of the "popular front," employed during most of the 1930's, shrewdly encouraged this naive supposition. The Hitler-Stalin pact of August 1939 most certainly damaged it; but in June 1941 the Soviet Union became, willy-nilly, the free world's ally in the great war against fascism, and at once the American Communists adopted a protective coloration of patriotism that temporarily reassured many doubters.

But the years 1945 and 1946 brought about a profound change in the situation of America's liberals. In April 1945 President Roosevelt died, and with his passing the great days of the doctrinaire left in Washington came suddenly and unexpectedly to an end, to be replaced by the kitchen-cabinet politics and pragmatic populism of Harry Truman. The war in Europe ended that May; Japan surrendered in August; and suddenly our former ally, the Soviet Union, emerged as America's chief remaining rival and major potential enemy. In Fulton, Missouri on March 5, 1946, Winston Churchill formally recognized the existence of the Cold War with Russia in his famous "Iron Curtain" speech. That November, the Republican Party captured control of both Houses of Congress for the first time in sixteen years.

The year 1947 thus opened on a far different scene from that to which non-Communist Marxists and other liberals had grown accustomed between 1933 and 1945; and to their discontent were soon added a vague sense of guilt and something very like fear. For the "hard left," the Communists and their immediate allies, now moved, in practised obedience to their Russian masters, to break with their old colleagues in the Democratic Party on the whole spectrum of issues related to the Cold War. While Truman proclaimed his Greek-Turkish aid program (1947) and launched the Marshall Plan (1948), Henry Wallace led (or more precisely was led by) the Communists into open opposition to the

President, culminating in Wallace's Progressive Party candidacy for President in 1948.

All this was upsetting enough, and many a non-Communist veteran of the popular-front days of the Roosevelt administration must have wondered uneasily just how wise it had been to allow the Communists to participate, even discreetly, in shaping and administering the New Deal. But there was worse to come. For the Republicans, in Congressional power again after their long exile, quickly opened an investigation by HCUA into the precise extent of Communist penetration of the government, and slowly the whole long, sordid story began to unfold before an astonished nation.

It would probably have been vain, in any case, for America's liberals to try to deflect the blow by arguing (quite accurately) that the climate of opinion in the 1930's was very different from that of the late 1940's; and most of them did not even attempt it. Instead, they took the position —less valid but more defensible, and one in which they soon came fervently to believe—that the whole subject was being vastly exaggerated for personal and partisan advantage. Out of scores and hundreds of hearings America's liberals pieced together—years before most of them ever heard of Joseph McCarthy—the villain he was one day to typify: ". . . a pitiless demagogue, callous, cynical, . . . [who], armed with the subpoena power of an investigative committee of Congress, . . . crushes those he can bring into the committee room and slanders those he cannot."

It is not my purpose here, and certainly not necessary to it, to pass judgment on the rights or wrongs of the bruising controversy that rocked America in the years 1947-49. No doubt the Republicans rode the issue for all it was worth. Few impartial students, on the other hand, would any longer attempt to deny that the domestic Communists effected a thoroughly impressive penetration of the American government during the Roosevelt years, and not only of the government, but of many other areas of our national life as well. What could or should have been done about this in the late 1940's has been the subject of many books; but it is not the subject of this one.

What matters for our present purpose is what actually happened: which was that the whole issue seemed, in the public mind, finally to resolve itself into the technically subordinate but heavily symbolic question of the guilt or innocence of Alger Hiss. Complex social issues often tend to become oversimplified in this way; witness the tensions between the Italian immigrants and the Brahmin aristocracy of Massachusetts in the 1920's, which imploded into the trial of Sacco and Vanzetti; or further back, the way in which the internal pressures of *fin de siècle* French society focused upon the Dreyfus case.

Hiss was far from being the only Soviet agent unearthed by HCUA in its investigations. He was not even the only such individual to risk a perjury conviction by denying espionage. But fortune had singled him out to be the symbol of much more. In his Brooks Brothers suit, with his splendid record and his apparently assured position, he seemed the very model of a young-old New Dealer—badgered now, and brutally mistreated, by reckless slanderers. When he strode into court, there went with him in spirit some part of many other, better men. And when, on January 21, 1950, he was at length convicted of perjury and sentenced to prison, America's liberals tasted a bitter and strangely personal defeat. It was, politically and emotionally, their nadir.

I do not think it is by any means a mere coincidence that history discovered Joseph McCarthy less than three weeks later, when he rose to address the Republican Women of Wheeling, West Virginia. What was so remarkable about his speech on that retrospectively historic occasion? Certainly it wasn't the first, or the longest, or the best, or the worst, speech on the subject of Communism in government. It had, in fact, just two significant attributes: it contained a seemingly vulnerable reference to a number of loyalty risks allegedly still in the State Department; and it was delivered at a time when, above all other times, *America's liberals desperately needed an issue upon which to base a counterattack against their tormentors.*

So Joe McCarthy got the full treatment—much, I am sure, to his own surprise. Ninety-nine politicians out of a hundred, observing the barrage, would have dropped the subject as soon as they gracefully could. Certainly there is no reason to believe that the liberals expected the episode to yield more than a gratifying and psychologically useful retraction by McCarthy. But Fate was working overtime that week, and the barrage had landed on a stubborn Wisconsin *naif* who didn't know when to quit. Far from retracting, McCarthy expanded his charges; and, when ordered by the Tydings Committee to name names, he—incredibly—named them.

That tore it. Even though the wiser liberals must have been far from sure that they could force McCarthy to eat that whole series of names, they had to try. Their own formidable propaganda facilities had focused the nation's attention on this one gladiator, that all might be edified by his forthcoming humiliation; it was unthinkable, now, to turn out the lights and refund the tickets without a show. Thus began "the McCarthy issue," a snarling battle which raged for five years over whole seas and continents of factual data and ultimately dragged into its vortex almost every man, woman and child in the Western world (except, of course, Richard Nixon).

If I am right in my analysis of the genesis of the great McCarthy controversy—the fateful counterpoint of liberal necessity and McCarthyian intransigence, the irresistible force and the immovable object—it is not hard to see why the Senate's condemnation resolution of December 1954 was, in a real sense, the last act of that particular drama, even though Congressional investigations of Communism were not to end with its passage and indeed have not ended yet. The nervous self-identification of the liberals with the larger implications of Hiss's conviction had become balanced and largely cancelled out, in their own minds and in the public mind generally, by the image of an overweening and unscrupulous investigator, of which McCarthy, thanks to his own ingenuous stubbornness, became the archetype. What was needed now, and all that was needed, was some symbolic act of judgment, in which the liberals would be seen to triumph over their supposed persecutor.

Unfortunately such a judgment in matters political is hard to obtain in America, short of a national election, and long years of shifting and uncertain struggle were first required. The liberals finally won President Eisenhower to their side in January 1954 by persuading him that McCarthy had gratuitously insulted General Zwicker. It was not until December of that year, however, that the Senate could be persuaded to pass Senator Flanders' resolution condemning McCarthy's remarks about Senator Watkins' committee. It did not matter that the resolution condemned McCarthy only for those remarks, and did not even purport to deal with any other aspect of his conduct over the years. It did not matter that, to pass it at all, its sponsors had to drop a section criticizing McCarthy for the very remarks to General Zwicker that had so annoyed President Eisenhower. All that mattered was that *the United States Senate had voted to condemn McCarthy*. Insofar as an act of judgment could be had, it had been achieved; the lights could be turned off; the show, at long last, was over.

It was, of course, the McCarthy of the post-condemnation period that I knew in Washington in 1956 and 1957. His interest in the question of domestic Communism was not (as some might suppose) obsessive, but neither did he in any sense abandon it, as long as he lived. As a senator of the minority party, however, without the facilities of a Congressional committee at his disposal, his opportunities for effective investigations were severely limited, and the liberals, shrewdly choosing to regard the Senate resolution as the final word on the hated McCarthy, naturally refrained from giving unnecessary publicity to his speeches and his other independent actions. It is probably also true that the American people in general, whose attention span had been severely tested by the whole five-year williwaw, were ready to forget about Joe McCarthy for a while.

I saw him on perhaps half a dozen private occasions in the last year of his life, sometimes with Bob Morris at McCarthy's own house on Capitol Hill, sometimes at dinner with the Bozells in their home in Chevy Chase. One of the unexpected rewards of knowing him was the opportunity to meet his wife, Jean (or "Jeanie," as she was universally called), without question one of the loveliest and most gracious women I have ever known. Fate deals its cards, for good or ill, with a curiously even hand. If McCarthy was made the fulcrum of ghastly, even fatal pressures in the years from 1950 on, the period from his marriage in 1953 to his death in 1957 was made bearable, even paradisaical, by the beauty, intelligence, and loyalty of his wife. She was born Jean Kerr, of Scottish descent, and had served as an administrative assistant in McCarthy's office before their marriage. A Catholic convert, with a fine instinct for politics, she was utterly devoted to McCarthy and made his cause her own. McCarthy, in turn, treated her with obvious affection and vast respect. In many ways, and perhaps especially in the fine coin of character, she was undoubtedly the stronger of the two.

One of McCarthy's most appealing qualities was his loyalty to friends under attack, another facet, I suppose, of the stubbornness that was so important a part of his personality. The obvious example of this fierce loyalty, of course, was Roy Cohn, the brilliant young (26) son of a Tammany judge, whom McCarthy had hired in 1953 as chief counsel to the Permanent Investigations Subcommittee of the Government Operations Committee when he became its chairman. Few appointments were ever better calculated to arouse resentment on all sides. Everybody over 26 resented Cohn's youth. Everybody less clever (and that included most people) resented his undeniable intelligence. Republicans resented Cohn because he was a Democrat, and a noisy one at that. Democrats resented him for "selling out" to a Republican. Many of his fellow Jews resented him because they were tremulously convinced that the whole so-called "Communist issue" contained the seeds of native fascism and a concomitant anti-Semitism, and accordingly regarded Cohn as little short of a traitor to his people. Many hard-shelled rightists around the country, whose innermost hearts contained a trace (or more) of anti-Semitism, resented him for being a Jew. Finally, it must be conceded that Roy Cohn's personality is no threat to, say, Bing Crosby's. Personally wealthy, addicted to flashy clothes, block-long limousines, and dizzy blondes, with an abrupt air that struck many people as intolerably overbearing, Cohn would have been a thorny problem in image-improvement for even the best PR firm; as counsel to the McCarthy committee he was a sort of Abominable-Snowman-in-Residence. When in 1954 he was accused of trying to browbeat the Pentagon into giving special favors to a close friend who had been drafted, not even Cohn's defenders argued that the charge was inherently out of character.

Yet the loyalty Cohn gave to McCarthy, and that McCarthy repaid to Cohn, reflected great credit on both men. The heavier the attacks on Cohn, the more stubborn—characteristically—McCarthy became. I especially remember one evening at the Bozell home, when someone mentioned Cohn and reference was made to his numerous defects. "I can understand why some people don't like Roy Cohn," McCarthy conceded, nodding reflectively, with just the trace of an indulgent smile. "I can understand that," he repeated, almost to himself. And then, with quiet finality: "But I like him."

And *that* was *that*.

It was on the same occasion, or during another evening at the Bozells', that I discovered McCarthy's aversion to cats. This well-recognized syndrome is technically known as ailurophobia, and is remarkably widespread; I believe there are even one or two half-serious organizations of people who just can't stand the sight of the genus *Felis*. McCarthy had a fairly mild case, I suppose, but he clearly wanted nothing to do with Brent Bozell's handsome collection of Siamese cats, which regally roamed the house. Brent, perversely, decided to tease the Senator by daring him to hold one of the cats in his arms. McCarthy protested, but Brent briskly picked one up and deposited it in McCarthy's lap anyway. The Senator tried to chuckle, but his arms were rigid with distaste; the cat, sensing it was unwanted, looked as miserable as McCarthy and soon jumped to the floor—to the latter's immense and evident relief. I asked McCarthy how he explained this odd revulsion, and he said he thought he could trace it to an episode when he was a boy on the farm, back in Wisconsin. He had watched a cat corner a rat in a barn, play with it, and finally tear it to bloody pieces, and the sight had left an indelible impression on him.

My last private conversation with McCarthy took place on the date of Eisenhower's second inauguration, Monday, January 21, 1957. I had spent most of the morning working in our office, ostentatiously ignoring the ceremonies taking place just a few hundred feet away on the East steps of the Capitol. In mid-afternoon Morris, his slender, bright-eyed wife Joan and I decided to cap our defiance of Eisenhower Republicanism by paying a visit to Joe McCarthy.

We found him with Jeanie in the living room of his house, watching the inaugural parade on television. He was in a somber, thoughtful mood. "Y'know," he remarked, gesturing toward the TV set, "I listened to his speech. And when he came to the part about Hungary and how brave those people had been, and how we can never turn our backs on them, and I thought of how he had let the Russian tanks roll over 'em last November. . ." He paused, shook his head, and was silent.

We had a drink together—the old ritual!—and then he invited us upstairs to see Tierney, the infant daughter he and Jeanie had adopted less than two weeks before. The little girl was sound asleep in her crib, and McCarthy motioned us to be silent. Dutifully we admired the one pink ear that was visible. I got the impression that McCarthy was thrilled but slightly awed by the baby; those hairy hands were unused to such fragility.

Back downstairs again, the Morrises and Jeanie went back to the kitchen on some errand, and I was left alone with the Senator. After a moment he said, rather conspiratorially, "Would you like to see my operation?" I knew from newspaper accounts that he had recently been in the hospital for surgery, but I was unclear as to its nature. He had long had trouble with his right knee, a problem variously attributed to an old war injury and other, less romantic causes. Anyway, not knowing any social precedent for a United States Senator's invitation to view his operation, I said I would be delighted. Thereupon he turned around, unbuckled his belt, pulled up his shirt and showed me a neat surgical scar, about three inches long, running vertically down the small of his back, on or near the center line. As with Tierney's ear, I mumbled my admiration. Then we heard the Morrises and Jeanie coming toward us down the long hallway from the kitchen. Quickly McCarthy rearranged his clothes and was sitting composedly in his favorite chair, smiling, when they entered the room.

I saw him once or twice thereafter, in the Senate chamber or greeting Wisconsin constituents in its ornate Reception Room nearby; but that was my last real visit with Joe McCarthy. In a general way I had known all along that his health was poor. There was clearly something bothersome about that knee, for he constantly favored it, and more than once I saw him limping as he walked along the hallways of the Capitol. Whether his back surgery was related to it, or completely independent of it, I simply do not know. After his death there were all sorts of rumors, many of them spiteful: he had died of cirrhosis of the liver; of acute alcoholism; of cancer. The medical certificate, I believe, blamed hepatitis, which is to say (in layman's language) "liver trouble."

I have no reason to suppose that the doctors were mistaken, or covering up. Like many other people in public life, he had been a hard drinker and may even, at one time, have had a "liquor problem," in the sense that he drank too much and then compounded the error by not eating properly. He was one of those vigorous and robust men whose basic response to any hint of physical illness is to ignore it as long as possible. This and the frantic, disordered life he had led for the previous decade, with its irregular hours for eating, sleeping, etc., had taken their toll. I should stress, however, that he was usually a very moderate drinker on the occasions in 1956 and 1957 when I was present and able to observe him.

Bob Morris has a theory that men can be killed by events, if the events are sufficiently crushing. He does not believe it is pure coincidence that Robert Taft died, technically of cancer, just a year after Dwight Eisenhower had thwarted, by the narrowest of margins, Taft's third bid for the Republican presidential nomination. And regardless of the medical record, Morris does not believe that Joe McCarthy, condemned by the Senate he loved and respected in December 1954, died less than two and a half years later, at the age of forty-eight, of anything but a profound unwillingness to go on.

I am less certain. Perhaps Morris is right. There are worse reasons for dying.

Joe McCarthy died on Thursday afternoon, May 2, 1957, in the National Naval Medical Center at Bethesda, Maryland. I was on my way back by plane from New Orleans, where I had been working on the contempt cases growing out of our Subcommittee's hearings there the previous year (see Chapter 2), and did not learn of his death until I reached my apartment that evening. I had been out of touch for some weeks with the McCarthys and their immediate circle, and had no inkling of how seriously ill he was, so I was profoundly shocked. The next evening I walked down to Gawlor's Funeral Home on Pennsylvania Avenue at 17th, to pay my final respects. Joe McCarthy seemed handsomer in death than he had ever looked in life, but the hairy hand that held a rosary was familiar enough. In the visitors' book, not far above my own signature, a woman had inscribed beside her name a quiet valedictory: "Well done, thou good and faithful servant."

The Requiem Mass was celebrated at St. Matthew's Cathedral in Washington on Monday morning, the 6th, and was followed at 11 a.m. by a funeral service in the Senate Chamber itself—a far from customary proceeding, and one that testified, not (to be sure) to any special regard in which McCarthy was held by the majority of his colleagues, but to the warm affection they knew he had inspired in many millions of Americans. Admission to the galleries for the Senate service was by invitation only, and the demand for tickets was so great that only my friendship with Brent Bozell at last enabled me to obtain one.

I had been in the Senate Chamber many times on Subcommittee business, but nothing I ever saw on the floor or in the cloakrooms could compare with the scene upon which I looked down from a seat in the gallery that morning. But where was the artist, graphic or literary, who could depict its ironies?

The closed gray casket rested in the well of the Chamber, in front of the Secretary's desk. All around it and high behind it were huge banks of spring flowers, lending an unaccustomed touch of outdoor beauty to the great room. Every senator, it seemed, was in his seat. Senator Watkins was there, staring down at his polished mahogany desk top, his honor vindicated in every eye (except perhaps his own) by his colleagues' resolution condemning the deceased. Senator Flanders was there too— the author of that famous resolution. I saw Senator Javits come in and take his place, already very much at home in these new surroundings; far behind him, now, were those earnest talks in Louise Bransten's sitting room overlooking San Francisco Bay. Friend and foe, they were there, almost all of them: Eastland, who had voted as a loyal Democrat to condemn McCarthy, and had lived to come to know him and regret his vote; Knowland, the leader of the Republican minority, who had led a narrow majority of his Republican colleagues in voting *against* the condemnation resolution; these and nearly seventy others, with varying records, varying memories, varying regrets. Around the walls of the Chamber stood their administrative assistants, proudly invoking their "privilege of the Floor" on this memorable morning.

Immediately in front of the first semicircular row of senatorial desks, a number of chairs had been placed. Vice President Nixon entered and took one; Speaker Rayburn and other ranking members of the House of Representatives took others; I. Jack Martin of the White House staff, "representing the President of the United States," was next. Then came Jeanie, in widow's weeds, and other members of McCarthy's family. Postmaster General Summerfield, Agriculture Secretary Benson and Marine Corps Commandant Randolph Pate were the last official guests to take their seats.

Now it was the turn of the clergy. After a brief and appropriate eulogy by the Chaplain of the Senate, Reverend Frederick Brown Harris, there rose to give the funeral oration a young priest of St. Matthew's Cathedral, Father William J. Awalt. He had received Jeanie into the

Catholic faith, and had officiated at her marriage to Joe. Now, far earlier than he could possibly have anticipated, he was called upon to commend Joseph McCarthy to the God in which they both believed. His voice filled the silent Chamber as he intoned the sonorous words:

> Go forth upon thy journey, Christian soul; go forth from this world, go in the name of God, the Omnipotent Father Who created thee.
>
> Go in the name of Jesus Christ, our Lord, Son of the Living God, who bled for thee. Go in the name of the Holy Spirit, who has been poured out on thee. Go in the name of angels and archangels, in the name of thrones and dominations, in the name of princedoms and powers; of cherubim and seraphim; go forth.
>
> Go on thy course, and may thy place today be found in peace, and may thy dwelling be the holy mount of Zion, in the name of Christ, our Lord.
>
> Be merciful, be gracious, spare him, Lord; be merciful, be gracious, Lord; deliver him from the sins that are past. From Thy frown and Thine ire, from the perils of dying, from the nethermost fire, from all that is evil, from the power of the Devil, Thy servant deliver, for once and forever.

In front of me, in the same section of the gallery, I could see J. Edgar Hoover looking down upon the scene. How much, I reflected, he must know, yet never be able to say! A few seats away was Roy Cohn, subdued at last. In another row were the brothers-in-law, Bill Buckley and Brent Bozell, the latter very close to tears.

Father Awalt continued, speaking of the dead man's faith and the Christian significance of death. Now he pronounced his final benediction:

> May the angels lead thee into Paradise; may the martyrs receive thee at thy coming, and take thee to Jerusalem, the Holy City. May the choirs of the angels receive thee; and mayest thou, with the once poor Lazarus, have rest everlasting.
>
> Eternal rest grant unto him, O Lord,
> And let perpetual light shine upon him.
> May he rest in peace. Amen.
>
> May his soul, and the souls of all the faithful departed, through the mercy of God, rest in peace. Amen.
>
> In the name of the Father, and of the Son, and of the Holy Ghost. Amen.

The hands of the clock stood at 22 minutes past eleven.

Through the swinging doors to the left of the rostrum stepped, two by two, six U.S. Marines in formal dress, with white hats held tautly under their arms. In slow-step, with metronomic precision, they took up their positions, three on either side of the casket. With infinite care they wheeled it, on its rolling table, toward the corresponding doors on the opposite side of the rostrum. The doors swung outward, and Joseph McCarthy left the Senate Chamber forever.

McCarthy was buried in Appleton, Wisconsin, his family home. From the Capitol the funeral procession had gone directly to National Airport, whence one military plane carried the mourners to Appleton, and another, with a detail of military guards, transported the casket. It was only some weeks later that I learned of an interesting footnote to that journey.

A day or so before McCarthy's funeral, three of his closest senatorial friends—Bill Jenner of Indiana, Herman Welker of Idaho, and George ("Molly") Malone of Nevada—were discussing the plans. They were all flying to Appleton for the interment, and arrangements had of course been made for them to travel in the plane with Jeanie, the other members of the McCarthy family, and the rest of the official party. But this doughty threesome suddenly had an idea that struck them as better. They, of all his colleagues, had been closest to McCarthy in life; why not be closest to him in death as well? And so it was arranged. When the plane carrying Joe McCarthy's casket lifted from the runway of National Airport on the afternoon of May 6, three living senators were in it. They had gone thus far with Joe McCarthy; they would go the rest of the way.

At the opening of this chapter, I stated my objectives carefully and (I hope) modestly: ". . . to set down here my comparatively few personal recollections of [McCarthy], and to offer a tentative appraisal of the roots of the great crisis with which his name will forever be identified."

Now that the chapter is written, I see how futile it was to hope that even today, more than a decade after McCarthy's death, any discussion of the man could effectively be limited to such relatively innocuous aspects of his story. This tells us nothing about McCarthy; but it tells us something about the present intellectual climate of America. It tells us, in brief, that we are still too close to McCarthy to discuss any aspect of his life objectively. To mention his loving awe of his baby daughter, or his dislike of cats; to describe his surgical scar, or the bare facts of his funeral—to do these things, even though I saw them with my own eyes, is to risk an outraged charge of special pleading. To go beyond such minutiae and offer an appraisal of his significance that does not depict him as either the martyred savior of his nation or the devil's own rag-baby is to tilt at windmills that will outlast us all.

So let us leave Joe McCarthy in the Wisconsin earth, for less im-pacted generations to assess. And let us remember, too, that in the truly long run—beyond even the final "verdict of history," whatever that may be—the praise or condemnation that really matters will be meted out by a Tribunal far higher, even, than the United States Senate.

11

Odds Without Ends

The Other Mr. Hiss

For me, as for so many other Americans, Whittaker Chambers' great autobiographical work, *Witness,** published in 1952, was and remains the most powerful single influence shaping my concept of the problem of domestic Communism.

Few Americans who join the Communist Party are ever asked to commit actual espionage on its behalf. Of those who do commit espionage, few subsequently defect from the Party, and very few indeed are willing or, if I may put the point delicately, able to tell what they know. Barring Gold and Greenglass (who did not start talking until they had been arrested on charges carrying the death penalty), perhaps the two most important individuals in this category were Elizabeth Bentley, who served as a courier for the so-called Silvermaster group in the early 1940's, and Chambers himself. Both testified freely, and the testimony of both has been confirmed independently again and again.

Of the two, however, only Chambers was a professional writer, very probably the finest non-fiction writer America has ever produced; and he undertook to tell in writing the story of his life as a final contribution, or "witness," to the truth as he had come to see it. His book is an authentic masterpiece: a wonderfully sensitive autobiography, which explains with great care and comprehension the forces that turned a middle-class American boy into a Communist and a spy against his country. It is

* New York: Random House, 1952.

also, quite simply, a superb spy story, complete with microfilm, secret inks, and all the paraphernalia of that sinister genre. Yet again, it is a brilliant journalistic account of the development, progress, and outcome of the historic Hiss case, very definitely from the inside. Last but far from least, it is a powerful testament by a man who had acted out, in his own life, the central crisis of the 20th century and made his decision "for the losing side."

It is not too much to say, therefore, that *Witness* is the beginning of wisdom for those who would truly understand the problem of American Communism. It is almost impossible to read those simple, eloquent pages and disbelieve the man who wrote them. Those who wish to persist in other views are best advised to leave the book unread.

The central theme of *Witness*, of course, is the story of Chambers' friendship with Alger Hiss: how they met as members of the "Harold Ware cell" of the Communist Party in Washington and became fast friends, how Hiss passed secret information to Chambers for transmission to the Soviet Union; how, after Chambers had defected, Hiss under oath denied giving him such data; how Chambers produced a long-forgotten microfilm, and Hiss was convicted of perjury. Along the way, however, are scattered many other names, and one of them is the name of Alger Hiss's younger brother, Donald, who, as I write these words, is a partner in Covington & Burling, Washington's best-known and most distinguished law firm.

According to Chambers, Donald Hiss was a member of the Ware cell along with his brother. In the early days of the 1948 confrontation between Chambers and Alger Hiss—when Hiss was still denying that he had even known a Whittaker Chambers, and many months before Chambers produced the documents that sent Alger to prison—Donald Hiss appeared before the Committee and flatly denied ever having met Whittaker Chambers under that or any other name. Through subsequent appearances before the Committee, before a grand jury, and at his brother's trial, he maintained this position firmly. Quite clearly, as in the case of Alger either he was lying or Chambers was. But perjury cannot be proved merely by persuading a jury to believe one of two contradictory statements; the law requires that an allegedly perjurious statement be contradicted either (1) by two independent witnesses, or (2) by one witness and corroborative documents. It was the latter combination that brought down Alger Hiss; his sworn denials of espionage were contradicted by Chambers *and* by the so-called "pumpkin papers." In the case of Donald Hiss, there were no witnesses available other than Chambers, and no documents, to place him in the Ware cell; so the contradiction merely stood there, grinning back at those who sought to resolve it.

It remains unresolved to this day. In 1957, however, the ISSC received and published certain documentary evidence which, at a minimum, shows that Chambers knew quite a lot about Donald Hiss for a man who (according to the latter) had never even met him, and that Donald Hiss's trial testimony was *prima facie* incorrect in at least one factual particular disputed between him and Chambers. The manner in which the press handled the item is, incidentally, a good example of the way in which news can be "managed."

Let us first review what Chambers actually said about Donald Hiss, and vice versa. As explained in *Witness*, Chambers defected from the Communist Party in 1938, but he did not take his information concerning it to the government until September 1939, just after Stalin signed his infamous pact with Hitler. Thereupon Chambers was taken by a friend to Adolph Berle, then Assistant Secretary of State for security. They met at Berle's home in Washington on the evening of September 2, the day after Hitler attacked Poland and the day before Britain and France declared war on Germany.

Berle took notes, which were introduced in evidence at the second trial of Alger Hiss. So far as they pertain to the Hiss brothers, they read as follows:

> Donald Hiss
>   (Philippine Adviser)
>   Member of CP with Pressman & Witt
>   Labor Dep't.—Asst. to Frances Perkins—
>   Party wanted him there—to send him as arbitrator
>   in Bridges trial—
>   Brought along by brother—
> Alger Hiss
>   Ass't. to Sayre—CP—1937
>   Member of the Underground Com.—Active
>   Baltimore boys—
> Wife—Priscilla Hiss—Socialist—
>   Early days of New Deal

To be perfectly fair, it was quite a lot to swallow, back in 1939. One of the early scoffers was President Roosevelt, to whom Berle took the story. As Chambers told it in his book, "The President had laughed. When Berle was insistent, he had been told in words which it is necessary to paraphrase, to 'go jump in a lake.' "

Nor did Berle have better luck when, in 1941, Dean Acheson entered the State Department as an Assistant Secretary of State and requested that Donald Hiss be assigned to him as an aide. Berle called on Acheson to advise him of the doubts concerning the Hiss brothers, but the new Assistant Secretary would have none of it. Calling Donald in, Acheson questioned him bluntly about possible Communist associations. When Donald flatly denied ever having had any, Acheson pronounced the matter closed.

The same purblind attitude seems to have characterized Dr. Stanley Hornbeck, State's Chief of the Division of Far Eastern Affairs, in dealing with a roughly contemporaneous but quite separate report on the Hisses. Testifying before the ISSC in 1952, former Ambassador to France William E. Bullitt described how French Premier Daladier had warned him in 1939 that according to French Intelligence two brothers named Hiss, employed in the State Department, were Soviet agents. Bullitt did not recognize the name, but on encountering Alger Hiss in Hornbeck's office one day in the winter of 1940, and ascertaining that he had a brother who also worked for the Department, Bullitt told Hornbeck of Daladier's report. Once again the warning was ignored.

So the years rolled on—to 1948. On August 3 of that year, testifying in public before HCUA, Chambers answered the questions of Committee counsel Robert Stripling concerning the Harold Ware cell:

> MR. STRIPLING. Who comprised the cell or apparatus to which you referred?
>
> MR. CHAMBERS. The apparatus was organized with a leading group of seven men, each of whom was the leader of a cell.
>
> MR. STRIPLING. Could you name the seven individuals?
>
> MR. CHAMBERS. The head of the group, as I have said, was at first Nathan Witt. Other members of the group were Lee Pressman, Alger Hiss, Donald Hiss, Victor Perlo, Charles Kramer. . . .
>
> MR. MUNDT. What was Charles Kramer's correct name?
>
> MR. CHAMBERS. I think his original name was Krivitsky. And John Abt—I don't know if I mentioned him before or not—and Henry Collins.
>
> MR. RANKIN. How about Harold Ware?
>
> MR. CHAMBERS. Harold Ware was, of course, the organizer.

When Alger Hiss thereupon denied knowing anybody by the name of Chambers, the Committee realized that one or the other had very likely committed perjury, and Congressman Richard Nixon of California was appointed head of a subcommittee to ascertain, if possible, which. On August 7 Nixon questioned Chambers in great detail. So far as pertains to Donald Hiss, Chambers' testimony was as follows:

MR. NIXON. When did you meet Donald Hiss?

MR. CHAMBERS. Probably within the same week in which I met Alger Hiss.

MR. NIXON. Did you ever stay in Donald Hiss's home?

MR. CHAMBERS. No, my relation with Donald Hiss was much less close. I can make that point now, if you will permit. My relationship with Alger Hiss quickly transcended our formal relationship. We became close friends.

MR. NIXON. Donald Hiss—what relation did you have with him?

MR. CHAMBERS. A purely formal one.

MR. NIXON. He knew you as Carl?

MR. CHAMBERS. Yes.

MR. NIXON. Did you collect dues from him?

MR. CHAMBERS. Yes.

MR. NIXON. Did you meet his wife?

MR. CHAMBERS. I think I met her once, not very often.

MR. NIXON. Where did you collect the dues from him, at his home?

MR. CHAMBERS. Probably in Alger's house. He frequently came there.

MR. NIXON. He came there to see you?

MR. CHAMBERS. Yes.

MR. NIXON. Do you recall anything significant about Donald Hiss, as to personal characteristics, hobbies?

MR. CHAMBERS. No. Something else is involved there, too. Donald Hiss was married, I think, to a daughter of Mr. Cotton, who is in the State Department. She was not a Communist, and everybody was worried about her.

MR. NIXON. Getting back to Alger Hiss for the moment, do you recall any pictures on the wall that they might have owned at the time?

MR. CHAMBERS. No; I am afraid I don't.

MR. NIXON. Donald Hiss—do you know any other characteristics about him, can you recall any?

MR. CHAMBERS. Except I can give you the general impression. He was much less intelligent than Alger. Much less sensitive than his brother. I had the impression he was interested in the social climb and the Communist Party was interested in having him climb. At one point I believe he was fairly friendly with James Roosevelt.

MR. NIXON. Did you have any conversations with him you can recall that were out of the ordinary?

MR. CHAMBERS. Yes; one I think I can recall. He was working in the Labor Department, I believe in the Immigration Section, and it was the plan of the Communist Party to have him go to California, get himself sent by the Government to California, to work in the Bridges case.

At that moment he had an opportunity to go into the State Department as, I think, legal adviser to the Philippine Section, which had just been set up.

It was the opinion of the party that he should do that and not the Bridges matter. It was his opinion that he should continue in the Bridges matter and there was a fairly sharp exchange, but he submitted to discipline and went to the State Department.

If true, this was testimony of considerable importance. It significantly expanded the disjointed notes Berle had made at the time of Chambers' report to him in 1939. Harry Bridges, the Australian-born labor leader who headed the Communist-riddled International Longshoremen's & Warehousemen's Union (see Chapter 6), would naturally be an object of Communist solicitude when threatened with deportation proceedings as an undesirable alien. What better "arbitrator" in those proceedings could the Communists wish for than Donald Hiss, if Chambers was telling the truth in naming him as a member of the Ware cell? The further fact (if it was a fact) that the Party subsequently changed its mind and ordered Donald to work instead at his new post in the State Department merely indicated the order of Communist priorities as World Was II drew nearer.

Six days later, however, Donald Hiss appeared voluntarily before HCUA and under oath gave Chambers the lie direct:

> . . . I flatly deny every statement made by Mr. Chambers with respect to me. I am not, and never have been, a member of the Communist Party or of any formal or informal organizations affiliated with, or fronting in any manner whatsoever for, the Communist Party. In fact, the only organizations and clubs to which I have belonged are the local Y.M.C.A., the Miles River Yacht Club of Maryland, the old Washington Racquet Club, the Harvard Law School Association, the American Society of International Law, and college fraternities and athletic clubs.
>
> I have no recollection of ever having met any person by the name of Whittaker Chambers, nor do I recognize his photograph which I have seen in the public press. I am not and never have been in sympathy with the principles of the Communist Party. Any interested person could easily have discovered these facts by inquiry of the distinguished, respected and unquestionably loyal Americans with whom I have been intimately associated.

Actually, Donald Hiss's testimony about not recognizing Chambers' picture was more significant than his failure to recognize the name, for Chambers had testified that the Hiss brothers, like all his other Communist contacts in Washington, had known him only as "Carl," in keeping with Communist practice (cf. Chapter 3). Congressman Nixon moved

to nail the point down: "As I understand your statement," said Richard
Nixon, "you have made an unqualified statement that you have never
known a man by the name of Carl who resembled that man." Donald
Hiss: "I have never known that man by the name of Chambers, Carl, or
any other name, sir." Later on he was to add, "If I am lying, I should go
to jail, and if Mr. Chambers is lying he should go to jail." Whereupon
Congressman Mundt observed drily, "There is no question about that."
But, in the absence of another witness or corroborating documents, no
perjury charge could be brought against either man.

As Chambers points out in his book, the very explicitness of this
testimony by Donald Hiss, who had lived near his brother during the
relevant years and had seen him frequently, was soon to inconvenience
Alger greatly. Up to this point, the latter had confined himself to insisting that "The name [Chambers] means absolutely nothing to me." But
just three days after Donald's sweeping denial, Alger Hiss conceded that
he himself had indeed known Chambers intimately in those years—
though under the name "George Crosley." Why, then, hadn't Donald
known "Crosley" too? In a later hearing, questioning Alger Hiss, Congressman Mundt probed this difference of recollection between the
brothers:

> MR. MUNDT. Let me ask this question. The possibility would seem very
> plausible to me that since Mr. Crosley, as you call him, lived in your
> home for a while, while he was getting his furniture transferred, that
> your brother Donald undoubtedly visited your home frequently. Have
> you ever conferred with Donald to see whether he knew this man as
> George Crosley?
> MR. HISS. I have asked him and he has no recollection.
> MR. MUNDT. He has no recollection?
> MR. HISS. No.

And there matters stood, as far as Donald Hiss was concerned, until
the second trial of Alger for perjury. At that trial, appearing as a witness
for his brother, Donald again denied ever meeting Chambers under any
name, and specifically contradicted one of Chambers' most explicit
statements concerning him: the assertion to HCUA that Donald had
once worked on "the Bridges matter" as an attorney for the Labor
Department. Nothing could have been more unequivocal than Donald
Hiss's denial, under questioning by his brother's counsel, that he had ever
done any such thing:

> Q. Mr. Hiss, did you ever at any time do any work on the Bridges
> case?
> A. I did not, sir.

It may seem strange that no prompt effort was made to get to the bottom of this flat contradiction between the testimony of Chambers and Donald Hiss on a factual point that, after all, might have proved fairly easy to check. But it was at best highly collateral to the central issue of the trial—the guilt or innocence of Alger Hiss—and Hiss's subsequent conviction seems to have stilled the investigatory ardor of the Chambers forces.

Thus the uncertainty remained. That a jury believed Chambers over Alger Hiss, with the crucial help of corroborating documents, did not necessarily mean that twelve impartial observers would have believed him over Donald Hiss as well, *without* documentary support. Moreover, Chambers never contended that Donald Hiss had committed espionage. In fact, in *Witness* Chambers stated that Alger, when questioned early in 1937 by a top Russian agent named Colonel Bykov (with Chambers acting as interpreter), had expressly said that his brother could *not* be persuaded to "bring out materials," i.e., spy for the Soviet Union.

Still, it was, to say the least, thought-provoking that a partner in Washington's most famous law firm had been identified under oath in 1948 as a member, some ten to twelve years earlier, of a highly influential Communist cell. But was Chambers telling the truth? On this question, verification of any circumstantial details was obviously important. That was why Congressman Nixon had probed Chambers' memory for recollections of "pictures on the wall" of Alger Hiss' home, and why he asked for "any conversations with [Donald Hiss] you can recall that were out of the ordinary." As to the latter, the only incident that Chambers could dredge up after ten years was the story of Donald's assignment by the Communist Party to "get himself sent by the Government to California, to work in the Bridges case"; the Party's subsequent change of mind, directing him instead to "go into the State Department as, I think, legal adviser to the Philippine Section;" Donald's initial sharp opposition to the change, and his final submission "to [Communist Party] discipline." Were any of these allegations capable of independent verification? As the years passed, many wondered.

Viewing the matter from the perspective of the mid-1950's, it certainly seemed unlikely. The Subcommittee had no easy access to the records of Donald Hiss's employment by the Executive branch of the government in the late 1930's, let alone to the inner deliberations (if any) of the Communist Party on the subject. To go into the matter at all, without probable cause, was to risk a potentially damaging hullaballoo far out of proportion to any light our investigation might shed.

Then, quite unexpectedly, the ISSC came upon certain documents which spectacularly confirmed that there *had* been some sort of intramural dispute within the Roosevelt administration in 1938 over whether Donald Hiss should be reassigned temporarily to the Labor Department to preside over the Bridges hearing or allowed to concentrate instead on a new assignment with the State Department's Division of Philippine Affairs. They strongly suggested, furthermore, that Donald had been somewhat less than accurate in swearing that he had never worked on the Bridges case.

First, in a letter dated April 15, 1938, we found Immigration Commissioner James Houghteling advising the San Francisco District Commissioner, Edward Cahill, that "Donald Hiss, formerly Assistant Solicitor of the Department of Labor and now a member of the legal staff of the Department of State, will preside at the Bridges hearing"—which was to be held in San Francisco. But this arrangement had plainly not sat well with somebody at State, for in a letter dated April 22, 1938, Secretary of Labor Frances Perkins sought to lay at rest doubts that had evidently been expressed to her in writing on April 11 by Assistant Secretary of State Francis B. Sayre, who was, by an odd coincidence, at that time Alger's superior. Madame Perkins wrote:

> Dear Mr. Sayre: I have your letter of April 11 with regard to Mr. [Donald] Hiss and can understand your difficulties in arranging for his temporary detail to this Department in view of the opposition of his superiors in the Division of Philippine Affairs.
>
> As you perhaps have heard, the hearing in the Bridges case has been continued pending the disposition by the Supreme Court of a petition for a writ of certiorari in another immigration case involving the same legal problem. Should the Court's decision make it necessary to hold further hearings in the Bridges matter, I should appreciate it at that time if you could arrange matters in your Department so that Mr. Hiss could be assigned to the case again. As you know, his transfer to the State Department was a source of serious concern to the legal staff here as he was the only member fully cognizant of the various aspects of this important immigration case.
>
> If the case is marked up for hearing again, I hope to be able to give you ample notice so that arrangements which will not inconvenience his division can be made in advance.

But despite Madame Perkins' reassurances, the fact was that Donald Hiss did *not* preside at the new Bridges hearing—exactly the denouement required by Chambers' account of the episode.

Of course, such evidence was only circumstantial and was far from constituting conclusive proof that Donald Hiss had once been a Communist. It was at least theoretically possible that Chambers had learned from Alger of a perfectly innocent wish on Donald's part to stay with the Bridges case, and then subsequently dragged it into a false account of Donald's alleged Party activities, using it as circumstantial straw for his mendacious bricks. In that case, however, what was one to do with Donald's flat denial, at the second trial, that he had ever worked on the Bridges case at all?

Hypotheses, in any event, are at best only hypotheses. The documents were real, and they established that Chambers had been quite correct in describing to the Nixon subcommittee, in 1948, the essential outlines (assignment—new assignment—opposition—acquiescence) of an important episode in the career of Donald Hiss ten years earlier. Moreover, they did grave damage (to put it mildly) to Donald's insistent assertion that he had never worked on the Bridges case. On the contrary, according to Madame Perkins' letter of April 22, 1938, he was "the only member [of the Labor Department's legal staff] fully cognizant of the various aspects" of the matter.

Accordingly, Morris decided that the Houghteling and Perkins letters deserved to be added to the public record of the Hiss-Chambers controversy. The Hiss case, after all, was much the biggest there had ever been in the field, and its embers were still glowing. What was uncertain was how the press would treat these documents. Would they be accepted as relevant evidence? Or would they be brushed aside as "just another smear?"

At this time (April 1957), the senior wire service reporter who ordinarily covered our hearings was John Chadwick of the Associated Press, whose hostility to the ISSC was apparent to any reader of his dispatches. The United Press was usually represented by a well-meaning young man who was content, and no doubt rightly so, to take his cue, in assessing a story, from the more experienced Chadwick. Other seats at the press table would be taken, intermittently, by reporters for the International News Service and for individual magazines and newspapers. (Two of the friendliest, whose stories accordingly covered our hearings accurately and in detail, were Willard Edwards of the *Chicago Tribune* and Jerry Greene of the *New York Daily News*.) In terms of nationwide coverage, it was apparent to Morris and me that whether the American people learned of the documents relating to Donald Hiss would probably depend on John Chadwick. It was a depressing thought.

On April 3, 1957, at the close of a public hearing before Senator Hruska on a totally different subject, Morris placed the two letters in the record:

MR. MORRIS. Before adjourning, Senator, I would like to offer for the record two letters we have gotten from the Department of Labor in connection with our inquiry in Communism in the Harry Bridges unions. We have been doing some followup staff work and we received from the Department of Labor a letter dated April 22, 1938, which purports to be a ribbon copy document on file at the National Archives and Records Service, from Secretary Perkins, who was at that time Secretary of Labor.

And we have a photostatic copy of a letter from James Hou—Mr. Rusher, could you spell that?

MR. RUSHER. H-o-u-g-h-t-e-l-i-n-g. James Houghteling.

MR. MORRIS. And this is dated April 15, 1938, addressed to the Honorable Edward Cahill, district commissioner.

These letters, while adding some light to our inquiry about the Harry Bridges case, Senator, tend to confirm some of Whittaker Chambers' testimony before the House Un-American Activities Committee with respect to the brother of Alger Hiss, Donald Hiss, which tends to refute statements Donald Hiss has made in connection with some of his assignments.

SENATOR HRUSKA. They will be accepted into the record.*

The hearing was adjourned, and we distributed copies of the letters around the press table. Chadwick picked one up between his thumb and forefinger, looked at it with obvious distaste, and—as his colleagues watched—said slowly: "I don't think I'll use this." That afternoon, checking the AP and UP wires over in the Senate cloakroom, I was able to confirm to Morris that Chadwick was as good as his word, and that the UP had followed suit.

The curtain fell once more around Donald Hiss. Today, ten years further on, the matter remains where Donald Hiss placed it, coolly and firmly, in 1948: "If I am lying, I should go to jail, and if Mr. Chambers is lying, he should go to jail."

The trouble with books like this one is, they don't always have such tidy endings.

The Case of the Missing Witness

The form notice of our scheduled hearing, distributed to the press the day before, had said only "Scope of Soviet Activity in the United States —2 witnesses. Caucus Room, Senate Office Building, 11 a.m." We had subpoenaed two individuals for that morning's hearing, a union offi-

* Part 58, "Scope of Soviet Activity in the United States," pp. 3813-4; ISSC, 1957.

cial and a man who, in the late 1930's, had served on the administrative staff of a famous Midwestern university. We had reason to believe that both had been, and might still be, members of the Communist Party. Although the two interrogations were not related, we felt that both, either by testifying or refusing to testify, might contribute materially to the record of Communist activity in America.

Both subpoenas had ordered the recipient to appear at our office at 9:30 a.m., a procedure that enabled us to question them first in executive session. First to arrive was the university official, and he immediately riveted our attention, for he was *not* accompanied by a lawyer. There is certainly nothing inherently incriminating about bringing a lawyer along when one is subpoenaed to appear before a Congressional committee, and many non-Communists did so during the seventeen months I served with the ISSC. But it was also indisputably true that a witness who did *not* bring a lawyer very probably intended to cooperate with the Subcommittee and thus felt no particular need for one. (Conversely, of course, the Communist Party maintained a whole battery of lawyers, both in Washington and New York, to represent its members when they were haled before the ISSC or HCUA. If a witness arrived in the custody of one of these—and we saw some of them so often we were on a first-name basis—it was a sure sign of non-cooperation.)

We quickly installed the unaccompanied witness in an office where prying eyes would not find him, and welcomed the union official when he arrived accompanied by one of the Communist Party's brightest attorneys. Leaving the latter two in an outer room of Senator Eastland's suite, we brought the university man into Eastland's own office by another door. Middle-aged and tweedy, the witness asked and was given permission to smoke a pipe. He was plainly nervous as Eastland administered the oath and Morris asked his name and address. The interrogation continued, roughly as follows (since the session was executive, I am not quoting verbatim):

> MR. MORRIS. Are you a member of the Communist Party?
> WITNESS. No.
> MR. MORRIS. Have you ever been?
> WITNESS. (After a long pause, and a pull on his pipe.) Yes.
> MR. MORRIS. (Quietly and unemotionally.) Will you tell us about it?
> WITNESS. (Another pause. The shoulders sag a little.) Yes. I've been wanting to get this off my chest for a long time.

Then, slowly and carefully, the witness began to speak. He told us how, in the late 1930's, he had joined a Communist cell at the university where he was then employed. With very little prompting, he described how he had been recruited; he described the meetings and activities of the cell; he named the others who had belonged to it. Soon, for it was now almost 10:30, Morris interrupted and addressed Eastland:

> MR. MORRIS. Senator, I think it is apparent that this witness is testifying fully and freely, and intends to cooperate with the Subcommittee. In view of the time factor, I suggest that he be turned over to Mr. Mandel, who can conduct a staff interview with him. Unless something arises that requires to be placed in the public record, I see no need to subject him to all the unfavorable publicity of a public session.
>
> SENATOR EASTLAND. Yes, it is so ordered.

I escorted the man out the way he had entered and turned him over to Ben Mandel for a comprehensive discussion. Then I hurried back to Senator Eastland's office and brought in the union official and his lawyer. As expected, this second witness grimly took the Fifth on every question having the remotest conceivable connection with Communism, and we soon adjourned the executive session and told him to meet us in the Caucus Room at 11. There he repeated his performance in public—while on the floor below Ben Mandel was making careful notes of the account being given by the cooperative former university official. At the close of the public hearing, one or two alert reporters asked us where our second witness was.

"What second witness, fellows?" we replied blandly. "Gosh, that notice must have been in error." I doubt we persuaded them, but there was little they could do. Later that day, the cooperative witness returned quietly to his home town, with the thanks of the Subcommitee still ringing in his ears. Unless he himself has told someone, nobody outside the Subcommittee knows to this day that he was ever subpoenaed by us.

In some ways, of course, it would have been more satisfying to skip the union official's monotonous invocations of the Fifth and put the cooperative witness on in public. But this would simply put a high premium on the Communist tactic of refusing to answer questions, and an equally high penalty on cooperating fully. It was, therefore—and I believe necessarily—the Subcommittee's rule to compel uncooperative witnesses to display their reluctance in public (a reluctance which, after all, gave rise to inferences that both the Subcommittee and the public were entitled to draw), and to avoid, where possible, requiring cooperative witnesses to confess their past Communist activities before the world. I say "where possible," for sometimes it was necessary to put on a cooperative witness in public, in order to round out the picture of some situation the Subcommittee was publicly investigating. (Cf., for example, Thomas Black's testimony, discussed in Chapter 3, which placed Amtorg's Gaik Ovakimian squarely in the leadership of the industrial espionage conducted in this country by the Soviet Union in the early 1930's.)

Luckily for the former university official, his testimony, while valuable, was not an essential aspect of some investigation then being conducted publicly by the Subcommittee. I am happy to be able to offer this evidence that, wherever it could, the ISSC was glad to be, not only a willing listener to the truth freely told, but a sympathetic and understanding friend of the teller.

The Battle at the Three Musketeers

Internal security is ordinarily a pretty grim business. Every so often, however, a little humor tinted the dark canvas of our daily concerns, and we always greeted its advent with relief. In the same spirit, after this long chronicle of spies, traitors, perjurers and suicides, I welcome the opportunity to tell a joke on the ISSC and on certain of the gumshoe agencies of the Executive branch. It is to our credit, I hope, that when the truth of this particular episode finally dawned on us, we at least saw the comedy in the situation.

It all began seriously enough, as an aspect of our investigation of the "Scope of Soviet Activity in the United States." My sharp-eyed boss Bob Morris had spotted, and was carefully documenting in a series of open hearings, an intensive Soviet drive to repatriate Russians and citizens of other Iron Curtain countries who had previously defected to the West and were now living in this country. These poor people, many of whom spoke little English, could be found in 1956 huddled in small emigré communities all over the northeastern United States, often unable to make a successful fresh start in a strange land but still terrified of the murderous and seemingly omnipotent despotism they had fled. Their very existence was, of course, a source of embarrassment to the leaders of the Workers' Paradise.

Evidently it occurred to Khrushchev, or one of his minions, that some of these people might be lured back to the Soviet Union by a judicious combination of the carrot and the stick. After all, Khrushchev was just then making a big point of the argument that things had changed for the better in the Soviet Union after the death of Stalin in 1953. Once the relative glamor of life in America had worn off and had been replaced by the grim necessity of earning a decent living in an unfamiliar country, it was reasonable to assume that an artful appeal to return to Mother Russia might be effective in some cases—with obvious collateral propaganda advantages to the Soviet Union. Most of the emigrés had relatives or sweethearts still behind the Iron Curtain, whose photographs and letters could be, and were, used to generate the pressure. A whole bureau was set up, in East Berlin, to supplement their personal pleas with letters to the emigrés from semi-official Soviet sources, promising forgiveness and good treatment to those who would come home. (What actually happened to those who returned was, of course, something else again.) Finally, Communist diplomatic and consular personnel, accredited to our government or to the UN, often approached the refugees directly, bringing letters and photographs of their loved ones and urging them at first hand to come home.

It was not all borscht and balalaikas, however. Every letter from a mother, child, sister or sweetheart in the Soviet Union was a reminder that the Communists could, if they chose, hold the writer of that letter hostage—or worse. Moreover, the dismaying ease with which the Communist bureau in East Berlin was somehow able to locate the refugees in this country (for many had changed their names and tried to cover their tracks) seemed only to emphasize the omniscience of the vast and terrible machine they were fleeing. After years in some obscure American town, living under a pseudonym, the frightened emigré would suddenly receive a letter from East Berlin, mailed to his current address, but addressed to him under his true Russian name! Or worse, a Soviet agent—from one of the consulates, or the UN delegation—would appear without warning and try to talk to him. It was terrifying, and sometimes it was effective.

This whole Soviet repatriation campaign was the subject of a careful investigation by our Subcommittee in 1956 and 1957, and those interested in pursuing the matter will find reports of the numerous hearings, and our recommendations for legislative action, in the published record of the Subcommittee for those years. All that concerns us at the moment is one small aspect of one of the many hearings on this subject.

On June 13, 1956, we questioned one Peter Pirogov, a young Russian who in 1948, together with a colleague named Anatole Barzov (also spelled Borzov), had flown a Soviet plane to the American Zone of occupied Austria and sought political asylum. This was granted, and both were brought to the United States. Pirogov seems to have adjusted nicely, and at the time of his interrogation in 1956 was earning his living as a taxi driver in Washington. Barzov, however, had left a wife and son in the Soviet Union and soon began to get homesick. He approached the Soviet Embassy, and told Pirogov he had been assured by Soviet Ambassador Panyushkin that he would receive only a two-year jail term if he would return to Russia. Furthermore, he was told, if he could persuade Pirogov to return with him, neither would receive any jail sentence at all. Pirogov declined the deadly bait, but Barzov took it; on August 15, 1949, he left for the Soviet Union.

Morris interrupted Pirogov's testimony at this point to read into the record a few paragraphs of a then just-published book by Vladimir Petrov, the Russian embassy official and secret agent who had defected from the Soviet Union in Australia in April 1954. It revealed the pathetic end of the story of Anatole Barzov (or Borzov):

> One day in 1950 at MVD headquarters in Moscow, my colleague Igolkin, who worked in the American section of the SK department, told me of Borzov's return and said that he was interrogating him in his cell in the Taganskaya Prison. Igolkin had a series of interviews with Borzov, who supplied a mass of valuable information. He was talking freely and was describing every detail of his experiences in American hands, in the hope of working his passage back to pardon, and of being permitted at least to see his wife and son again. Igolkin described it to me, "Each time I go to see him he looks at me like a dog that wags its tail and gazes at you in the hope of a bone."
>
> They kept Borzov about 8 months in prison because he had so much interesting information to supply and because so many senior MVD officers wanted to check up on various points in his story.
>
> Of course, no one told him that he had been sentenced to death while he was still in America. When they had finished with him they shot him without letting him see his wife and son again.
>
> If this story helps some waverers who are hesitating on the brink of returning to their Soviet homeland, it will have been worth the telling. (From *Empire of Fear*, by Vladimir and Evodokia Petrov, Andre Deutsch, Ltd., 1956; p. 341.)

Pirogov's testimony had then concluded with a spirited challenge to the Soviet repatriation bureau in East Berlin to produce Barzov alive, if it could, as a means of reassuring prospective repatriates about the possible dire consequences of a decision to go home.

Back in our office, however, Pirogov for the first time mentioned one other episode, concerning him and Barzov, which struck us as so unusual and so full of ominous implications that we decided to add it to the record. It was too late to schedule another public hearing that day, however, so we took the story in private that afternoon and released it to the press in mimeographed form two days later. It began as follows:*

> MR. MORRIS. Mr. Pirogov, since you have been in the United States have you been approached on any other occasions by persons you recognized as Soviet officials?
>
> MR. PIROGOV. No; except one case which happened after Mr. Barzov decided to return to Russia, at which time we met.
>
> MR. MORRIS. Where was that?
>
> MR. PIROGOV. In a restaurant here in Washington.
>
> MR. MORRIS. What happened at that time?
>
> MR. PIROGOV. Well, it is hard to say. I still don't understand today what actually happened.

That, as we later found out, was the understatement of the year. But to continue:

> MR. PIROGOV. This is what happened. Barzov had gone from New York to Washington for good, planning to return to Russia.
>
> MR. MORRIS. He had left Washington and gone to New York?
>
> MR. PIROGOV. No; he left New York and went to Washington, to see officials in the Embassy and to receive tickets for his ship or airplane on his way to Russia. And then after one week I decided to send him a letter and meet him once more before he left the United States, to try to help him to change his decision about that.
>
> MR. MORRIS. You had advised him, had you not, not to go back?
>
> MR. PIROGOV. Of course, but this particular time I wanted to have one more meeting with him. Well, I sent a letter. The next morning, I was not in my room in the hotel, but somebody—the manager—told me that some man was there and had left a letter for me. That letter was from Barzov—from Washington, from the Russian Embassy. In the letter he said, "I want to have a meeting with you, on one condition: that it must be without any witnesses; just you and me."
>
> MR. MORRIS. This is what the letter said?
>
> MR. PIROGOV. Yes; his letter said that.
>
> MR. MORRIS. Do you still have the letter?
>
> MR. PIROGOV. Oh, I think somebody has it. I don't. I think the FBI people; I don't know who. Then Barzov's letter said, "I want to meet you in the Three Musketeers Restaurant," and he put in the same letter a small clipping from a newspaper, advertising that restaurant.

---

* Since Pirogov's English was notably fractured, and he was a friendly witness, I have taken far more liberties in the interest of clarrifying his testimony—adding punctuation and words, correcting grammatical errors, revising sentence structure, etc.—than has been customary elsewhere in this volume. The original transcript appears in Part 25, "Scope of Soviet Activity in the United States" (ISSC, 1956), at pp. 1370-74.

Finally the letter said, "I want to see you tomorrow at 5 o'clock."

After receiving the letter I called a friend of mine in Washington and asked him if he thinks it is okay for me to go and see Barzov. He said okay. So the next morning I took a train and came to Washington.

Pirogov's "friend" in Washington was obviously a CIA contact, with whom he had been told to get in touch whenever necessary. His casual reference to the final recipients of Barzov's letter ("Oh, I think somebody has it. I don't. I think the FBI people; I don't know who") was another attempt to shield the CIA; in 1956 that agency had not yet received the publicity that has rained down on it in recent years, and was not supposed to be mentioned in public at all. Pirogov knew the rules and, with our understanding and consent, was playing the game.

MR. PIROGOV. Well, I was afraid to go just by myself to that restaurant and see Barzov. I asked my friend if he will come with me. He said, "No; I don't want to go with you, but don't be worried. I will be there, or somebody will be there whom I know." Then he give me a plan of that restaurant.

MR. MORRIS. Who gave you the plan of that restaurant?

MR. PIROGOV. My friend. He said, "You are to meet Mr. Barzov in the dining room, not the barroom." Well, then I took a taxi and went to the restaurant, and waited on the street. In about 5 or 6 minutes Barzov came. He looked strained and tired and completely different in appearance from what he was before.

And he said, "O.K., let's go in the restaurant and have a talk." But when we arrived in that restaurant and that barroom, there were too many people there; it was almost impossible to find a table. Then a waiter came to us and said, "You looking for a table?" We said, "Yes." He said, "For two?" and we said, "Yes," and he said "Come with me."

And that table was already reserved for us—by whom, I don't know.

MR. MORRIS. By whom, you don't know?

MR. PIROGOV. Yes. The table was close to the wall. He showed me to the chair next to the wall. I was afraid to sit there and decided to sit on the chair opposite the wall. Then a waiter came and Barzov ordered two drinks. Then I asked the waiter if I could have dinner, because I had just come from the train and I wanted to have some dinner. The waiter said, "No, sir; this is not the dining room. We have a dining room just across the hall."

Then I recognized I had made a mistake. I was not supposed to be there [in the barroom] but where friends of mine would be sitting, in the dining room. So I just got up and said, "Well, I am sorry. Let's go to the dining room; I want to have my dinner. And you can order drinks from here and they will deliver them to the dining room."

For those who may be having difficulty following the action, Pirogov's "friend" had told him to sit with Barzov in the dining room of the restaurant rather than in the bar (which was separated from the dining room by a corridor). In the dining room they would be under surveillance by a number of Pirogov's "friends." However, the dining room was crowded when they arrived, and the waiter had seated them in the bar instead, without the edgy Pirogov realizing at first that they had been put in the wrong room. As soon as he discovered this, Pirogov moved (as already quoted above) to correct the error.

All that Pirogov and Barzov needed to do was to cross the corridor from the bar into the dining room. But suddenly it appeared that Barzov, too, was accompanied by "friends." As Pirogov described what happened next:

MR. PIROGOV. Well now, the bar—the King Cole Room—is on the right side; between the two rooms is a small corridor. I was going first. Just as I reached the corridor I saw 3 or 4 men from another side, you know, just in the center of that corridor. Without our talking or saying anything, or there being any questions, somebody hit me. Then, you know, another man took my arm and put it behind me and put handcuffs on my right hand. In front of me a small man—I would say about 5 feet tall—brought out a pistol. I didn't know what he intended, so I kicked him with my foot. Then another man took that pistol from his hand, and knocked me in the head.

Well now, that happened in the corridor between the two rooms. The door leading into the dining room was closed. I tried to give a signal to a friend of mine who was sitting in the dining room. I was sure he was there, but since it happened—you know, just too quickly. Finally I got close to that door and knocked on it and the door opened and then, you know, suddenly there were many people there. I don't know, maybe 10 or 15 men stood up and came out of the dining room. I understand that the people who came from the dining room were people whom my friend asked to be there.

MR. MORRIS. In other words, this other episode—where someone tried to put handcuffs on you and pulled the gun on you—was in the corridor concealed between the dining room and the bar?

MR. PIROGOV. Yes.

MR. MORRIS. It was all concealed and hidden in there?

MR. PIROGOV. Yes. And then when these people came—this friend of mine and his friends—well, a fight started. I couldn't tell who was who and who hit whom. I know one thing: I was hit a couple more times on my head and face, and one man tried to do everything to put that second handcuff on my wrist, but he couldn't.

MR. MORRIS. In other words, somebody was trying to forcibly kidnap you?

MR. PIROGOV. Yes. Well, it looked that way. That is how it looked to me.

MR. MORRIS. You know whether these men were Russians?

MR. PIROGOV. Well, I don't know.

Pirogov didn't know, but he certainly had his suspicions, and one could see why. Barzov had agreed to see him, no doubt to try to persuade him to return to Russia. Barzov had evidently also brought along some "friends," quite possibly to shanghai Pirogov if he refused. Fortunately Pirogov's own "friends" were also on hand, and the scuffle that broke out in the corridor had been a distinctly two-sided affair. When it was over, Pirogov found that he was still safe with his own "friends":

MR. PIROGOV. And then my friend and his friends came to me, and we took a taxi and went to some house—I don't know, I think it was some hotel. Then we had some trouble, because they couldn't remove the handcuff from my arm.

MR. MORRIS. They couldn't take the handcuff off your arm?

MR. PIROGOV. No; and it took about 1 or 2 hours, because they tried a lot of keys. At last they found one that worked.

MR. MORRIS. Who were these people who tried to remove the handcuff?

MR. PIROGOV. They were my friends.

MR. MORRIS. Have you any reason to believe that the management of either the Three Musketeers restaurant or the King Cole bar, or any of the employees, such as the waiter, were a party to this thing that happened?

MR. PIROGOV. I am sure now, because the same waiter came up to me when I first arrived there looking for Barzov.

He immediately came to me and asked if I want to have a table. I said, "No, I am waiting for a friend of mine."

Then, when I came in with Barzov, the same man came over and offered us table. Yet there were too many people; it was impossible to find a table.

MR. MORRIS. In other words, there was no other empty table in the whole restaurant?

MR. PIROGOV. No; that was the main point that I was surprised about. It seems to me that somebody must have ordered that table in advance or asked the waiter to keep that table empty.

MR. MORRIS. Did the waiter seem to know Barzov?

MR. PIROGOV. Yes.

MR. MORRIS. What makes you say that?

MR. PIROGOV. Because of the way he looked at him. We just came in, you know, and the waiter seemed so familiar, you know—like you meet somebody who knows you. But at that time I assumed it was because Barzov had been staying for a week in the Russian Embassy. The Russian Embassy was very close to the restaurant, to the Three Musketeers.

MR. MORRIS. What street is the Three Musketeers on?

MR. PIROGOV. Connecticut Avenue.

MR. MORRIS. In other words, it is near the Soviet Embassy?

MR. PIROGOV. Yes. And I supposed Barzov often came to that restaurant and that was why the waiter knew him. But I don't know; it was so—everything was prepared.

All in all, despite certain minor loose ends, Morris and I were satisfied with Pirogov's account and felt that it warranted inclusion in the public record. If Soviet agents were prepared to try to kidnap a Russian defector right out of a Washington restaurant, Congress and the public ought to know about it—and could take comfort from the fact that, thanks to Pirogov's alert "friends," the Communists had been thwarted. Two days later therefore, on Friday the 15th, at the opening of a public hearing on another subject, mimeographed copies of the additional Pirogov testimony were distributed to the press. Less than an hour later I was called from the hearing to take an urgent phone call from an official of the Immigration and Naturalization Service of the Department of Justice with whom Bob and I had discussed the Pirogov-Barzov case.

"Has Pirogov's testimony about the fight in the Three Musketeers been released yet?" he asked anxiously.

"Yes," I replied, "at 9:30 this morning."

"*Oh no!*" he groaned, from some unutterable depth of his soul. And then he told me why—the script for an *opéra bouffe* heretofore unpublished.

He had just discovered that *Barzov*'s "friends" that day at the Three Musketeers had been agents of the Immigration Service. The Service was aware that Barzov was planning to redefect and had thought it wise to put a tail on him to see whom he would talk to in his last weeks here. They learned of his plan to meet with Pirogov, and, like Pirogov's own "friends" in the CIA, were on hand in strength for the festivities. Unfortunately, whatever recognition signal was then in use between American secret agents failed to work, and each mistook the other for Russians bent on kidnapping Pirogov. Hence the fisticuffs and assorted mayhem, during which one of a pair of Immigration handcuffs got clamped protectively over the wrist of the baffled Pirogov, whose CIA "friends" subsequently had the very devil of a time finding a key that would fit it. We later learned that, after Pirogov had been taken away and the dust had settled and introductions had been made all round, the suit of one of the CIA men was found to have been torn and Immigration punctiliously paid for its repair.

To make the irony still richer, the restaurant itself reported that later that evening some *bona fide* Russians from the Embassy (tipped off by Barzov, no doubt) did drop in and survey the wreckage. What they made of it all, one can only conjecture. One newspaper reporter who tracked down the real story, the veteran *Chicago Tribune* correspondent Willard Edwards, speculated that they went away muttering, "Those crazy Americans!"

So, Mr. Pirogov, there at last is the truth about what happened to you on that evening in the summer of 1949 at the Three Musketeers. I am sure that you, who have endured so much and chosen so wisely, will forgive me for having told the whole truth, even though it makes just about all of us, with the regrettable exception of Ambassador Panyushkin, look a little ridiculous. Better ridiculous than dead—as Barzov would no doubt have put it.

Far Out—and Still Further

Like all agencies dealing with internal security problems, from local police to the FBI and HCUA, our Subcommittee was the object of a steady bombardment by private citizens who believed they had some legitimate grievance within our power to ameliorate. Very occasionally they did; far more often they didn't. One of my jobs, as Morris' associate counsel, was to screen their letters and phone calls and talk to those who came in person, to sort them out and where possible refer them to some appropriate agency. Often I would simply advise them to report the problem to their local police; occasionally I would pass them along to the FBI. If no other recourse suggested itself, I would usually urge them to take the matter up with their Congressman, that, after all, being one proper function of a member of Congress: to act, knowledgeably and influentially, on behalf of constituents with meritorious claims.

Certain borderline cases continued to trouble me as long as I served with the Subcommittee. Twice, for example, we were approached by former employees of the CIA who had been fired by that agency. Despite their own naturally self-serving accounts, it was not hard to recognize them as quarrelsome personalities and quite possibly near-unemployable neurotics. I certainly did not take at face value their pitiful

descriptions of how some CIA superior had mistreated them and finally
engineered their unjust discharge. Yet it was impossible not to sympathize with their predicament, which they brought to us, not because they
believed or alleged that the CIA was infested with Communists, but
simply because they did not know where else to turn. In both cases, the
employee had been dismissed on the vague but deadly ground of "the
good of the service." Since this in the circumstances somehow (though
wrongly) smacked of "security risk," it was almost impossible for the
luckless individual to get a decent job in civilian life. Whatever review
procedures were available to the dismissed employee within the CIA
itself were obviously and rightly suspect of being biased against him, all
the more so because the whole review was necessarily carried out in
secrecy, out of sight of independent-minded critics. By law and regula-
tion, on the same ground of necessary secrecy, no appeal could be taken
by the employee to the courts or to any other outside reviewing authority. All in all, to a security-conscious lawyer who fully recognized the
need for secrecy in CIA affairs and yet was trained to believe that every
wrong should have its appropriate remedy, it was a thoroughly unsettling dilemma. Even if these particular individuals richly deserved to be
fired, it was inevitable that some day—error being human—an injustice
would be done; and I could not see then, and cannot see now, what the
victim would be able to do about it.

Let me add that I by no means necessarily endorse the various proposals of Senator Mansfield, over the years, for an independent body to
review the whole sphere of action of the CIA. Still less did I favor
Senator Fulbright's 1966 attempt (happily defeated) to bring the CIA
partially under the jurisdiction of his hot-eyed Foreign Relations Committee. Such a cure would be worse than any disease of which the CIA
can fairly be accused. But some provision, in my opinion, ought to be
made for an independent review of administrative discharges from the
CIA "for the good of the service."

Further out, and if possible still more pathetic, were the cases of
individuals who, by reason of profound neurotic problems, incipient
psychosis, or (in one case that I especially remember) sheer senility,
were being eased out of government jobs for which they could not
possibly find adequate substitutes, and who had come to the tragically
mistaken and characteristically paranoid conclusion that secret Communists were at the bottom of their problem. It was impossible—at least
I found it so—to tell the old gentleman who sat so trustingly beside my
desk that his Army employers were *not* concealed Communists; that the
truth was that he was just getting too old, too crotchety and too slow to

go on translating documents efficiently. He shook his massive head and sighed in genuine bewilderment: "I just—don't—know—what—to do." I am ashamed to say that I referred him to his senator.

Numerically the largest group of all, of course, consisted of true psychotics: mentally disturbed people who persisted in seeking rational remedies for the sick fancies they confused with reality. Scarcely a day went by without a letter or a phone call from some desperately unhappy individual who was convinced that he was the victim of a monstrous plot, usually Communist in origin, and that we alone could save him. It was usually not hard to spot such cases. They would write us (for example) on paper towels filched from washrooms of Veterans Administration hospitals, begging to be saved from a gigantic conspiracy of Communists and psychiatrists. In a surprisingly large number of instances, they charged that their tormentors were assaulting them with mysterious vibrations, often electronic in origin. (So common was this particular syndrome that FBI agents, I am told, invented a simple cure for similar cases. While the complainant recounted his story of radio-wave attacks, the listening agent would thoughtfully splice together a long chain of paper clips. When the account ended, the agent would attach the chain to the man's lapel and say soothingly, "There! Now you're grounded.")

A psychiatrist friend once told me that people with paranoid symptoms (i.e., a "persecution complex") often, though not invariably, identify their imaginary persecutors with whatever happens to be the public symbol of evil at that particular moment. During World War II American paranoiacs by and large believed they were being hounded by the Nazis. With the advent of the Cold War, Nazis went out of style and Communist villains became all the rage. It would be interesting to know whether Chinese Communists are now more in vogue among these unfortunate people than their Russian counterparts.

Our most persistent correspondent in this category was a woman then living in New York City. From various references in her innumerable long and neatly typed letters, it was possible to deduce that she had been in and out of mental hospitals in the past. At the time, however, she was out and living with a sister in a small apartment on the East side. Her persecutors included just about everybody, and she believed they had installed "machines" of some (electronic?) sort in the apartment over hers, to torment her. She was an avid reader of newspapers and magazines, and everything she read was grist for her mill. Consider these opening paragraphs of her long dispatch to Bob Morris dated May 15, 1957:

Dear Judge Morris:

Last fall I reported an incident to J. Edgar Hoover regarding the operations in this house in which a United Nations man and his wife were actively used, and I reported that the fellow seen in that apartment through the open door, was the same one who had used a female stooge who boasted in Dec. 1948 that she had the $3,000,000. That night the wife of this UN man disappeared and was said to have gone to South America. This involved the Philippine Embassy, because a registered letter handed HERE from them had several bankbooks in it, which could be felt and seen through the envelope. The postman MAY have made an honest mistake, but after I reported this to Hoover there was a big shakeup in the post office here. In fact, I believe such elements are still used, because it was through that method the letter sent here in December was stolen.

My reason for reporting this now, is the fact that the forces that are still in operation here that worked with the UN man in the past are still acting the part, operating the powerful machines 24 hours a day. These in turn are also linked to the Montgomery operations and was part of the Winchell participation.

We had scarcely digested this fascinating if slightly addled information when the following letter, which I set forth in full, arrived under date of May 23:

Dear Judge Morris:

Yesterday I started to write you a letter. The snoops and chiselers at the machines overhead have reflected the attached in the *News* Chinese cartoon, which has been used for years by this gang.

The inference here that I have "fear" is a vicious libel, but one which has been used by such as Winchell and Gordon Fine in the Police. The lie is tagged to THEM because they constantly intercepted the letters which would have given me the chance to go to Washington and clean it up.

The violent reaction of Winchell when I wrote to Sen. Jenner for a hearing last winter, was ample proof.

I shall, however, be in Washington next week. The evil people who pulled these actions have been keeping a 24-hour watch at the powerful machines all around this apartment. They did this, with foot-guards outside the house all winter during the period I went to Washington.

The person who was behind the letter theft May 17 is a person who has gotten money out of this, known to myself and Hoover among others. That is why Hoover jumped when I wrote him of it. The same persons deny any money or works.

I would have come this week, but I have had a very upset stomach, and you get no sleep around here from these rackets. It is these actions which indicate the intense corruption covering up the chiselers. The *Readers Digest* piece by Brownell amazes me, after what they said to me!

There was much, much more of the same from this distraught woman, over a period of many months. Not long after mailing the letter just quoted, she actually appeared at our office and asked to see Bob. For once my fearless boss funked out; with a fiendish grin he assigned me to the task of talking with her, and subsequently insisted she had fallen in love with me and was henceforth my responsibility!

A more difficult problem, precisely because it was so well written and coherent, was presented by a communication from a former WAC. It was dated July 18, 1956, and the only note of early warning was sounded by the fact that she was writing from a VA hospital. But her typing and syntax were impeccable:

> I know that your time is precious, as well as your attention. Yet, I must try to claim a measure of both without offering you any authority other than my own to vouch for the significance of what I have to say.
>
> I am inclosing copies of some communications in which I have tried to make my experience here in the Veterans Administration Hospital useful to people who are concerned with the internal security of the country.
>
> If I could think of any way to magnify the import of what I am here saying to these people I should be glad; but I can only offer you the copies of what I have written to each, trusting that you will be open-minded enough to weigh their significance.

Enclosed were copies of memoranda the author had written to various people in authority, from the hospital engineer all the way up to the Secretary of the Army. Although couched in the form of attacks on the security of our military installations, they betrayed a remarkable similarity to the charges about "machines" by the New York woman quoted above. To the Secretary of the Army, for instance, the ex-WAC had written:

> During my first years here, 1948-1949, pulsing, battering energy waves were focussed upon this area, from some source, particularly at night, while military planes cruised leisurely overhead. There seemed to be no fear of disclosure on the part of those responsible, for the frantic display of violence on the part of disorganized patients was being continually rationalized by a corps of psychiatrists. Meanwhile, doctors were kept busy "reducing tension" by subjecting scores of patients each day to

electric shock convulsions, with even occasionally a prefrontal lobotomy for emphasis.

Volunteers from service organizations came and went, giving out candy bars and cigarettes. Sunday church services were conducted by Chaplains who, looking down from the pulpit into the disfigured faces of hundreds of once-human creatures, equated Sin with Sickness in their prayers. The hired workers took their cue therefrom and behaved toward the patients accordingly.

Months and years of this caged suffering ensued. Battering, pulsing waves of energy, heat or sound (I am not a physicist) continued to scorch and un-hinge the nervous machinery of regimented human beings, who, at night, tossed and turned without rest. Exhausted, but too miserable to sleep, or even to lie still in bed, many tried to roam the corridors, shouting and screaming their discomfort, having finally to be put under sedation or "in restraint". . . .

Mr. Secretary, my experience here has clinched a hundred times over a conclusion I had reached during service in the Army, that there are now means at hand by which human nervous systems may not only be disorganized at any level, but ferocious, unreasoning hate may be incited and directed to pre-chosen targets. That is a fact which is hard to learn, and one might die of despair before it finally comes through into the light; but so it is.

Not all the complaints, of course, came by mail. One day an agitated lady phoned from Hartford to beg our help; her house, she said, was completely surrounded by Communists.

"Have you phoned your local FBI?" I asked.

"Yes, I did."

"And what did they say?"

"They couldn't help me."

"Then, madam, neither can we."

Sometimes, purely as an intellectual exercise, I would go out of my way to treat these irrational performances as if they were, or might be, descriptions of actual facts, i.e., I would assume the truth of the statements made and resolve all doubts in favor of the report, like a judge considering a motion to dismiss a complaint in a lawsuit. Forget the letters of the New York woman, as too incoherent to cope with. But what if that house in Hartford really *was* surrounded by Communists, and the local FBI, out of sheer sloth or worse, *had* simply refused to do anything about it? Or worse yet, what if some irresponsible person or group was in very truth possessed of a device "by which human nervous systems may not only be disorganized at any level, but ferocious, unreasoning hate may be incited and directed to pre-chosen targets"? Such things were to say the least highly unlikely, but what if—*just if*—they were true, and our Subcommittee was a sort of Court of Last Resort?

Fortunately for my peace of mind, such hypotheses always collapsed under their own weight. If Hartford was really in the grip of a Red Terror, and the local FBI was too paralyzed or lazy to react; if great nerve-ray machines actually existed, and were in the possession and control of sinister forces—then how was it that life in Washington was still going on around me so normally, and Old Glory was still flying so reassuringly atop the Capitol there, just across the park? Moreover, if all the Communists and psychiatrists in America were in fact (as another writer charged) in league to destroy one hapless wretch in a federal insane asylum in California, why on earth hadn't they destroyed him? Wasn't it fatally implausible that he had nevertheless somehow survived, even if only barely, to indite these long letters of protest to the Senate Internal Security Subcommittee?

Similar considerations are, as far as I am concerned, the most serious objection to the durable demonologies that are so popular in various quarters on the extreme right: the notion that our national ills are the fault of the Elders of Zion, or the Illuminati, or Force X, or the Bilderberg Society, or that just about everybody—Nasser, de Gaulle, Eisenhower, you name him—is conspiring with the Communists to bring about our downfall.

Such speculations are for summer afternoons and late-night college bull sessions, and not to be taken too seriously. A little perspective, a little common sense, is indispensable when dealing with such serious matters as America's internal security. All is not lost. If it were, the battle would have been over long ago. Instead, it is being fought, and sometimes well fought, on a hundred fronts around the world.

12

Summing It Up

At last a day came when I decided it was time to be moving on. I had left my law firm to go to work for the Subcommittee without any understanding, express or implied, that I would be coming back. My own original notion had been that I might work for the ISSC for two or three years, then return to the private practice of the law with a congenial business or firm. In the spring of 1957, however, Bob Morris intimated to me that he would be stepping down as chief counsel later that year, to enter the Republican primary for the Senate seat of retiring Republican H. Alexander Smith of New Jersey, and although I liked my work, I did not want to stay on after Morris had left. I had come to Washington with him early in 1956, and had worked for over a year at his side. Much as I admired his logical successor, Jay Sourwine (who had served as chief counsel between Bob's first and second hitches), I knew that it would be a different job—almost a different Subcommittee—without Bob Morris.

So I began putting out cautious feelers, as one does when casting about for a new job. As it happened, one of my earliest approaches proved successful, though not exactly in the way I had visualized. I knew that the family of my friend Bill Buckley was in the oil business, and it occurred to me that the business might be able to use a young lawyer. I tossed out the idea over lunch with Bill and Pat in their handsome Connecticut home overlooking Long Island Sound one Sunday in June 1957. Buckley, who had launched *National Review* in

November 1955 and had served as both its editor and its publisher since, surprised me by countering:

"How would you like to work for *National Review*?"

He well knew how highly I thought of the magazine; I believed it was the most important and responsible voice in the new conservative movement that was then just getting under way, and as such represented the most significant single development in contemporary political thought. But what did he want me to do at *National Review*? Surely it didn't need a full-time lawyer? So I responded cautiously:

"Well—er—as what?" Buckley thought a moment, then replied:

"As publisher."

At the time I knew very little about just what a publisher is expected to do. In point of fact, it is a pretty vague title—the French, I have since discovered, don't even have a word for it. In some publishing enterprises it is the title taken by the owner. In others (the most famous example is Time Inc.) it is given to the man in direct charge, under the owner, of the business aspects of the publication. As Buckley outlined to me the job he had in mind, it seemed to correspond to the latter description, with the important addendum that I would also participate in all major editorial conferences and decisions.

I deliberated for five weeks before making up my mind. After all, it is no small matter for a man to leave altogether the profession for which he has been specially trained, and to which he has devoted the first nine years of his working life. Moreover, shaky new magazines, especially of the "opinion" variety, are a dime a dozen; what assurance did I have that this one would survive? Finally, I had an uncomfortable, vaguely Calvinistic feeling that anything I wanted to do so much must be bad for me. Nevertheless, I finally decided to take the plunge. In July 1957 I resigned from the staff of the Internal Security Subcommittee to become the publisher of *National Review*—and lived happily ever after.

In the seventeen months I served on its staff, the Internal Security Subcommittee interrogated nearly 300 witnesses in public hearings and held an almost equal number of executive sessions as well. Of the witnesses heard in public, over 80 pleaded the Fifth Amendment in response to one or more questions. Two refused either to answer *or* to invoke the Fifth, and these (Pauline Feuer and Herman Liveright) were duly cited, indicted, and convicted for contempt of the United States Senate, though the appellate courts ultimately spared Liveright on a technicality (see footnote, p. 42.). In addition to holding hearings, the Subcommittee conducted "staff investigations" of many subjects within its field of interest, research projects formidable in scope and highly important to the Subcommittee's basic task.

The eleven preceding chapters of this book hardly begin to suggest the vast array of subjects investigated by the ISSC during those seventeen months. I have described our probe of the New Orleans professional group; our investigation of Harry Gold's introduction to the world of espionage; our staff study of the ruin of the Chinese Nationalist currency by Communist agents in the Treasury; our look at Jacob Javits' activities in the mid-1940's; our survey of the Communist grip on the life of the Hawaiian Islands; our talks with the important redefector, John Santo; our scrutiny of the American Foreign Service officer, John Emmerson; and (in passing) our inquiry into the Soviet repatriation campaign—because these particular inquiries were exceptionally dramatic or more than ordinarily interesting, or because they have some special significance for contemporary readers. But a glance at the ISSC's annual reports for 1956 and 1957 will show that the Subcommittee also investigated such disparate topics as: Communist control of the American Communications Association (certified bargaining agent for 5000 Western Union and RCA Cable employees in New York City); attempted validation in New York, in 1956, of prewar German bonds stolen by the Red Army on entering Berlin in 1945; the *non*-atomic espionage of Julius Rosenberg; the activities of Tass, the Soviet news agency, and its employees in this country; ownership of important American corporations by anonymous foreign interests; American citizens who were (and in some cases still are) working for the Chinese Communist regime; the 25-year American career of J. Peters, formerly the top Soviet espionage agent in this country; Communist influence in the "American Forum for Socialist Education"; NKVD agents in churches of the Soviet Union and other Iron Curtain countries, and among their emissaries to the United States; various illegal uses of numbered Swiss bank accounts; and, of course, the administration and effectiveness of those internal security laws already on the books, and the consequences of their ongoing interpretation by the courts.

But it may be asked, what was the impact of all these various inquiries on the specific area the Subcommittee was mandated to investigate—namely, the administration, operation, and enforcement of the Internal Security Act and America's other internal security laws? Were any new laws proposed, or changes in any old ones recommended, as a result of these wide-ranging investigations?

The answer is: definitely, yes. But, before we review some of the recommendations, let us remember that a Congressional committee ought not to be judged primarily by the sheer yardage of new or amending legislation it proposes. Ordinarily, in any field over which Congress exercises legislative power, there is already on the books a body of basic statute law. The wise Congressional committee will not be unduly eager to add to it, or duplicate it, or festoon it with pointless amendments. Rather, the efforts should be to prune it, lubricate it, modernize it and in general help it to do more efficiently the job it was designed to do.

Beyond this, moreover, it has long been recognized that the investigative powers of a Congressional committee may be exercised most usefully without immediately resulting in any new legislation whatever. Just as only an informed Congress can legislate intelligently, so only an informed public can make known to Congress its considered views on national problems. And not even their severest critics, I think, will deny that the investigations of the Senate Internal Security Subcommittee and the House Committee on Un-American Activities have played a large role in shaping American public opinion on internal security problems. The public opinion thus formed has, in its turn, stimulated much additional legislation.

The basic federal statutes in the internal security field in 1956-57 were: the Subversive Activities Control Act of 1950 (Title I of the Internal Security Act), the Communist Control Act of 1954, the Foreign Agents Registration Act of 1938 (as amended), and various provisions of Title 18 of the United States Code (the Criminal Code). In addition, of course, many other statutes in such fields as immigration, atomic energy, intelligence, national defense, passports, and even the postal service touched in one way or another on the matter of internal security.

My seventeen months with the Subcommittee happened to extend over two Congresses, the second session of the 84th Congress and the first session of the 85th. Since any bills that have not completed the lengthy legislative process when a Congress finally adjourns, die at that moment and must be introduced afresh at the beginning of the next Congress, my direct experience with internal security legislation consisted, during 1956, of watching the progress of bills that had been introduced before I was hired and, during 1957, of helping to launch bills that did not become law (if at all) until long after I had departed.

During the 84th Congress of 1955-56, seventeen bills were referred to the Internal Security Subcommittee. Of these, three were still pending unreported in the Subcommittee when the 84th Congress adjourned in July 1956. Of the remaining fourteen, all of which were reported (i.e., recommended) by the Subcommittee to the full Judiciary Committee,

S.2375 became Public Law 254 and H.R.3882 became Public Law 893. The former set the term of members of the Subversive Activities Control Board at five years; the latter required the registration of certain persons who have knowledge of or have received instruction or assignment in the espionage, counterespionage, or sabotage service or techniques of a foreign government or foreign political party. (A third bill, S.750, was identical with the latter and was therefore postponed indefinitely upon its passage.) A fourth bill, S.2887, prohibiting the recording of deliberations by grant or petit juries in federal courts, became Public Law 919.

In addition, two other bills (S.1392 and S.547) were postponed indefinitely when the full Committee approved instead, without referral to the Subcommittee, two substantially identical bills already approved by the House: H.R.4753 and H.R.2854, which became Public Laws 173 and 766. The former increased in certain respects the standard prescribed in the Subversive Activities Control Act with respect to the past affiliations of individuals conducting the effective management of organizations alleged to be Communist-infiltrated. The latter increased the penalties for seditious conspiracy, and for advocating or conspiring to advocate the overthrow of the Government by force, to a maximum of 20 years' imprisonment and a $20,000 fine.

A seventh bill (S.2171), providing that a member of the Subversive Activities Control Board should continue in office after the expiration of his term until his successor was appointed and had qualified, was passed by both Houses of Congress but vetoed by the President. Another (S.1273), making certain technical changes in the Foreign Agents Registration Act, was passed by the Senate but failed to reach the floor of the House of Representatives before adjournment.

Of the remaining six bills reported by the Subcommittee to the full Judiciary Committee, the latter approved three, but they were still on the Senate Calendar when Congress adjourned and therefore failed to become law. One of these (S.3617) would have extended, and in certain cases suspended, the statute of limitations on perjury by federal employees with respect to subversive activities and connections. Another (S.782) would have prevented Americans of questionable loyalty from working for the United Nations. The third (S.3617) proclaimed the intent of Congress not to preempt the field of sedition legislation—and would thus have restored the effectiveness of forty-two sedition laws on the books of individual states, which had been struck down by the decision of the U.S. Supreme Court in *Pennsylvania* vs. *Nelson* (1956).

The remaining three bills reported by the Subcommittee (S.4047,

S.4050 and S.4051) were essentially similar bills designed to contravene the Supreme Court's decision in *Cole* vs. *Young* (1956), which held that Executive Order 10450 could not extend the provisions of the Summary Suspension Act of 1950 to all departments and agencies, but only to "sensitive" positions, in keeping with the supposed intent of Congress. None of these three bills, however, had been acted on by the full Committee when Congress adjourned.

I have dealt above only with bills referred to the Judiciary Committee, and by it to the Internal Security Subcommittee, and in many cases the nexus between the proposed legislation and preceding investigations of the Subcommittee (or in some cases HCUA) is apparent to any student of the full record. In addition, however, it should be remembered that the Subcommittee's investigations also frequently gave rise to bills that were referred to other subcommittees of the Judiciary Committee (for example, the Subcommittee on Immigration) or to other standing committees of the Senate—and even prompted the introduction of bills in the House of Representatives. To establish the inspiration and trace the legislative history of all these bills, however, is beyond the scope of this book.

The convening of the new (85th) Congress in January 1957 naturally resulted in the introduction of a flood of new bills, a fair proportion of which dealt with one or another aspect of the problem of internal security. During the first session, no less than sixty were introduced in the House of Representatives, and twenty-nine more in the Senate. Of the latter, twenty-one were referred to the Judiciary Committee, and six of these twenty-one were referred by the Committee to the Internal Security Subcommittee. They were:

S.337, providing that no act of Congress shall be construed as invalidating (by "preemption of the field") an otherwise valid state law, unless there is a direct and positive conflict between their express provisions. (Once again, aimed at *Pennsylvania* vs. *Nelson*.)

S.654, providing that federal laws relating to criminal subversion and sedition shall not prevent enforcement, in state courts, of state laws making such acts crimes. (Same purpose.)

S.1140, providing special procedures for the protection of "defense facilities" from sabotage and espionage.

S.1254, granting preference in federal courts to proceedings involving treason, espionage, censorship, sabotage, sedition, and subversive activities, and increasing to fifteen years the statute of limitations on the prosecution of such offenses.

S.2401, restoring the effectiveness of state laws on subversion and sedition where not in conflict with federal statutes, and limiting the appellate jurisdiction of the federal courts in cases relating to the public schools.

S.2646, revoking the jurisdiction of the Supreme Court to review (1) functions of Congressional committees, including contempt proceedings, (2) actions of the executive branch with regard to security cases, (3) statutes or regulations of state governments controlling subversive activities, (4) school board rules concerning subversive activities, and (5) rules of any board of bar examiners pertaining to the admission of persons to the practice of law in a state. (This was the famous Jenner-Butler Bill and expressed the exasperation of its sponsors at the series of Supreme Court decisions that had recently been handed down in the five specified categories: (1) *U.S.* vs. *Watkins,* (2) *Cole* vs. *Young,* (3) *Pennsylvania* vs. *Nelson,* (4) *Slochower* vs. *Board of Higher Education,* and (5) *Konigsberg* vs. *State Bar of California.*)

Of these six bills, S.337, S.1254, and S.2646 were reported by the Internal Security Subcommittee to the full Judiciary Committee before the close of the first session of the 85th Congress on August 30, 1957, but in none of these cases had the full committee itself acted by that date. The other three bills (S.654, S.1140 and S.2401) were still pending unreported in the Subcommittee when the session ended.*

So much, then, for the quantitative record of the ISSC, so far as concerns both investigations and legislation, during my stay in Washington. All in all, I think the Senate and the people had, and have subsequently continued to have, every reason to be satisfied with the over-all performance of the Internal Security Subcommittee. And if that is true, then it is difficult not to feel a profound sense of gratitude to those few hardy senators who, in the teeth of all the opposition that can be mustered by a frightened Communist Party and an apprehensive Liberal Establishment, hold it steadfastly to its tremendously useful course.

It would appear that the Senate itself may agree with this view, for the Subcommittee's appropriation is renewed each year with little opposition or none. As for the opinion of others, I have already mentioned (in Chapter 1) the special commendation conferred upon the Subcommittee in 1959 by the House of Delegates of the American Bar Association, a noteworthy tribute by a highly knowledgeable and judicious body of men.

I have no particular desire to revive here the argument that has raged, ever since the creation of the Dies Committee in 1938, over the desira-

---

* Although several of them advanced further up the legislative ladder during the second session of the 85th Congress in 1958, none of these six bills was destined to become law.

bility of Congressional investigations of Communism. Manifestly, I favor them. In the last analysis, however, each of us must decide for himself whether, on balance, we think the problem of domestic Communism in the era of the Cold War merits this particular sort of attention of the part of Congress, or whether the alleged defects and disadvantages of the method outweigh whatever value it may have.

However, I probably owe it to the reader to set forth a few of the considerations that govern my own thinking in this and various related matters. With apologies, then, for what will undoubtedly seem obvious to some, and very far indeed from obvious to others, I offer herewith a few random reflections:

1. International Communism is not an imaginary danger, like the radio waves that assailed the lady quoted on pages 281-282. It is a dynamic and highly aggressive force in world affairs, and its importance is not diminished in the least by the fact that it is subdivided into Russian, Chinese, and still other factions.

2. All of the major Communist factions have domestic American affiliates, whose comparatively small intrinsic importance is multiplied many times by their international connections—just as the minuscule American Nazi movement of 1938-41 was rendered vastly more significant than it would otherwise have been by the existence and the aggressive policies of Nazi Germany.

3. The evidence is by now conclusive that domestic Communists made substantial inroads into many fields of our national life, including the government itself, beginning in the early 1930's, and that their efforts along this line are continuing today.

4. Insofar as the activities of domestic Communists violate existing laws, they are properly dealt with by law-enforcement agencies: the local police or (in the case of federal laws) the FBI, and the appropriate prosecuting attorneys. But the modification of existing federal laws, and the enactment of any needed new ones, is the function of Congress; and for this purpose it is essential that Congress be given broad investigative powers, including the subpoena power and contempt power.

5. The rules of procedure for investigating committees have been hammered out over a period of years, by the two Houses of Congress themselves* and in a series of Supreme Court decisions. Every witness, for example, has long been entitled to be accompanied by counsel, and to consult him before answering any question. It is, however, not only

* For a comprehensive study of the Senate rules as they existed in 1955 and the years immediately following, see "Rules of Procedure for Senate Investigating Committees," published by the Subcommittee on Rules of the Senate Committee on Rules and Administration (83rd Congress, 2nd Session).

impractical, but surely illogical as well, to throw around every hostile witness before a Congressional committee, whose greatest peril is an embarrassing question, the same intricate network of protective procedures that are rightly required when the state seeks to deprive a defendant in a criminal case of his life, liberty, or property.

6. Similarly, in the field of government security regulations, it is entirely proper to remove an employee from a government job if he is demonstrably a security *risk*, without requiring the government to prove that the employee has already committed a crime. Life, liberty, and property are *rights*, not to be taken away without meeting a heavy burden of proof of wrongdoing; but government employment is a *privilege*, and doubts concerning fitness for it should properly be resolved in favor of the government.

7. It would theoretically be possible to divide all government jobs into "sensitive" and "non-sensitive" categories, and to require quite different standards of security for the two categories. Alternatively, it would be possible (and I personally believe better) to apply a single high standard of security to all government employees, but to vary in practice the intensity of the security investigation conducted. For example, a skilled employee in a secret atomic installation would presumably be a prime candidate for what is called a "full field investigation" by the FBI, whereas a rural letter-carrier, while quite rightly expected to be just as loyal, might be subjected to only a comparatively perfunctory name-check, unless this turned up information requiring a deeper probe.

8. Bear in mind the distinction between a *disloyal* employee and the one who is merely a *security risk*. Many people who have never been the least disloyal to this country are, by any fair test, grave security risks; i.e., because of some personal weakness or special vulnerability they possess, there is a larger than average risk that they *may* some day succumb to one of the vicious pressures that Communists know so well how to bring to bear.

9. Do not be deceived by the glib contention that so-called "loyalty oaths," of the type that require a person (a teacher, a labor union official, a federal scholarship recipient, or whatever) to deny Communist Party membership on pain of perjury, are ineffective because a secret Communist "would be perfectly happy to swear falsely." It is not a fear of God's vengeance, or even a simple distaste for dishonesty, that makes concealed Communists dislike these oaths so intensely. Rather, they know very well that the FBI may already be watching them, ready to act if they commit perjury.

10. On the other hand, do not expect miracles from either loyalty-oath requirements or any other kind of anti-Communist legislation. The

Communist Party is an extremely agile organization. It can, like Shakespeare's Richard III, "add colours to the chameleon, change shapes with Proteus to advantages, and set the murderous Machiavel to school." It can be, and has been, severely inconvenienced by sound laws vigorously enforced, but it can never be put out of business altogether by the legislative route. The impulse that will one day write *Finis* to Communism can come only from the hearts of men.

Such observations lead inevitably to far wider reflections, having to do with the true nature and significance of Communism and its probable place in the ongoing history of mankind. I believe with the late Whittaker Chambers that Communism is the modern form of "man's second oldest faith"—the most serious effort yet made to organize and direct human society without reference to transcendental considerations. As such it demands our careful attention. But because it is based on a fundamentally inadequate and mistaken concept of man's nature, I believe it is doomed to final failure—for the same reason that the proposition that two and two make five is doomed to final failure.

It does not follow, however, that the free world as we know it will necessarily prevail in its present mortal struggle with Communism. Free men are divided among themselves, and profoundly unsure of their course. When God is "dead" in the hearts of many good men, and Science is our king; when even conservatives find it difficult to synthesize and express in modern terms the traditional wisdom of the West—in times like these, it is impossible to feel that the prospects for the victory of free men are very bright, still less that their victory is inevitable.

But, having said this much, let me stress that since the real problem is not our adversary's strength but our own weakness and irresolution, the remedy lies within us. Communism's absurd and primitive scientism could not possibly prevail against a free world sure of its own meaning and destiny. That is why I agreed so thoroughly, from the very first, with the basic contention of *National Review*: namely, that what America has most to fear is not the Communists either at home or abroad, but our own good-hearted, well-meaning fellow citizens of the liberal persuasion, whose unintended effect has been to sap the survival powers of free societies everywhere. And that in turn is why, when I left the Subcommittee to become *National Review*'s publisher, I had no feeling that I was giving up the struggle. On the contrary, I believed—and still believe—that I was turning my attention from one crucial battlefield to another that is, if possible, more crucial still.

But that too is another book.

On Tuesday morning, July 23, 1957, I attended my last session of the Subcommittee as its associate counsel. The witness was William A. Wallace, an impressive young Negro who had been a member of the Communist Party from 1949 to 1955 and who had cooperated with the FBI for the last three of his six years in the Party. At the end of the morning session the chairman, Senator Hruska, who had evidently been tipped off by Morris that I was leaving, had a few characteristically generous farewell words for me:

> SENATOR HRUSKA. Before we adjourn, I would like to call attention to the fact that this is one of the last hearings that will be attended by Mr. William Rusher as a member of the staff of the subcommittee.
>
> I understand he has resigned, effective the middle of next month, to accept new employment to go into a new field.
>
> Do you want to tell us what it is, Mr. Rusher?
>
> MR. RUSHER. Publisher of the *National Review* magazine, in New York City.
>
> SENATOR HRUSKA. Well, that is fine.
>
> I understand you have been here with us a year and a half, and from my experience in the last seven and a half months, I have been very gratified. From what I hear from the other members of the staff, they likewise enjoyed a benefit from your working along with them, and we are sorry you are leaving.
>
> We hope you will find your new job both beneficial and interesting.
>
> MR. RUSHER. Thank you. It has been a great pleasure for me, Senator.
>
> SENATOR HRUSKA. If there is no further business, the subcommittee stands adjourned.
>
> (Whereupon, at 12:20 p.m., the subcommittee adjourned.)

The next day I left Washington aboard the 11 a.m. "Midday Congressional" for New York, to take up my new job—and once again a new life. In the cab on the way to the station, with my hand luggage piled around me, I reviewed it all. Seventeen crowded, fantastic months with the Subcommittee were behind me now. Hunter O'Dell and his New Orleans comrades; the stately palms of Waikiki; sad-eyed little Harry Gold; John Santo shrinking back into the shadows along the Ringstrasse; razor-voiced Jack Javits; Herbert Norman gazing down from a Cairo rooftop; Joe McCarthy in his gray casket in the well of the Senate Chamber—all these memories, and many more, came flooding back.

Had it been worth it? Had we done our very best? Would the cause we had fought for triumph in the end, or fail? I recalled, and softly repeated to myself, a reassuring little quatrain by Coventry Patmore:

For want of me the world's course will not fail:
When all its work is done, the lie shall rot;
The truth is great, and shall prevail,
When none cares whether it prevail or not.

The taxi swung into the great plaza before Union Station. Away to the south I caught a last glimpse of the Capitol, its cool gray dome floating above the midsummer greenery: graceful, majestic, serene.

Index